DIVIDED WE STOOD

A Tale of the Lost Orders

as told by

John F. Crosby

Copyright © 2015 John Fulling Crosby

ISBN: 978-0-9915282-9-5

Published by Holon Publishing
& Creative Community

Collective for authors, artists, and creative professionals -
Holon exists to create symbiosis between artists of all kinds,
businesses, non-profits, and their communities.

www.Holon.co

719 Virginia Ave.
Indianapolis, IN
46203

Other works by John F. Crosby:

Sons and Fathers: Challenges to paternal authority -
Published by Routledge, 2013

*To learn about the author and his works, visit this book's
website:*

wwwDividedWeStood.com

* * *

Printed in the United States of America

Acknowledgements

Thanks to my early writing partner when I first created the book, Robert W. Bailey. Bob's imagination served as stimulus to my story telling and balance to my academic bent. Janet Hasson of the Belle Meade Plantation, Nashville, Tennessee, helped me appreciate the importance of physical descriptions in the service of settings and character development. A critical review by Dana Huebler Hinrichs stiffened my resolve. Great thanks to my life-long friend, David Albert, who always gave me great encouragement over the twenty some years during which this work evolved. I appreciate the work of Larry Wilkerson on the Historical Setting and Chapters One and Thirteen. Thanks also to the Civil War Roundtable of Cape Cod and the Monroe County Civil War Roundtable of Bloomington, Indiana. These "Roundtable" experiences gave germination and incubation to my thoughts and ideas. Further, exposing my work to the Revisionist writing class taught by Cara Prill served as impetus to the final push toward revision and publication. Thanks to Paige Rasmussen for her diligence in copyediting. Finally, deepest thanks to my publisher and producer, Jeremy Gotwals, who adopted the story and shepherded the work to fruition as if it were his own.

Table of Contents

Chapter 1 1

Chapter 2 10

Chapter 3 17

Chapter 4 30

Chapter 5 40

Chapter 6 51

Chapter 7 60

Chapter 8 69

Chapter 9 81

Chapter 10 89

Chapter 11 99

Chapter 12 109

Chapter 13 122

Chapter 14 132

Chapter 15 141

Chapter 16 150

Part 2

Chapter 17 163

Chapter 18 177

Chapter 19 192

Chapter 20 205

Chapter 21 217

Chapter 22 228

Chapter 23 242

Chapter 24 256

Chapter 25 268

Chapter 26 280

Chapter 27 293

Chapter 28 307

Historical Setting 316

DIVIDED WE STOOD

A Tale of the Lost Orders

as told by

John F. Crosby

This work is dedicated to:

Charles Thomas Shanner

Comapny A, 63rd. Regular Indiana Volunteers, USA
by his Great, Great, Grandson, John Fulling Crosby.

PART I

CHAPTER ONE

"Gentlemen, gentlemen!" Tad barked. "It's early! One more round—while I tell y'all what's gonna happen." Loud and boisterous, he loved regaling a rapt audience.

Tad and other staff officers weren't supposed to mix and mingle with the junior officers—mostly sergeants. Their socializing was officially frowned upon, but none of them cared.

After each evening mess, the troops would retreat to chairs fashioned from wooden barrels. Grousing and gossiping, they'd pass a whiskey bottle to fuel their banter as cigar smoke began clouding their tent like fog settling in a bottom.

Dominating and intimidating, Second Lt. Taylor Arvin Dwyer, Lee's Headquarters, Army of Northern Virginia, could hold his liquor and the men's attention. His call to stick for another round drew no objection from the other staff officers, certainly none from the junior staff aware of their inferior rank.

They all liked Tad, who at 6'2" was taller than most and had sparkling blue eyes and thick, curly black hair that always seemed to be in place. Clean-shaven, he'd worn a full beard only briefly. Itched, he said, and made him feel old. Besides, he thought, covering the shape of his face detracted from his good looks. With his broad smile and slightly droopy jowls, he was a bull terrier of a man, one that could scare a stranger up a tree but was down-home friendly to anybody who'd just say *Good boy!* to him.

Tad was a great storyteller, unsparing in his use of hyperbole. When he started on a yarn, the men listened up. They never knew which path he'd taken at the fork of fact and fiction, but they always took him seriously on military matters. He had good ears, the

1

couriers said, and he always seemed to be on top of things, especially those involving troop movements.

Still passing the bottle, the men quieted down—all except one. "All right, Tad, sir, dazzle us with your customary brilliance," said Staff Sgt. Red Dawkin, nicknamed Talker. His appropriate given name was Isaiah. His smooth, freckled face seemed engulfed by a big smile, and his sense of humor was contagious. Red loved his pranks and horseplay, but he had a serious side. An imposing figure, at 6'5" towering over even Tad, he stood ready to mix it up with his big fists over any little thing. "You bound to have some 'portant news," Red continued, "or you wouldn't be so hell bent on us havin' another round."

After a short look around, one which both commanded and confirmed attentiveness, Tad spoke. "Well, I'm not positive about all this, but I'm telling you we're up to something big," he said. "And if you ask me, I think we'll be staying with Lee."

"*Staying with Lee?*" Red asked. "What'n the hell does that mean?"

Tad let the suspense build as he poured himself a drink.

"Look here," he resumed, "we all know Lee's itchin' to get at McClellan, right? But Lee, he wants to be the one to say where and when he'll do it. He wants to surprise McClellan and force him to take a stand. But of course, any stand Lee would take would be at McClellan's disadvantage."

"Aw, get on with it, Tad," said Red, already impatient. "What's your big news?"

Tad paused for effect. "Gentlemen," he announced, "Lee is going to divide the army, and we're going to take this war to the North!"

"Bullshit," Red said flatly. "I don't believe that for a *minute.*"

"Me, neither!" declared Lt. Bert Weatherly. Usually quiet and reserved, he seemed agitated, almost offended. "That's just plain too risky. Lee'd never do such a thing, least not this far north."

Weatherly, *much* shorter than Red, had huge ears that he tried to cover with shoulder-length hair. His full beard blended well with his dark green eyes, and despite his high-pitched voice, he was soft-spoken.

As if to challenge them both, Tad straightened to his full height and spoke again: "How much you put on it?"

Weatherly retorted: "How'd you know?"

Pleased with the stunned reaction he had anticipated, Tad

flashed a knowing smile at both Dawkin and Weatherly. "I ain't about to tell you—but mark my words, boys: We're fixin' to move north."

"You been stickin' your nose where it don't belong," Weatherly said. "You privy to some orders you're not s'posed to know nothin' about, ain't you, Tad?" At this point Tad looked at his friend, Second Lt. Billy Dean Tanner, as if to invite Tanner, a fellow courier, to give confirmation. Tanner sat dead still, communicating neither yea nor nay.

"Listen," Tad said. "Lincoln replaced Pope with McClellan as commander of the Army of the Potomac. You boys know Pope didn't do much of nothin' right at Second Manassas, so Lincoln's gone back to McClellan. You remember how McClellan lost his nerve in the Peninsula campaign last summer, and everybody knows he's slow as cold molasses."

"So what?" Red took a swig of whiskey and glared as he wiped his mouth with the back of his hand. "What are you tellin' us here, Tad? What are you gettin' at?"

"We'll be leavin' Frederick, clear out of Maryland, then march into Pennsylvania and raise some hell in Yank territory. Lee's gonna leave McClellan so far behind that Little Napoleon won't be able to catch us 'til it's too late.

"Way I see it, Lee's been wantin' to take this army northward ever since way back in early June, and our victory at Manassas gives him his chance. He's sick 'n' tired of the talk about him not being the fighter that Joe Johnston is."

Weatherly's face reddened as his voice rose: "I wouldn't be so sure about that," he protested. "Most people think Lee's a *lot* better general than Johnston."

Tad glared at him. "Bert, if Joe Johnston hadn't been wounded, Lee would still be military adviser to Jeff Davis. You know as well as I do that Lee really hasn't proved himself in battle. Hell, it's common knowledge that he had more setbacks than he did successes early on, in western Virginia—even got outsmarted by Little Napoleon a time or two."

Rather than try to argue Tad down, Weatherly opted to change the subject and started griping about something the duty officer had done or said. Paying little attention to the lieutenant's harangue, Tad set down his cup of whiskey and reached into his top left coat pocket for a cigar. Not feeling any, he quickly reached into his right inside coat pocket and found nothing. Then he patted his empty shirt pocket, and finally dug into his trouser pockets. No cigars! Tiny beads of perspiration formed on his forehead. Feeling hot and nauseated, he sagged to his knees on the damp earthen floor.

"What the hell you doin' on your knees, Tad—prayin' or boot lickin'?" Red teased him. Laughing, he pointed at his own muddy boots. "If you want to practice your boot lickin', you can start with mine."

Rising as quickly as he could, Tad chuckled nervously. "Uh … I lost my cigars … need to find 'em … see you in a little while," he mumbled, and bolted out of the tent.

"Damn fool!" said Red, grinning as he reached for Tad's abandoned drink. "Ain't *no* cigar worth leavin' good likker to go lookin' for." The men laughed appreciatively as he emptied the cup.

Outside the tent, Tad pressed his palm against his clammy forehead. His mouth was as dry as cotton, and he felt as if he were vibrating. With every beat of his pounding heart, he heard a surge of blood in his eardrums. A cold wave of fear and panic swept over him. He'd heard tell that a shiver like that meant someone was walking on your grave. Oh, my God, he thought. They'll be digging my grave this time tomorrow if I don't find … Hearing footsteps, he turned abruptly to find Billy Dean Tanner walking toward him.

"You all right, Tad?" Befitting his calm demeanor, Billy Dean had been sitting quietly next to Tad and was bewildered by his rambunctious friend's abrupt departure. The two had been close ever since First Manassas. Billy Dean had been a great comfort back in April, when Tad learned that his brother Art had been killed at Shiloh. Tad stayed drunk for three days and was on his way to becoming a bang pitcher when his soft-spoken fellow lieutenant straightened him out.

Billy Dean knew a couple of missing cigars wouldn't make Tad take off the way he had. "I don't understand," he said. "You've prob'ly got half a dozen boxes of cigars hid away, along with your good bourbon. Now, what's going on?"

Like most of the men, Billy Dean was shorter than Tad. He had brown eyes and a medium complexion, kept his hair short and his face smooth, and was always neat in dress and appearance. None of the men knew him well, but they felt comfortable around him. Neither judgmental nor opinionated, he maintained an air of reassurance and a commanding posture but demanded nothing of them.

Billy Dean had little in common with Tad. Mild-mannered,

4

he kept a low profile and didn't smoke, drink, gamble, or chase women. Yet, their enduring friendship wasn't really surprising: Tad would've resented anyone who tried to outshine him or best him in anything, and Billy Dean would be bored in the company of someone like himself. They knew one another inside out, and the bond between them was strong.

As Tad turned, Billy Dean saw the concern in his friend's eyes. Tad shook his head in a gesture of disgust. "Oh, God," he moaned. "I've really done it this time. You won't believe what a mess I've made, Billy. I'm gonna get court-martialed for sure."

Billy held up his hand as if to ward off the outburst. "Whoa, whoa! Hold on here, and tell me the hell what you're talking about. I've seen you act dumb as a tree stump, but I've never heard you talkin' like this."

Many a time, Billy Dean had retrieved Tad from the drinking holes and brothels that spring up around an army's flanks and rear. "Come on Tad," he'd always insist. "Gotta get you outta here."

"Oh God, Billy, I need your word of honor that you won't repeat any of this, even at a court-martial."

"You have my word, now hush all this about a court-martial and tell me what's going on."

"Well, I really did want a cigar, but it wasn't 'til I reached for one that I realized what I'd done. Lee's going to have a rope around my neck for sure."

Billy Dean's patience was gone.

"*Dammit*, Tad! What did you do that was so terrible?"

"I … I lost the orders I was supposed to deliver to General Hill. I wrapped 'em around my cigars and put 'em in my coat pocket, and I reached for 'em and they was gone."

"You mean that special order early this afternoon?"

"Yeah," Tad replied, sighing heavily.

"Like the ones I delivered to McLaws?" Billy asked, as calmly as he could.

"Yeah, those," Tad said. "Did you look at McLaws' copy? Tells all about Lee dividin' the army." Though still a churning vat of fear, guilt, and desperation, he felt the pressure ease as he confided in Billy, and the details came pouring out. "I got a message at about 2 o'clock to get my butt over to Chilton's tent. Then Chilton gives me these orders and tells me to get them to D. H. Hill. So, I took 'em and folded 'em, and wrapped 'em around the cigars, and put 'em in my top left pocket. I *know* that's where I put 'em, it's where I *always* keep 'em. Anyhow, I walked over to the livery and put my name in for a mount. Sergeant says none was available because all the couriers had 'em out, then he tells me they could get me one from cavalry but it would take about forty-five minutes.

Tad paused, looked down, took a deep breath, and continued. "I was walkin' around to kill time and come upon a crap game. For a little while, I just watched, but then this feller motions for me to join in. Hell, you know how it is, Billy. Somebody passed a bottle around, time kinda got away from me. I had me a few snorts, and the next thing you know I'm hittin' it big! I reckon I just got caught up in it and forgot about everything except how I was winnin'. I guess I must've played for over an hour."

"You never went back to get your mount?" Billy asked evenly, almost softly.

Tad kept staring at the ground, unable to show his face. "Plumb forgot all about it. Never gave it a thought 'til I reached for a cigar back there. *Damn*, Billy! What am I gonna' do?"

In stark silence, Billy Dean formed a mental picture of the cigars wrapped in white paper. He remembered exactly the outside heading on the copy he'd delivered to McLaws: *Sept. 9, 1862. Special Order 191, Headquarters, Army of Northern Virginia.* "You're right, Tad," he said. "You're in real deep."

"Billy, you've got to help me figure out what to do."

"All right, listen: Ain't much daylight left, so let's hightail it back to where you were shootin' craps and look around. Do you know any of the other men there? If you do, we need to talk to 'em. Somebody must've found that packet."

"Not by name, but I'd know 'em if I saw 'em," Tad said, appearing to be regaining his composure.

From the livery, they retraced Tad's steps until they came to a trampled area amid a stand of trees, mostly maples with leaves turning to yellow and red.

"This's it!" Tad said excitedly. "This here's the exact spot we was throwin' dice!"

"If you dropped that package in a place like this, somebody surely would've seen it..." Billy Dean's voice trailed off. "Let's ask around and see if we can find anybody else that was here."

Over the next half hour Tad and Billy asked at least fifteen men if they knew of anybody who'd been shooting craps that afternoon. Just as their hopes began to fade, they got lucky. "Yeah, I remember hearin' this one feller complainin' about how much he'd lost," a corporal told them. "Said it seemed like he couldn't roll nothin' but snake-eyes."

"Can you find him for us?" Ted implored the young soldier. "It's important."

Within minutes they were in the presence of a gruff sergeant with a scraggly beard and a scowl on his leathery face.

Tad got right to it. "Look, this afternoon while we were shootin' craps I lost some cigars wrapped in a couple of pieces of paper. Don't know how they dropped out of my pocket. I was on a roll."

"You sure as hell were. I don't feel sorry for you losing some damn *cigars*. I lost good *money* while you're rollin' nothin' but deuces and boxcars. Now here you are worried about what you're gonna *smoke?*"

"No, sergeant, I don't really care about the cigars. Y'see, they were wrapped in letters I got from my brother who was killed at Shiloh. That's *real* important to me. You know the name of anybody else who was around there?"

"Naw, don't know any of 'em. Fact, I got into the game just 'fore you showed up ... Now that I think about it, though, I believe somebody *did* light up a cigar after you left."

Tad started to feel sweaty and queasy again.

"Thanks," he said half-heartedly, and motioned to Billy for them to get moving.

Tad started off at a rapid pace but soon slowed, sat down on a log, and put his head in his hands. "Sweet Jesus, I feel like a pig on a spit," he told Billy. "Between feeling guilty and worrying about gettin' court-martialed, I can't even think straight. What do I do now?"

"Well, this has to be reported to Chilton," Billy said matter-of-factly. "We need to rectify things by gettin' him to make another copy of the orders for Hill."

"Hill?" At first Tad didn't get the connection. "*Shit!* Forgot all about *him* not having orders. Now Hill won't know what the hell he's supposed to do. Damn, Billy, I still can't believe I forgot those orders. My life won't be worth two cents after I tell Chilton what I've done."

"I don't know about that, but for now just be thankful that those orders are still somewhere in camp. At least they can't fall into enemy hands. They're lost on *our* ground."

"*The enemy!*" Billy's words pierced Tad's consciousness like

7

a dagger. What if the Yanks get hold of those orders? Even briefly considering the ramifications of it pushed him further into despair. Then, a quiet spell later, he began to think a bit more clearly.

"A package like that wouldn't lie around long, no matter where I dropped it. And whoever found it would rip off the paper and put the cigars in their pocket. Being a gambling man, I'd bet my life on that. So it's gotta be one of two things: Either those orders have been returned to headquarters or they've been torn up, maybe thrown away."

Billy, sensing an uplifting in Tad's morose spirit, picked right up on his logic. "Y'know, you're probably right. Let's say you are. If the orders *have* been found and returned to headquarters, then it stands to reason Chilton has notified Hill and he knows what to do. Of course, it also means they're probably looking for you this very minute. On the other hand, if the cigars were found and the wrapper was thrown away, General Hill won't know what he's supposed to do or where he's supposed to go. We'd best be on our way to Chilton."

Silence shrouded them on the fifteen-minute return to headquarters. As they drew closer, Tad spoke. "If I get outta' this in one piece, I'll be a changed person," he vowed. "I swear to God."

"Sure you will, Tad." Billy was sarcastic. "Better be careful when you take an oath. Besides, what would you do different? Quit drinkin' and smokin'?' Give up gamin'—or women? I know you better'n that."

"Yeah, you're right," Tad said despondently. "This here is pointless talk anyhow. We both know I'm headed for court-martial."

Billy didn't say so, but he knew Tad was right. A court-martial probably was inevitable. Knowing what Tad had to be thinking, he cautioned him. "I think you should fess up to Chilton. I know it sounds scary, but it's better than runnin' and tryin' to get away without tellin' anybody."

"Yes, it's scary as hell. You're probably right Billy, but it's just not in me to do that. There's *got* to be a way around this. If I confess they'll *hang* me."

Billy Dean fell silent. He could add nothing.

They heard the faint noise of men and wagons in the distance and they figured part of the army was pulling out.

Not Hill's division, Tad thought. He was hit by another wave of nausea, feeling fright and panic at the realization of the horrible thing he'd done. For the first time, he understood why a man would take his own life. Tad thought of his father back home in LaVergne, and his mother, dead now for almost twenty-five years. He thought about the shame he might bring upon his brother Louis, and his sisters, Lucy and Jane. He thought of his brother Arthur, who'd given his life for the Confederacy. The family handled Art's death better than they will mine, he thought. Art died honorably.

The more he thought about all this, the sicker he became. His legs felt weak and rubbery, as if they would buckle under him at the next step. The nearby trees loomed like gallows. There was the limb the rope would be slung over, its vines entwined into a noose. Up ahead another line of trees stood tall, like his buddies at attention, all eyes focused on the stupid officer who let a crap game overshadow his duty. I'm as good as dead, Tad thought.

CHAPTER TWO

After the twelve-minute walk to headquarters, Tad walked into the tent summoning every ounce of energy he could muster to look sharp and poised, as if nothing in the world was wrong. Within seconds, his superior, Major Edward Wilson, caught a glimpse of him. "Where the hell you been Tad? We need you on courier."

Before Tad could respond, the major continued. "Get your gear packed, secure a mount, and be back here in one hour sharp." Major Wilson wasted no words, nor did he wait for any reply from Tad. No mention was made of any lost orders.

Tad had trouble finding Billy Dean, who was at the far end of the HQ tent. When he finally spied him and caught his eye, Tad motioned to Billy to follow him outside. They pushed and shoved their way through the crowd. The army was preparing for immediate departure. Officers were everywhere and the noise level was rapidly increasing. The clanging of metal against metal, the whinny of horses, and the brazen voices of sergeants barking orders combined to make for a scene of controlled chaos. Tad need not have been concerned about anyone overhearing his conversation with Billy.

"I don't understand it, Billy. Nobody acted like anything was wrong. I sure as hell wasn't going to ask if General Hill was all set to move out with the others. Somethin's goin' on I don't understand. How would Hill know what to do without orders?"

Billy wasted no time in replying: "Maybe your luck's changed. Know what I mean? Maybe somebody found the orders and got them to Hill. Or maybe Hill really didn't need the orders cause he was in meetings with Longstreet and Jackson and the others."

Billy made one last attempt to persuade Tad to come clean and confess: "Are you sure, Tad? Are you sure you don't want to make a clean breast of things right now, before lies and circumstances stack up against you?"

"No way, Billy. They'll hang me."

"Well then if I was you—if you're not plannin' on fessin' up—I'd just follow orders and say nothin'. Don't borrow trouble. Know what I mean? If something is wrong you'll find out soon enough. Until that happens keep a tight rein on your emotions, and do what you've been told."

Billy rarely gave advice to anyone, but now he sounded like a domineering father or a stern Dutch uncle. Tad knew Billy was right. As they walked toward their tents in silence, Tad reminded himself how lucky he was to have a friend like Billy.

With nothing left to say, Billy took his leave and headed toward his tent. Tad continued on and noticed that rows and rows of tents had already been dismantled. "Damn," he mused to himself. "Why can't these guys just let us do our own packing?" He hated it when those guys took it upon themselves to pack up his gear without his being there. Tad was thinking mostly of the two bottles of bourbon he kept well hidden.

The exodus from the campground just south of Frederick on the night of the ninth of September and in the early morning hours of the tenth was an exercise in logistics. Moving these divisions out of the Frederick encampment was a task of the first order. There was no room for error. Men, horses, and wagons were moving out. Ordnance was being readied for transport.

Activity was becoming more intense. Tad overheard a colonel of cavalry having it out with a colonel of artillery about who should form column first. "If I don't get my cannon and limbers on this road within an hour I'll be hopelessly behind the infantry. Tell me, colonel, what good is artillery after a battle's already been fought?"

The colonel of cavalry retorted, "Yeah, and I suppose the cavalry can deal with skirmishers by following the artillery." Exchanges like this didn't surprise Tad because each branch of service thought itself less expendable than the others.

Relieved to see his tent still standing, Tad wasted no time packing his gear. He'd done this many times, or so it seemed, and he'd learned long ago to travel light. He had very few clothes and a minimum of personal possessions and paraphernalia. The bourbon and cigars presented the biggest challenge. He carefully wrapped the two bottles of bourbon among a few of his clothes and stuffed them into his knapsack, after which he placed the two letters from Art and

11

Jane into a side pocket. He put his remaining clothes and two boxes of cigars into his haversack. He rolled his two blankets into a long bundle secured at his waist, slung over his right shoulder, and then down his backside to his left hip. In addition to his officer's sword and scabbard, Tad always carried a holstered sidearm attached to his belt, along with a tin of caps and an ammunition box. He also carried another small leather bag in which he kept the remaining loose cigars and a few eating utensils.

After he was packed up, Tad growled and muttered under his breath. "All I have to do now is secure a mount. All right, Dwyer, do you think you can remember to get a horse this time?" Then he found himself mumbling that he owed Billy Dean big time. "Billy thinks I should confess, but he's not in my shoes. It's not his hide. Just can't bring myself to turn myself in. I'm gonna lick this thing. Damned if I turn myself in long as nobody's hurt."

Daybreak was now but four short hours away. Lee wanted to have all forces on the road by noon on the tenth, but now this appeared to be unlikely. Jackson confided in Turner Ashby: "If we march swiftly to a position just east of Martinsburg, we'll be ready to spring forth on the Feds at daybreak tomorrow. I plan to have this part of the operation completed by early afternoon on the eleventh. Then we'll beat a march to Bolivar Heights. We've got to be ready to join with McLaws and Walker as they close from Loudon Heights and Maryland Heights. Their divisions should be in position late on the eleventh and certainly no later than dawn on the twelfth."

Meanwhile, General Lee was going over his plans with Chilton: "Invasion of Pennsylvania depends on the early surrender of the feds at Harpers Ferry. I'm taking a big risk here—dividin' our forces into four parts. If the plans get muddled, or if defenses are stronger than I anticipate, this entire operation could end in disaster." Chilton listened, but made no response. Lee continued, "If something goes wrong we may need to stand and fight McClellan, but I'm counting on McClellan being his usual slow-poke self."

Chilton thought it best not to comment on Lee's remarks. He hadn't been asked to comment. The general, after all, was only verbalizing his thoughts and doubts. Chilton was acutely aware that Lee was in constant distress because of the injury to his hands. Back on August 31, after the second battle of Manassas, Lee had been standing near his horse Traveller as he often did, holding the reins while talking to several staff officers. Suddenly, Traveller was spooked. He reared up and Lee fell. Instinctively, Lee broke his fall with his hands, spraining one and breaking a small bone in the other. Because both hands were in splints, he was unable to ride and had to be transported by ambulance. Chilton would often hear Lee expressing hushed complaints about his hands. "If it weren't for these hands..."

Only two days ago Lee had expressed himself to Chilton: "I hate dictating orders. Feel more secure writing them out. At this rate I'm afraid it'll be another couple of weeks before I can handle the orders and the daily correspondence with the president. I know it puts a burden on you, but please bear with me."

"No problem," General Chilton responded, "but please allow for my slowness in taking dictation. I also wish you'd double-check everything. Make sure I get things straight."

Plans for the invasion of Pennsylvania had come to fruition on the evening of September 3, shortly after Lee's accident with Traveller. Lee had summoned General James (Pete) Longstreet to his private tent. Lee felt a strong urge to talk over his plans with Pete, who was never one to hide his disagreement or to pretend agreement like a sycophant.

Longstreet was slow to reply. He was a contemplative type, not given to impetuous outbursts or quick retorts, but on this issue he disagreed with Lee. "I'm concerned with what you hope to gain from it. What's the immediate objective?"

Lee looked Longstreet squarely in the eyes and without any hesitation replied: "First, we need to live off the land of the northern farmers and give our Virginians an opportunity to lie in their crops for the winter. We've devoured much of the Shenandoah Valley and the longer we can keep action away from the valley the better.

"Of key importance we need to provide an opportunity for the Confederate sympathizers in Maryland to show their true colors by coming into our ranks.

"Then, as long as we're moving northward, McClellan and the Union headquarters have got to be worried about the security of Washington. With us up north there's no way McClellan will go back toward Richmond. Richmond is safest when we draw Union armies in pursuit of us.

"And, Pete, you know I want to engage McClellan on a field of battle of my choice rather than his.

"Mostly though, I'd like to make a move that would persuade France or England to recognize the Confederacy. If we can threaten the eastern seaboard around Philadelphia and Baltimore we might weaken the resolve of the Union, especially those who've never agreed with Lincoln's stance against the South."

Then Lee surprised Longstreet: "We need to put Baltimore under siege."

Now Pete challenged his superior: "How are we going to have enough ordnance to put Baltimore under siege?"

It was Lee's turn again. He spoke slowly and with great deliberation: "With Bedford Forrest and Jeb Stuart, we can form a constantly moving semi-circle of cavalry around Baltimore, from the northeast, to the west, to the south. We have a fair bit of artillery with us. By spreading it out I'm counting on McClellan to overestimate our strength. At the same time Hampton and Morgan will head toward Wilmington and the Delaware, and feign toward Philadelphia. I'd expect very little opposition in that area because of the concentration of Union forces down to the south around Washington."

"What about the Chesapeake?" asked Longstreet. "I don't see how we can put the squeeze on Baltimore if we can't control the Chesapeake."

"You're right on that count," Lee retorted. "We won't be able to stop activity on the port side of Baltimore, but I think our forces on the other three sides can tie up communication and commerce. The railroads will be key. I'm countin' on Stuart and Forrest to disrupt all rails leading south out of Baltimore toward Washington. And I'm countin' on Hampton and Morgan to take out all the rails leading north out of Baltimore toward Philadelphia and Wilmington."

At this point, Longstreet was silent. He had tremendous respect for Robert Lee. That they often disagreed only pointed to the fact that Pete Longstreet felt secure enough to tell his commander exactly what he thought. Longstreet believed that he didn't have to guard his words or disguise his thoughts. This was, of course, a credit to both men, but especially to Lee.

Lee was pensive. He frowned in silence. His eyebrows furrowed. He hesitated as if he had left something out, but he didn't know what. "See something I've overlooked?"

Longstreet remained silent for a few more seconds and then replied: "It's a daring plan. Risky as hell. The big thing as far as I'm concerned is our line of supply. You planning a constant line of supply?"

"I don't see how we can." Lee replied. "I think our best bet is to live off the Union, cattle, game, clothing, shoes, you name it. I won't stand for plundering or laying waste, understand, but we must forage just as Yanks have foraged."

Longstreet became silent again. Longstreet knew well that sooner or later these two armies must meet and square off in a battle the likes of which had never been seen on the American continent. Longstreet was thinking deeply, trying to shoot holes in Lee's plans. Playing the devil's advocate was part of his job. "Where do you aim to encounter McClellan?"

Now Lee was the quiet one. After a few seconds he started to speak, then stopped. After another few seconds he shook his head from side to side, as if he were saying *no* to one of his own inner thoughts. "This is the key to everything. I must trust McClellan to be McClellan."

At this, Longstreet quickly interrupted: "What is that supposed to mean?"

"Means he'll take his good sweet time in getting ready and organized to meet us on the field. He won't move against us until he's satisfied everything's in order. Even if Lincoln and his cabinet demand it, McClellan simply won't take risks. He'll be slow to pursue us into Pennsylvania for no other reason than McClellan is habitually slow. He fidgets around making sure everything is just right. He waits until all is ready, taking no chances about not having adequate supplies, equipment, and provisions. And he's very likely to overestimate the size of his opponent."

Longstreet commented: "There's no way you're gonna surprise him. Mustn't kid ourselves. Our army's being watched and scouted daily." Longstreet began stroking his beard and fidgeting with a wayward hair.

Lee was quick on the retort: "I think our best bet is to keep him guessing. If battle is to be joined I want to pick the time and place. Go after him before he can strike us. Do all the damage we can, feign a quick retreat, and then come at him with everything we have."

Lee stopped speaking, but before Longstreet could make any comment, he continued. "My best guess is we'll join battle somewhere south of Baltimore. I'll bet my life McClellan won't attempt to get to our north or west because he'll figure he must keep his main strength to the south of us, between us and Washington."

Once more Longstreet was silent. He rubbed his brow, tugged at his mustache, and squirmed in his chair. Pondering a few more seconds, Longstreet finally laid his cards on the table. "You know me. I much prefer the defense even when we're on offense. I agree your plan is sound except maybe for the last part in attacking McClellan. Certainly need to work the northerners into a frenzy. Scare the tar out of them. Still, I prefer a defensive strategy. Let him come at us."

Longstreet paused, as if to invite Lee to rebut. But Lee remained silent. Longstreet continued, "What makes you think we can overpower McClellan? His troops will surely outnumber ours. If the outcome is no better or worse than a draw, we'll have lost our edge. We need more than a strategic victory. We need a tactical victory."

Lee was slow to speak. He was hoping Longstreet wouldn't ask this question, at least not in such a direct manner. "Your question is a painful one. It points to the weakest part of my plan. We're sure to achieve strategic gains and create divisions. Yet I can't say I'm confident of tactical victory. We're speaking here of defeating superior numbers who command unending reserves of men and ordnance. A clear victory will require some daring generalship with swift and efficient maneuvering, to say nothing of valiant soldiering. If we win, it could spell disaster for the Union. If we lose, it could be the end of the Confederacy."

Now both men fell silent. Each knew there was little left to be said. Each knew the issue at hand was an all-or-nothing proposition. Each knew Lee was contemplating a gamble which could backfire and spell ignominious defeat for the Confederacy. Or it could spell glorious victory. Common belief held that Union victory demanded the unconditional surrender of the Confederacy. But the only necessary condition for the Confederacy to be victorious was the Union's recognition of secession.

Lee looked directly at Longstreet and nodded his head. "That's it Pete. It's done! I've made my decision."

Lee started to extend his hand to Longstreet in a gesture of warmth, but he suddenly realized his bandaged hand was not able to withstand even the pressure of a handshake. "These damn hands will be the death of me yet." He lifted his right hand in salute. "Thanks, Pete. You've been a great help."

Longstreet returned the salute. "I only hope there's nothing we've overlooked."

CHAPTER THREE

After the surrender of Harpers Ferry on Monday, September 15, Jackson, Walker, and McLaws were again on the march. They headed north to reunite with Lee, Longstreet, and D. H. Hill at Hagerstown. Jackson left General A. P. Hill behind to supervise the surrender and parole of the Union prisoners. By mid-day Tuesday, the sixteenth, the Army of Northern Virginia—except for A. P. Hill at Harpers Ferry and the three regiments guarding the South Mountain gaps—was encamped just outside Hagerstown. Lee did not anticipate that McClellan would pursue him, but as a matter of precaution the three regiments at the South Mountain passes would perform a rear guard action.

Just north of Hagerstown, Lee sat in his headquarters tent surrounded by his top aides. They had been up most of the night. Outside the bugle call of reveille sounded and the camp stirred to life. Today the Confederate army would press farther north, leading to an attack upon Harrisburg. Lee's plan was to move as many men as possible on railroad cars from Hagerstown, this small town on the Maryland-Pennsylvania border, to Carlisle, just west of Harrisburg. Hagerstown, in the north central part of Maryland, was the southern terminus of the rail spur running north and south through Greencastle, Chambersburg, Shippensburg, and Carlisle to Harrisburg. On the fifteenth, one of Longstreet's divisions seized the Hagerstown rail station and secured the surrounding area. Lee intended to use the cars as much as possible in the movement toward Harrisburg.

A half hour ago Lee startled everybody at the headquarters tent when he called out "General Stuart, I need you." Lee was fuming

17

because he could not locate his cavalry commander, the colorful and sometimes dashing James Ewell Brown Stuart.

Red-haired Jeb Stuart had just finished polishing his boots. Now, having arranged his uniform and submitted himself to his own admiring inspection, he was in the far corner of the headquarters tent conversing with several of his lieutenants. That's when he heard Lee's voice ring out over the din and bustle of the host of officers gathered in the huge tent. In no time the red-bearded Stuart, with his plumed hat cradled in his arm, stood in front of General Lee.

"General Stuart, I must find out exactly where General McClellan is. Almost every move I plan depends on my having up to the minute detail on McClellan's whereabouts. According to the latest information from the three regiments at South Mountain, McClellan shows no signs of giving pursuit. I don't understand this. I know McClellan's slow and deliberate, but I just can't believe he would permit invasion of Pennsylvania without pursuit."

Before heading north to Hagerstown, Lee had dispatched couriers to deliver orders to the colonels of the three regiments still guarding the gaps at South Mountain: "Break camp and follow the army north. Keep vigilance in guarding your flanks and rear. Communicate twice daily with headquarters. Employ constant recognizance as to the whereabouts of McClellan."

"Stuart, I want you to set out to the south and east toward South Mountain. You need to do alert recognizance at the three gaps—Turner, Fox, and Crampton's. Follow every promising lead, even if you have to go beyond South Mountain. Remember, as far as we know McClellan is still west of Frederick. Report back to me twice daily by courier without fail. Am I making myself perfectly clear?" At times, Lee felt he had not been precise enough in issuing verbal orders such as this, especially to Jeb Stuart.

Stuart gave a snappy reply, not asking for any further detail. "Yes, sir."

Lee was still undecided about whether to destroy the Cumberland Valley Railroad. Lee confessed to Longstreet, "I'm having difficulty deciding whether or not to destroy the rails. The railroad will soon be behind us. Destroy it and thwart McClellan. Preserve it and McClellan will have the means to transport his army northward very quickly. Destroy it and we have no quick means of escape. Preserve it and we have a built-in line of supply to the north end of the Shenandoah Valley. What do you think?"

Longstreet replied forcefully: "You know me. Keep my

defensive options open. Don't destroy the rails at least till we have it confirmed that McClellan's in pursuit."

Lee was pensive, staring down at his wounded hands. "If I were in McClellan's shoes I certainly wouldn't stand still for an opposing force heading toward Harrisburg. On the other hand, maybe Lincoln's intent on keeping McClellan between Washington and us. That's fine with me. I'll go with you on this one, Pete. Let the railroad be."

Lee turned to Chilton, "Write up orders for D. H. Hill to keep everything under as much guard as possible until we secure the rails to the east and south of Harrisburg."

Lee assigned Jackson's, McLaws', and Walker's divisions to the cars. This, of course, tended to create dissension among the other divisions, especially Longstreet's. Longstreet's men thought they should have been on the cars. Longstreet had great respect for Jackson, but at times he was downright jealous of the reputation that had been pinned on Jackson ever since the first battle of Manassas when Brigadier General Barnard E. Bee shouted to his men about Jackson standing there *like a stonewall.* No one was quite sure if that meant Jackson was standing firm in anticipation of repulsing an attack, or if, as some say, Jackson was standing there doing nothing. Regardless, the name became attached to the more flattering interpretation, endowing Jackson with a reputation of strength, power, and determination, and his brigade gloried in being known forever after as the Stonewall Brigade.

Even General Lee did not enjoy the powerful and positive reputation that surrounded Jackson. Lee still ruminated with resentment following the biting words of an editorial he'd read recently:

Lee was appointed commander of the army only this past June 1862, just before the Seven Days battles. Before that he proved a failure in his campaigns in western Virginia. Jackson has been with the Army of Northern Virginia since a year ago May 1861, shortly after the voters of Virginia ratified the Ordinance of Secession. Jackson knows how to march, how to fight, and how to lead. Lee has yet to demonstrate these qualities.

Daniel Harvey Hill was also very critical of Lee, at least in his private conversation with his brother-in-law, Thomas Jackson: "I don't care what anybody says, Lee's tactics at Malvern were terrible.

19

He gave little thought to the consequences of open field assault on a battery or a line of infantry making an open field charge in the face of entrenched infantry with strong artillery support."

Hill and Jackson were good friends as well as brothers-in-law, being married to the Morrison sisters. They were both strong-willed and resolute in their beliefs and ways. While Jackson always kept his own counsel and was very careful not to speak his mind, Hill was constantly expressing his unhappiness and dissatisfaction with almost everything. People attributed Hill's temperament to the fact he was in constant pain due to a spinal problem in his years at West Point.

Hill greatly admired his brother-in-law and honestly felt that if the war evolved into a prolonged struggle, one day Thomas Jackson would be in command of all the armies of the Confederacy. Both men were very religious and held firm to their conviction that the sacred *Cause* of the Confederacy was just and right and blessed by the Almighty. Hill's brand of Presbyterianism permitted him to proceed fearlessly and defiantly in battle. "If my work on earth is finished, I'll fall in battle, but if the Almighty still needs me, it means nothing can bring me down. So what's to be afraid of?"

Hill had recently been denied promotion. He complained to Jackson, "I feel strongly that I should have been promoted. Deserve to be a Lieutenant General. Know I'm outspoken at times, so what? I reckon the higher-ups are down on me because I was critical of Jeb Stuart's antics, especially his ride around McClellan's army during the peninsular campaign. Well, that's just tough. Still think Stuart's a show-off."

"You've got to understand," Jackson counseled Hill. "Big brass don't like people like us speakin' our minds. You've got to play the system. Do what you're told. Can't be criticizing your peers and still expect to be promoted."

"You know something I don't?" Hill said as he looked at Jackson.

"Well, almost everybody knows you and Longstreet weren't particularly fond of each other while you were at West Point. Whatever you say or do, don't be bad-mouthin' him. I'd like to see you promoted but you must learn to keep your own counsel. And that means keeping your mouth shut."

*****

Lee issued strict orders about troop behavior and deportment while in northern territory. Lee placed his generals under strict orders. "Foraging is necessary and expected, but there shall be no intentional laying waste to land, houses, or property. Civilians are to be treated with respect and left alone. If the locals taunt the army it must be endured. Only if troops are physically assaulted or attacked are we justified in exerting authority, making military arrests, or taking prisoners."

Hill's troops disregarded Lee's orders. His division was the last of the divisions to make the northbound trek. Only the regiments coming up from the South Mountain gaps were behind. Hill's troops were spoiling for confrontation with Yanks. The confrontation could be military or civil—it didn't matter. All they wanted was a chance to vent pent-up anger and frustration at the Northern devils who were responsible for the present misery of the Southerners. If Hill's men found blankets, shoes, shirts, pants, or drawers, then too bad for the locals.

Hill's men spared nothing. The rebels did not torch buildings or rape women, but little was spared along a mile-wide line, following the railroad northward from Hagerstown to Chambersburg. No Northerner ever dreamed of such devastation. Up until now most of the North had been spared, except for Washington. Only in Washington and north toward Frederick, Maryland, was the civilian population under threat.

Lee issued orders to Bedford Forrest to move his cavalry northward to Chambersburg: "Proceed to Chambersburg and capture the military supply depot. We can make good use of their provisions and supplies." It did not take long for Forrest to secure the surrender of the Pennsylvania militia, taking the entire company as prisoners. "We'll hold 'em until the entire army passes north. After that we'll parole 'em," Forrest reported to Lee.

The supply depot proved to be a horn of plenty. From this point on there would be no justification for stealing clothing from local people. Even for the Yankee haters in Hill's division there could now be no excuse. The depot yielded overcoats by the thousands, shirts, pants, drawers, and socks. The only disappointment was there were not many shoes, but rumor had it that shoes could be found in Gettysburg.

Upon setting up camp that evening about ten miles north of Hagerstown, Lee issued a call for a meeting of his generals. This would be the first time he took all his generals into his confidence

21

concerning plans for the invasion of Pennsylvania. While the army was resting after the long day's march, Tad, Billy Dean, Bert Weatherly, and the rest of the couriers were busy notifying the generals of the meeting at Lee's headquarters.

Once courier duty was accomplished, Tad sat relaxing outside his tent. He was thinking about how nice it would be to go to a local tavern, but then his conscience began to bother him. He scolded himself and then sulked for a minute as his mind wandered back to the events leading to the lost orders. As he gazed downward toward his filthy shoes he muttered to himself, "Still don't understand it. A week's gone by and there's no hint of trouble. Hill seemed to know exactly what to do." Since the beginning of the march northward, Tad had not ceased thinking about the lost orders. The old feelings of panic and nausea would return whenever he would review the events of the craps game. Tad still couldn't believe he'd completely forgotten about those orders. As unpleasant and alarming as all these feelings were, he felt it was better than a court-martial and the severe punishment that would follow. Tad concluded as he had countless other times, "Only one thing for me to do and that's keep my mouth shut."

Had it not been for General Daniel Harvey Hill's penchant to secure his own reputation, and his tendency to be overly sensitive to what he imagined to be slights, Tad might never have heard another word about those orders.

Hill hadn't seen Jackson since September 9, and therefore hadn't had an opportunity to question him about the orders. This he certainly intended to do. About a half hour prior to the meeting of the generals, Hill caught sight of Jackson and immediately went over to him. After a brief greeting, Hill said, "It was you, wasn't it, who wrote out my copy of orders 191?"

"Yeah, wrote a copy as soon as I read 'em. Sent 'em by courier. Lee was removing your division from my command and I wanted to be certain you knew 'bout it. I didn't know if Lee intended to have Chilton send you a copy. Why ask? Somethin' wrong?"

Hill, now visibly upset, answered abruptly:

"Yeah! Somethin's wrong all right. I swear Lee's got something against me. He figured I'd hear from you, so he didn't bother to have me officially notified. It's like I'm not important to him. Doesn't think enough of me to send me a copy of the damned orders. I swear he seems to have it in for me. Wish I knew why."

"Now, Dan'l," said Jackson, "you don't know all that to be

fact. I've told you before you're just too darn sensitive. Lee always has his reasons. Why don't we ask him about it right now, before the meeting?"

Buoyed up by Jackson, Hill agreed.

They walked over to the headquarters tent and sought out Lee, who was busy preparing the maps for the meeting. "Sorry to interrupt you, general, but we'd like a quick word with you."

"Certainly, but please make it brief," Lee replied, obviously displeased at having his train of thought broken.

Hill spoke right up: "General Lee, I'm troubled by the fact that all my information about our move northward came to me from General Jackson. Jackson copied the 191 orders to make certain I knew my division would be detached from his. What I'm troubled about is, well, I ... I ...'"

At this point Hill felt himself ill at ease and was filled with anxiety as he considered confronting his commanding officer with what amounted to personal criticism. To his credit, Hill looked straight into Lee's eyes as he spoke:

"Well, sir, I'd've appreciated a copy of those orders directly from you instead of hearing about everything second-hand from Jackson here."

There! He'd said it. He'd confronted Lee and expressed his concern. Hill was sure that nothing Lee could possibly say would make him feel differently.

"What's that you say, Hill? Why of course I sent you a copy of those orders. I had Chilton make seven copies. Let's see."

Lee paused as he began to recall methodically the various generals to whom he had sent Special Order 191. Lee lifted his left hand and started to count fingers with his bandaged right hand: "One, Longstreet, two, McLaws, three, Walker, four, Jackson, five, Hill." Then, running out of fingers Lee began again: Six, Stuart, and seven, the file copy. Yes, seven copies. You say you didn't get yours?"

Hill was outwardly composed, but he could hardly believe what he heard. Lee had not slighted him.

"No, sir. I didn't receive them." Hill replied.

"Better look into it, Hill. First double-check with Chilton. Then look to the couriers. Be sure to check your own operations. We can't have things like this getting lost. Is that all, Hill?" Lee asked, indicating that their meeting was concluded.

"Yes, sir. Thank you, sir." Taking leave of Lee, Hill smiled at Jackson. "Hear that, Thomas? Lee intended for me to have my own copy!"

Lee opened the meeting without fanfare: "Gentlemen, our immediate objective is Harrisburg. We will shell munitions factories near the Susquehanna River. Pennsylvania militia shouldn't be difficult to contend with. I figure McClellan is at best two days behind, if he's even in pursuit. General Stuart is presently on reconnaissance trying to find out exactly where McClellan is."

During the meeting, Tad, Billy Dean, and about seven other staff officers were assigned posts outside the headquarters tent to ensure security. Although they weren't allowed inside during these top-level meetings, they were considered trustworthy enough not to reveal any information they might overhear. Tad enjoyed being privy to such information. He always liked to think that he knew more about what was going on than anyone else.

Tad and Billy stood just outside the side entrance to the headquarters tent. They could not see the huge map Lee uncovered at the conference table, but they listened with rapt attention as Lee went on to explain his reasons for sparing the Cumberland Valley Railroad between Harrisburg and Hagerstown, reviewing the advantages and the disadvantages either way. Then, pointing to the roads and rail lines surrounding Harrisburg, Philadelphia, and Baltimore, he continued.

"I want the rail center in Harrisburg destroyed, but we'll safeguard the Northern Central Railroad because we need it as we head southward to Baltimore. Everybody clear on that? Put all rolling stock on the Northern Central. However, I want the Pennsylvania destroyed. Destroy all trunks and spurs extending eastward from Harrisburg to Reading and from Reading to Philadelphia.

"By October 1, I want Wade Hampton along with Morgan's Raiders, to've blocked all traffic on the Philadelphia, Wilmington & Baltimore between Philadelphia and Wilmington. Bend the rails. Torch all rolling stock. Destroy as much motive power as possible."

"Morgan, you take the Philadelphia-Wilmington district," Lee said, nodding at John Hunt Morgan, who had a penchant for destroying rails and cutting telegraph wires faster than the Yankees could repair them.

"I want Forrest and Stuart to possess and control the Northern Central from Harrisburg to Baltimore," he continued. "I intend to form a crescent around Baltimore extending westward from the Chesapeake on the northeast around the west side of the city and then southeastward to the Chesapeake again. I want John Pelham to lay siege to the entire area with his heaviest artillery. If his guns can reach the Port of Baltimore so much the better."

Lee revealed his timetable: "I want to begin these operations by Friday, October 10. Everything should be completed and in place by October 14. The siege of Baltimore will begin on October 15. It will extend until sometime in November."

"By then the Union forces will certainly be located somewhere between Washington and Baltimore. I'm guessing the decisive battle will be fought somewhere south of Baltimore. Perhaps near the junction of the B & O with the Philadelphia, Wilmington & Baltimore, or perhaps a few miles further south. I can't be certain just where the battle with McClellan will take place, but I'm quite positive the Union will make its greatest effort of the war.

"Questions?"

At this point an anxious officer confronted Lee. Neither Tad nor Billy Dean knew who it was, but whoever it was seemed to radiate an air of arrogance, even impatience.

Sounding more like a newspaper reporter than an officer, he asked: "General, what are our goals, our objectives?"

At first Lee looked aggravated by the question. Then he paused, as if deliberating, grabbed each of the lapels on his military jacket, and holding an authoritative military bearing, launched into a short review of his intentions and purposes.

Lee seemed unperturbed: "I see the goals of this campaign as three in number: undermining northern morale; winning English and French recognition of the Confederacy; and pressuring the Lincoln administration to bring an end to the war."

Lee then began to talk in a more strategic and political tone. "England, France, the Netherlands, Spain, Brazil, and several other nations have granted us the status of a belligerent. But belligerency isn't good enough. We need the sense of legitimacy that recognition affords. We need our sovereignty to be officially recognized."

As the meeting neared adjournment, Lee made a brief statement concerning policy in acknowledgement of receipt of orders. "By the way, I've been informed that a set of Special Order 191 was not received by General Hill. Henceforth, all Special Orders and specified General Orders will be verified as having been received by giving acknowledgement via return courier in writing. You generals need to make sure you receive verification."

As a last item of business, Lee reiterated his policy about

foraging and stealing. "Foraging will be increasingly necessary, but stealing, plundering, and unnecessary threatening of civilians will not be tolerated. I'll not tolerate such behavior. Now are there any further questions?"

After the meeting adjourned, General Hill felt deflated. Once again he believed he'd been slighted by Lee. Just as he was beginning to feel better about things the old fires of doubt were rekindled. "Why'd Lee have to go and mention my name in connection with the lost orders?" Hill asked Jackson.

As Hill thought about these things he felt somewhat mollified by having learned that Lee had sent him his own copy of the orders, but he still felt there was something not right in the relationship between Lee and himself. "I admit," he said to Jackson, "that maybe I'm acting a bit over sensitive, but I still feel things aren't right between Lee and me."

Then, eyeballing his brother-in-law, he vowed, "I intend to get to the bottom of the lost orders business. I just can't let go of such carelessness. Besides, Lee himself said I should follow it up."

Hill began looking around for Lee's chief of staff. Chilton would know which courier was responsible for the delivery of the orders to Hill. He made his way over to Chilton.

Robert Chilton was a self-composed person, who exuded an air of having things well in hand in spite of his scraggly appearance. His medium height and somewhat disheveled appearance belied his command of memory and events. Chilton was truly well prepared for his role as Lee's chief of staff. No detail escaped him. No item of business was too unimportant or too trivial for his attention.

Hill minced no words with Chilton. "Colonel Chilton, can you tell me which courier was responsible for delivering my copy of Special Order 191? I swear I never received my copy."

Chilton was quick to assume an intimidating stance. He stood up to his full height, at almost six feet tall. Then he cleared his throat and spoke in a deep baritone: "I don't remember. Hang on for a minute and I'll check the records. I usually make a note of these assignments."

Hill waited nervously for Chilton to go over to his dispatch file, yank open the sticky drawer, and find the 191 file.

Chilton thumbed through. "Hmm...looks like I gave your copy to Tad Dwyer."

"I don't place Dwyer. Is he here at headquarters right now? I'd like to get this matter resolved once and for all," Hill pressed.

"He was here a few minutes ago, a tall, husky man, about my height, curly black hair. Follow me. I think he may be over in the staff headquarters tent."

With Hill trailing by several paces, Chilton went quickly to the nearby staff officers' tent. Sure enough, Tad was there, along with Billy Dean and several of the other yaller dogs.

"Dwyer."

Tad looked up and when he saw Chilton he immediately stiffened. Tad began to feel nauseous, as though he'd just been kicked in the groin. After all this time, he dared to hope the incident had been forgotten.

"Dwyer, General Hill wants to speak with you. Over here," Chilton said brusquely.

Before Tad had a chance to ponder his situation, he was in the presence of Major General Daniel Harvey Hill.

"Damn," Tad cursed to himself.

"General Hill, this is Second Lieutenant Tad Dwyer."

Tad saluted.

Hill just nodded. "Dwyer, Colonel Chilton just informed me that you were the courier assigned to deliver Special Order 191 to me, back on the ninth of September, at Frederick, Maryland. Is that correct?"

Tad thought, Mustn't look scared. Keep calm. It's the end, Dwyer. Truth will be out. I'll feel better after I confess and get it off my chest. Gawd, I'm feeling sick with dread.

Tad had gone over his confession a thousand times. There was nothing left to do but come clean. Poker was fine when you had some cards, but he no longer had any cards.

"Yes, sir, that's correct. I was supposed—"

Hill cut him short.

"I just now found out that the orders I received were a copy sent to me by General Jackson. General Lee intended for me to have my own copy of those orders, but I never received them. Chilton here says you were the courier. I want to know what happened. Did you deliver those orders to my headquarters or did you not?"

Hearing Hill's spiel, Tad's mind was ablaze. He thought, "Wait. What was …? What was that Hill just said? *Jackson* had sent *him* a copy of the orders? So that's how Hill knew what to do. That puts a whole new light on things. Nobody's been hurt or killed because of my stupidity. Hell, why should I get crucified when no real harm's been done?"

And suddenly, without any hesitation or further forethought Tad Dwyer put his entire future on the line: "Yes, sir. That's correct. I most certainly did."

Tad answered without any forethought of the possible dire consequences. Armed with new conviction and a faith in his ability to convince anyone of anything, Tad fabricated his reply. "Yes, sir, gave 'em to a sergeant at your headquarters. Late afternoon. Remember it well. The livery didn't have a mount for me but said they'd try to get one from the cavalry. I didn't want to sit around waiting so I walked. Must have taken me most 'bout an hour."

Tad could hardly believe the words that seemed to flow effortlessly out of his mouth. He certainly hadn't rehearsed his lines. He flat out lied through his teeth. The words gushed straight out just like that, and Tad set himself on a path that could dog him forever. Tad didn't know what'd come over him. He certainly hadn't planned to tell a bold-faced lie. The thought occurred to him that he'd just sentenced himself to the gallows. It would take no time at all for Hill to check out his story with his own staff officers and aides, and they would say that they'd never seen either Tad Dwyer or the orders.

"You're sure about it, Dwyer? Sure you didn't get them to the wrong division or something?" Hill asked sternly.

"Yes, sir. Positive, sir," Tad replied.

Hill turned to Chilton and spoke in a harsh tone of voice. "Of course I'll check this out with Sergeant Stoesser and the rest of my staff. There'll be hell to pay once I get to the bottom of this. Losing those orders made me look bad in Lee's eyes. I've warned Stoesser about being careless and sloppy, and not paying attention to detail."

All Chilton could do was nod assent. Tad stood silent at Chilton's side.

Realizing that he was still detaining Dwyer, Hill excused him, "That's all for now, Dwyer, thank you."

Hill turned to Chilton. "I've no reason to doubt Dwyer. He seemed straight forward. Looked me right in the eye. The man would certainly remember making such a delivery, and anyway, why would he lie?"

Realizing that General Hill was deep in thought, and not wanting to embarrass him by standing around expectantly, Chilton said to Hill. "General, will that be all?"

"Yes, Chilton. Thanks for finding Dwyer."

Hill was engrossed in his thoughts. At one point he thought to himself, half audibly, "I just can't seem to impress upon Stoesser the importance of running a tight ship and paying attention to details. Seems like my staff's always in a state of disarray. Those orders are probably still unopened and lying in some file. Maybe even thrown out. Who knows? Then again, maybe Stoesser opened the orders, realized that they were the same as the ones Jackson sent, and didn't want to bother me with 'em. Thank God for Jackson. If it hadn't been for him this could have been a tragic mistake, the kind that tips the scales of fortune in war."

As he made his way back to his divisional headquarters, Hill began to think that perhaps he'd overreacted to this whole thing. His staff had undoubtedly made a mistake, but now there were more important matters to attend to and prepare for. The march to Harrisburg would resume in a few hours. Hill, as was his practice on such occasions, laid the matter in the hands of the Almighty and told himself not to think about it anymore.

Meanwhile, back in his tent, Tad lay on his cot and stared at the canvass wall. His body was awash with perspiration and he felt light-headed and a bit dizzy. "What've I done now? Made a bad situation worse," he muttered, answering his own question. Dereliction of duty was bad enough, but blatantly lying under questioning by General Hill would certainly bring the death sentence. What would he do under oath? Commit perjury? The thought crossed his mind that they might even accuse him of being a spy, claiming he turned the missing orders over to the Yankees. His stomach was churning again and he felt cramping in the bowels.

Well, he thought, there's no turning back now. He rehearsed his story to himself: Any change in my story will destroy my credibility and bring everything crashing down. Maybe I can't prove I delivered those orders, but nobody can damn well prove I didn't. I can't prove I'm innocent, but they can't prove I'm guilty. It's my word against Hill's staff, and didn't I just hear Hill admit clear as day that his staff and that Stoesser guy were careless and sloppy?

Having supreme confidence in his gambling ability, and having been able to liken this situation to a poker game, Tad suddenly felt much better. He decided it was now time to seek out his confessor, Billy Dean.

CHAPTER FOUR

President Lincoln slammed his fist on the conference table and glared at the men sitting around him. Secretary of State William H. Seward and Secretary of the Treasury Salmon Portland Chase had requested this special meeting of the cabinet.

Lincoln got to his feet and began pacing back and forth. "Tell me how General McClellan can say he's not ready to pursue the enemy when all he's been doing since he took command is make preparations. Preparations for what? McClellan is the only general I know who has a bodyguard instead of an army."

The cabinet sat in a state of raptured silence. No one moved or attempted to interrupt Lincoln's harangue. "What did McClellan want that he didn't have? What on earth was he waiting for? Why didn't he follow Lee's army immediately? Surely the vanguard of the Army of the Potomac could've overpowered Lee's defenses at the South Mountain gaps. Surely he wasn't worried about being outnumbered by Lee? What was it?"

All of Washington was in a state of anger and confusion about the spate of military failures that began with First Bull Run, then the Peninsular campaign, and then Second Bull Run. Newspapers all over the North were beginning to question not just the strategy of the Northern army and its commanders, but more importantly, the reasons underlying the war itself. Lincoln's cabinet was no exception.

The president finally sat down and called the meeting to order. "As you probably know, Chase and Seward called for this meeting. Mr. Seward, you wanted to share some thoughts with us."

"Thank you, Mr. President." Seward dared not stand inasmuch as the president was now seated. Seward was always an imposing presence and he would intimidate his listeners if given half a chance. "The people in southern Pennsylvania are demanding an armistice. War is foolishness to increasing numbers of Northerners. Without the southern eleven there will be increased unity and solidarity. The rebs have always been different. Ever since colonial days, they've embraced a way of life quite foreign to ours."

Seward paused, took a sip of water, and again eyeballed his audience. "Who's kidding whom? We don't need the rebels and they don't need us. The Southern states can do very well on their own. They have their cotton and tobacco, and plenty of corn, not to mention their masters and slaves. No wonder they're determined to cut themselves off from us.

"The Southern armies have their *cause* writ large before them. In their eyes, that *cause*, freedom from the domination and authority of the Union, is the purpose of the war as it has filtered down to the rank and file of the confederate soldier. The Southern rebel knows, or thinks he knows, the reason for which he is fighting.

"Our Northern soldier's cause is far less clear, far less articulated, and far less accepted than that of the Southern soldier. For some Northerners it's the issue of slavery. They're the radical abolitionists. Then there are the more moderate emancipationists. Still others, probably the majority, care nothing about the slave issue but hold tough against secession.

"Although our Northern cause is defined as preservation of the Union, the logic behind the war is not always obvious to those on the firing line. It doesn't grab them the way the Southern privates are grabbed by their *cause*. As in any enterprise, the closer one is to knowing and believing in the *why* of one's endeavor the greater is the likelihood of success. If one doesn't know why or, in knowing the why does not really believe in it or make it one's own, then the end result is more likely to be disaster and defeat."

Seward wanted to continue, but he sensed he had gone on too long. The secretaries were fidgeting and showing signs of restlessness and boredom.

Lincoln listened courteously but would have none of it. Standing again, he was adamant. "This nation was franchised by the Constitution, which was ratified by every state that entered the Union. In this sense the United States created itself. The many gave birth to the One and now the One would see to it that the many remained One. May I remind you of what I said in my inaugural address, that I have no intention of interfering with the practice of

31

slavery in the present slave states. I have but one overriding purpose in this conflict and that is my most solemn obligation to preserve, protect, and defend the Constitution."

Lincoln waxed eloquent in the presence of the cabinet.

"If we give in now we'll be forever divided. We'll be gravely crippled, unable to stand erect among the nations of the world. Worse, what will we do when a Massachusetts or an Illinois comes to us twenty years from now and says 'We want to leave the Union.' Will we say good luck and Godspeed? Will we act the parent who knows his child's request to leave home is legitimate and timely and therefore give the child our blessing? I submit to you, gentleman, the present situation is *not* like a parent submitting to its child's request for freedom. Rather, it is like a hand or a leg saying to the body, 'Let me go free, I can do better without being attached to you.'

"This war is not about the unhappiness of the South. It's a war to determine once and for all if a nation can govern itself. Can a democracy stand up to the forces of anarchy? Can a government that belongs to the people ensure both equality and freedom?"

Seward was quick to counter.

"Mr. President, please tell us just why you're so adamant that the future of democracy depends entirely on whether or not the Southern states remain in the Union. For the purpose of discussion I want to ask you a pointed question. Why can't the South be permitted to form its own experiment in democracy? Why can't we let the secesh go and instead of one nation at war with itself, have two nations rooted in democracy and the principles of liberty? Your words, Mr. President, are very lofty and emotionally persuasive, but they fail to consider the fact that the Confederates are capable of establishing themselves as a democracy. In the long run we may all be stronger and better off if we grant them their freedom."

The room was quiet. Attention was rapt. The members sat on the edge of their chairs, sometimes nodding in agreement and sometimes whispering inaudibly to the person next to them.

Before Lincoln could reply, Seward continued.

"And one last thought in reference to your point about Massachusetts and Illinois wanting to secede in twenty years: We could go for an amendment to the Constitution to specifically spell out the impossibility of secession as a future option once and for all. The lack of such an article is probably the greatest glaring weakness in the Constitution as it now stands."

At long last Seward went silent. A couple of the cabinet

members mumbled assent and several exchanged knowing glances.

Lincoln was pensive, collected, and determined to nip this thing in the bud. Although modest in demeanor, he wasn't shy in expressing his opinion of Seward's logic.

"Mr. Seward, I invited you and each of your colleagues to serve on this cabinet because I believed you to be the best minds available. I'm frankly amazed and disappointed that you would consider seriously the course of action you describe. This war sickens me as it does you. I feel responsible for every one of our young men who falls in battle. The cost may grow larger and larger, but, gentleman, we mustn't lose sight of the basic principles for which we are fighting. Our forefathers labored arduously over other plans of self-government, especially the Articles of Confederation."

Lincoln now straightened up to his full stature and somewhat tightening his facial muscles continued. "I wonder if it has ever occurred to any one of you to ask why the Articles of Confederation failed. Why did Virginia, Georgia, and the Carolinas, like most of the other states, find the Articles unworkable? Each of them was free to secede at a moment's notice.

"Have you also never asked yourself about the states admitted into the Union since its establishment? How they knew the rules when they petitioned for statehood? Perhaps we all need to reread the Constitution.

"My response to you, Mr. Seward, is that loose confederations of states have never really worked. They sound good on paper, but they'll always get hung up on the issue of authority and sovereignty in the areas of foreign policy, taxation, defense, conscription, banking, and finance. What body of authority has the power to summon young men to arms, to formulate and enforce international policy, to create fiscal and tax policies, and to defend the individual as does our Bill of Rights?

"What we have in question here is the issue of state sovereignty versus federal sovereignty, state's rights versus a strong constitution holding these states together." Lincoln's face reddened, his eyes seemed to bulge, and the arteries in his neck tightened. "The very nature of our Constitution comes down on the side of a strong central government. I was elected by the majority of the states to defend that great document and I aim to do just that."

Without giving pause for questions or rebuttal, Lincoln proceeded with his own agenda for the meeting.

"Before I remove General McClellan from command I'd like

to hear from you concerning your opinions of our other generals. Do you know of anyone who has demonstrated solid military leadership along with the personal courage and audacity to exercise that leadership? I want a general who has the passion to fight to win rather than simply to avoid defeat?"

Lincoln continued, "I'm so tired of McClellan telling me that he doesn't have enough of this or of that, or that he's grossly outnumbered. McClellan has 110,000 men at his disposal. At best Lee has 64,000. McClellan seems to be preoccupied with the fear that if something goes wrong he'll be blamed for it. He keeps saying that he can't be held responsible for the performance of his army as long as the army is denied additional ordnance, supplies, and manpower. I've never known a man so intent on creating excuses and reasons for defeat in advance of the event."

Chase spoke up. "I think Burnside and Grant are possibilities, although rumor has it that Grant likes to drink."

"I think Hooker's worthy of consideration, although I've heard that he and Burnside are personal enemies," Postmaster General Montgomery Blair said with little conviction. "Besides," he asked, "what's so wrong about McClellan being conservative and cautious?"

Stanton countered: "I'm with Mr. Lincoln on McClellan. When the time comes I vote for Meade to replace him."

"Me too," said Secretary of the Navy Gideon Welles, who could be counted on to back Lincoln.

Lincoln listened attentively. "Contrary to what several of you might think, I do appreciate McClellan's organizational abilities. He's done a superb job of getting the army into fighting shape after Pope's embarrassing defeat at Second Bull Run. And I think I've some feel for the esteem in which his men hold their general, their Little Mac. But I don't think McClellan should remain in command any longer. The war will not be won by occupying territory. It will be won either by destroying the army of the enemy or by rendering it unable to continue the fight, and I don't think McClellan has the commitment or the ability to spearhead such an endeavor."

Every man in the cabinet, except Stanton and Welles, voiced opposition to Lincoln's suggestion to remove McClellan. By standing behind McClellan they'd once again forced Lincoln to ignore their counsel.

The meeting seemed to accomplish nothing. Further exchanges seemed futile, and Lincoln abruptly adjourned the meeting. "That's all, gentlemen, we don't seem to be getting anywhere."

Later that day the president met with Secretary of War Stanton and General-in-Chief Halleck. Lincoln came right to the point: "Gentlemen, I propose splitting the Army of the Potomac into two separate fighting units. McClellan will retain overall command of the V and VI Corps, a fighting force of approximately 70,000. The V Corps will be under the field command of Joseph Hooker and the VI Corps under George Meade. I want Hooker and the V Corps responsible for the defense of the capital. I want Meade and the VI corps to move northeast toward Baltimore and be ready to take on Lee if Lee should have a mind to circle eastward."

"The second segment of the army will consist of the III Corps under the command of Ambrose Burnside and will march through the South Mountain gaps westward to Hagerstown in pursuit of Lee's forces in Pennsylvania. III Corps will have about 40,000 men. I want Burnside to do what McClellan hasn't done. Approach Lee from the rear and give battle whenever he catches up.

"By giving immediate pursuit we'll force Lee either to give battle or to beat a retreat. If he retreats back toward Hagerstown and the Shenandoah he'll run into Burnside. And if he retreats toward Baltimore he'll run into Meade. I don't see a third alternative. Lee doesn't like to be on the defensive. He'll want the initiative. We should be able to come at him from two sides."

Stanton questioned Lincoln, "What's the latest on Lee's position? Is it confirmed that he's heading toward Harrisburg?"

"Yes, the latest intelligence reports indicate he is. That's why I want Mead up near Baltimore. We'll draw orders instructing McClellan to divide his army immediately so as to get Meade and the VI Corps moving as soon as possible and give independent command of the III Corps to Burnside.

"Mr. Halleck, please arrange for a special courier with protection of cavalry to leave as soon as possible to catch up with McClellan and present him with detailed orders in person.

"I want McClellan to turn over the III Corps to Burnside as soon as he gets these orders. Impress upon Burnside the extreme urgency of the situation and the need for haste as he approaches Lee from the rear. Then have Hooker and Meade use the B & O to expedite their return eastward. Have McClellan return to Washington with the courier and the cavalry. I want him to meet with us as soon as he gets here. I want to see him face to face."

Halleck looked tired. He gave the appearance of being overwhelmed with the details of his job, almost as if it was too much for him. He wiped his brow as he looked over to Stanton and then turned his head to address the president. "It'll take me a while to write out all the orders. And I think you both should double check them."

Lincoln, appearing pensive and distressed, went into one of his long pauses. He was silent for nearly a minute. What this all boiled down to was Lincoln deciding he'd test McClellan. He eyeballed Stanton. "If McClellan fails to get Meade's VI Corps toward Baltimore or if he gets the army there and then proceeds to dig in and create all kinds of elaborate defenses instead of moving northward to head off Lee, as he's been ordered to do, then by god I'll sack him."

Stanton and Halleck didn't say a word. Lincoln continued, "Damn McClellan! Damn him! Why is he so slow in giving pursuit? Does he really want the Union to win or does he secretly want some kind of compromise with the South?

"I'm caught in a double bind. I'm damned if I remove McClellan. I risk the wrath of the congress, the military, and a good many Northern supporters. On the other hand, I'm damned if I stay with McClellan much longer because the military situation could deteriorate and become hopeless in a matter of weeks or even days."

Stanton and Halleck nodded agreement.

"I've come to a firm resolution. I won't stand by a lack of aggressive pursuit and confrontation. I'd rather be crucified than meekly sit back and watch the South win the war because of lack of resolve."

*****

Lincoln had been alone for barely twelve minutes before an aide ushered in Mr. Reginold Gilmartin, carrying a portfolio of official looking papers. Gilmartin was a man of medium build, about six inches shorter than Lincoln, with dark, thinning hair. He had high cheekbones and a huge, bulbous nose.

"Good afternoon, Mr. President."

"Welcome, Mr. Gilmartin. Welcome. I'm glad to see you're back. I trust your mission went well. I'm most anxious to have your report."

Gilmartin removed one of the folders from his portfolio and

handed it to the president. Lincoln glanced at the title: *An Assessment of the English Position Regarding Intervention in the American Civil War.*

"Please have a seat and tell me as much as you can. I won't have time to read this whole report until later this evening or even tomorrow."

"Well, Mr. President, England is very close to extending recognition to the Confederacy. Lord Palmerston, according to my latest information, is about ready to take the matter up with his cabinet. My assessment is that the British appear to be in sympathy with the South. Since the official stance of your administration is that the central issue of the war is *not* slavery, but rather the issue of secession, the British feel they are not bound to side with the Union. From all I can ascertain, the Brits go with their feelings and their emotions, and from the common man to the House of Lords, their feelings and emotions appear to be in sympathy with the Confederates."

The two men faced each other as if one was responding to the questions of the other, much as a mentor facing a student.

"Are these sentiments widely expressed?"

"Yes. I encountered strong opinion most everywhere I went. As I understand it, England has had many quarrels with the United States and one way for the British to release pent-up anger about past indignities is to side with the South. Further, although there is presently a glut of cotton available to the British mills, this will not always be the case. Lastly, and perhaps of even greater importance, the British consider the Southern gentry to have a great affinity to their empire because their lifestyle is similar to the English aristocracy and nobility, at least to their way of thinking."

"Do you think the English cabinet will actually offer official recognition to the South?"

"It's difficult to say. My guess is yes."

"How soon?"

"My best guess ... within the next two, maybe three, months."

Lincoln stared at the floor, his elbows resting on the arms of his chair, and rubbed his temples as if he had a nagging headache. He stared for several moments at the opposite wall with its paintings of the American Revolution. He was pensive and his brow was furrowed. He inverted his hands and wrung his fingers out. The question of recognition was constantly on his mind. He often pondered whether or not the Union could hold if England recognized the Confederacy. He always came to the same conclusion: Yes, the

Union could hold as long as England did *not* provide materiel and manpower. If the British intervened militarily the situation would be well-nigh hopeless. France would likely follow England and then the odds would be overwhelming.

"Mr. Gilmartin, are your conclusions based on conversations with government people, on newspaper accounts, or what?"

"Both, Mr. President. My report lists all the sources from which I've gleaned information. I had occasion to talk privately with several members of Parliament. Of course, there'll be no Parliamentary debate until the cabinet deals with the issue. One member told me he would wager the odds were three to one—three in favor to every one opposed. Most important is Prime Minister Palmerston. From all indications, he's just biding his time and will soon bring the issue before the cabinet. If the cabinet favors recognition, well, that's it. The Parliament will follow lockstep.

*****

Late that evening Lincoln shared some thoughts about the activities and developments of the day with his beloved Mary Todd. Mary listened attentively as he unburdened himself of his feelings of anger and frustration connected with Seward, Chase, and most of all, McClellan. Almost as a confession, he confided in her, "From now on I must carry on only with Stanton, Welles, Halleck, and other strictly military personnel. I can't count on my cabinet for support. Most of them want to let the secesh go."

Mary was straightforward in her response.

"I hesitate to be blunt, Abe Lincoln, but people are seeing you as depressed and almost beaten. For the sake of your staff, the Congress, and especially the news people, you need to do a better job of covering over your discouragement. Your depression is contagious."

Lincoln fixed his eyes on the pattern of the rag rug. The blacks and the blues seemed to overwhelm the yellows and the reds.

"They study you, Abe! More than you think. They read your moods and they draw conclusions. And another thing—I know you pride yourself on your endless stories, but please don't tell so many. Don't you see they're indulging you, even patronizing you?"

With these last comments, Lincoln nodded his assent as he buried his head in his knees with his long arms clutching his gangling legs.

After a long silence he spoke: "I must be permitted to show my despair in our private rooms and in your presence. I think your advice and admonition is well taken, but please don't insist I put on a tough exterior in front of you. You're the one person who gives me strength by just listening to me and being with me. The course I've set upon may cost me my life, but I won't give in to secession. You know this better than anybody. Of all people, you must understand this and accept it. I should rather die than give in to losing this war."

As if listening for the proper time to knock on the door, Halford, the Lincolns' most trusted house servant, knocked and presented a sealed envelope to Mr. Lincoln.

"I'se sorry, sir," Halford explained, "but this was just delivered by some messenger. I couldn't find any of your aides or clerks. I would've waited till mornin', but the messenger say it was urgent so I thought I best bring it right to you."

Halford, formerly a domestic slave, had been given his freedom by Mary's father, Robert S. Todd, a banker. Mary had brought Halford to the Executive Mansion from her childhood home in Lexington, Kentucky, where he had been serving the Todd family as a free man. Halford was graying and balding, yet he was still keen of mind and wit as he slowly settled into his declining years.

Thanking Halford, Lincoln read the note with rapt attention and then handed it to Mary.

IF YOU STAY YOUR PRESENT COURSE YOUR GRAVE WILL HARDLY HAVE SETTLED BEFORE HANNIBAL HAMLIN SUES FOR PEACE. HE WHO HAS EARS TO HEAR, LET HIM HEAR.

CHAPTER FIVE

Early autumn in the mountains and foothills of southern Pennsylvania was a time of pristine beauty. The leaves were slowly changing their color. Shades of green were giving way to oranges, reds, and brilliant yellows. With daytime temperatures reaching the eighties the men were tempted to discard their overcoats and warmer outerwear. But by early evening the air became quite chilly and by nightfall the men were very glad to wrap themselves in any warmth at hand. Frosty mornings greeted friend and foe alike.

The great bulk of the Army of Northern Virginia would arrive in Carlisle on the night of September 19. Lee had done a lot of thinking since the staff meeting on the seventeenth and had come to a decision. He didn't very often reverse himself, but he decided to play a hunch.

Lee's hands still bothered him, but he managed to scratch out three brief paragraphs: "Colonel Chilton, please make these orders operational. I think they're clear, but make sure I've missed nothing. I slept on it all night. Changed my mind and decided to destroy the Cumberland Valley Railroad. I just can't take the chance that McClellan would use it to transport his army." Lee continued: "The first order of business is to transport all motive power and rolling stock northward toward Harrisburg so it can be put on the Northern Central tracks. Then, after dealing with details of the Cumberland Valley Railroad, write orders to destroy about five miles of track on the Pennsylvania to the east of Harrisburg, heading toward Reading and Philadelphia. Transfer as much of the rolling stock as possible to the tracks of the Northern Central between Harrisburg and Baltimore. And make sure rapt attention is paid so that no one confuses the Pennsy tracks with the Northern Central."

Then Lee added a last-second directive: "Better remind the couriers I want confirmation."

The orders went out swiftly—straight down the line to Hill's division, which immediately reversed itself and headed southward, beginning the arduous task of destroying the rails from Shippensburg to Chambersburg. The three regiments that had been guarding the South Mountain gaps were still one day's march behind Hill's division. When the three regiments caught up to Hill they would give added muscle to the task.

Hill's division dug in. Tearing up rail was a backbreaking chore. Up and down the line the men created huge fires. Daytime heat in mid-September was bad enough, but the fires had to be hot enough to make the rails pliable. Work was parceled out by company. One detail would tear up the rails and throw the ties onto the fires, and then another detail manned both ends of a rail section and carried the rail into the heart of the fire and allowed it to heat to the red-hot. The ends of the rails weren't hot like the center, but they would still get plenty warm, especially for the men closer to the middle. When the center was red-hot, the men quickly backed off with the rail, approached a nearby tree and proceeded to wrap the rail once around, allowing it to fall to the ground after forming a loop, or as the men called it, a necktie.

Some of the men were lucky enough to have gloves, but most used pieces of old clothing or whatever rags or burlap they could muster. No one could find the special arm-length hooks used in the placement of rails. These would make handling the hot rails much easier. There was considerable cursing, especially by those nearest the center portion. Every once in a while a terrible shriek could be heard when some unlucky soul got too close to the hot center.

It was still possible for McClellan to catch up with Lee at Harrisburg. If so, Lee welcomed the showdown. He'd hoped to engage McClellan south of Baltimore, but if McClellan pursued Lee would certainly give battle.

Later in the day of the 19th, Lee received a dispatch from J.E.B. Stuart. "Be advised Union forces have cleared South Mountain gaps and are moving quickly toward Hagerstown." Lee sent the courier back to Stuart with revised orders to scout further toward Frederick and Baltimore in order to determine Union strength in that vicinity.

Lee estimated he still had a two-day advantage over the

advancing Union army. Knowing Hill was without cavalry, he dispatched a company of cavalry under the command of Wade Hampton to scout the size of the forces in pursuit.

Next, Lee directed Major John Pelham to make comprehensive plans for an artillery fusillade upon the industrial complex of Harrisburg to begin the following afternoon, Saturday, September 20. Since Harrisburg was the key transportation center for all of northern, western, and central Pennsylvania, Lee was determined to destroy its transportation potential.

Lee decided to give Harrisburg a chance to surrender before he unleashed his artillery. Tad drew the courier assignment along with Bert Weatherly and Red Dawkin. Lee addressed Tad with a calm, yet firm tone of voice: "Dwyer, first thing tomorrow morning you'll go into Harrisburg under a white flag of truce and deliver this message to the mayor or other local authorities and available military personnel. After you present this to them your only task will be to wait for their official reply. Make sure they do not draw you or your companions into any kind of conversation. Is this clear?"

"Yes, sir." Tad saluted smartly.

By about 8:15 a.m., Tad, Red, and Bert were on their way to Harrisburg. Tad could not contain himself.

"Hey, we really got ourselves a peach of an assignment. Hard for me to believe Lee knows my name."

"Maybe he doesn't," replied Red. "Could be Major Wilson gave Lee our names."

"Don't know 'bout that. All I know is he called me Dwyer."

They moved quickly over the terrain. The mountains were well behind, and the roads were fairly level and in excellent condition. As they approached the bridge over the Susquehanna, they hoisted a large white flag.

Tad was very much aware that if they were shot at he could lose his life in a matter of seconds with no chance to defend himself. The offending party need only claim that he thought it was a ruse by the enemy, or that he hadn't seen the white flag until it was too late. "Red, keep your head straight forward and your eyes a bit downward. Don't you be makin' eye contact with anyone and whatever you do, don't open your mouth."

Tad rode first followed by Weatherly and Red. They moved unchallenged across the bridge. However, on the other side of the bridge was a military contingent consisting of a captain and two lieutenants, forming an imposing presence as they stood guard at the north entrance to the bridge.

"We're under orders to deliver a letter to the mayor and any other local authorities and available military personnel," Tad said only to the captain, with no further comment.

"Just follow the lieutenant yonder. He and one of the corporals will escort you to City Hall." The lieutenant appeared to be a smartly dressed Pennsylvania Militia, and he and the corporal formed escort for Tad, Red, and Bert as if these three were long-awaited visiting dignitaries. Word of this brief visitation spread quickly and it didn't take long for crowds to gather. Before long there were hundreds of people lined up along the street to give vent to their curiosity, which quickly turned to anger.

As they passed through a residential area, just before reaching the stores and shops leading to City Hall, they could hear the jeers getting louder.

"You secesh go home. Got no business up here. We don't need you. Don't want you."

"We'll whip your butts. Just you rebs wait till Burnside catches up."

Tad couldn't be certain but he imagined the hostile group of people included fanatical abolitionists. Tad was certain any show of arrogance or belligerence might result in a fatal shot being fired. At point blank range they were inviting targets. He was grateful for the Union lieutenant and corporal escorting them.

Tad tried to ignore the taunts and curses hurled at them, but certain phrases stood out. The remark about Burnside bothered him. Before long Tad saw a woman waving a newspaper and yelling, "Burnside'll teach Bobby Lee a lesson." Although his mind was on his mission, those remarks remained troublesome.

Tad couldn't help but notice the way people looked at him. It was, he thought, as though he was a foreigner, or a member of an alien race, which spoke an unknown language. "Well," he thought, "I suppose I do represent a culture that is alien to them. I've no personal feelings of animosity toward these people. I wish they'd understand I'm only doing my duty." Then, upon further reflection, he concluded they saw him as an invader in their unfortified city. Why wouldn't they be hostile?

Once safely inside City Hall, Tad spoke to an attending major. "Major, we've been sent by Commanding General Robert E. Lee of the Confederate States of America for the purpose of transmitting a sealed letter to your mayor and the highest available

43

civil and military authorities."

"Would you like to speak with the mayor?"

"Yes! Err, no! Just need to deliver this message and wait for a response. We have no authority to speak for General Lee." Tad surprised himself with his crisp response.

Standing over six feet tall, Tad assumed a powerful stance. Although he displayed no arrogance, neither was he intimidated by the presence of this Union major who outranked him.

The major led Tad, Red, and Bert to the office of the mayor of Harrisburg, the Honorable Roger D. Blackledge.

"I'm Second Lieutenant Tad Dwyer, Confederate States of America. We've been sent here under flag of truce to deliver this letter to you and other civilian and military authorities."

Tad handed the letter to the mayor.

"Thank you, lieutenant. Of course you know we don't recognize the so-called Confederate States of America, but as a matter or courtesy we shall read the letter." Blackledge was small in stature, but he had a commanding presence. He had a scar on his left cheek. His reddish hair was unkempt, but his beard was trimmed neatly and he was dressed impeccably. Apparently, thought Tad, he was one of those successful merchants that found it both expedient and profitable to be involved in local politics.

Lee's letter was conciliatory and to the point:

Saturday, September 20, 1862, 6:00 a.m.
To the Mayor of Harrisburg and ranking military authorities:

We propose to shell and destroy all rail centers and industrial and manufacturing plants in and around Harrisburg. We do not intend to shell residential areas.

It would be in the best interest of all concerned if you would surrender the city immediately, thereby eliminating the terrible hazards and destruction due to artillery bombardment.

If you choose not to surrender I strongly advise you evacuate the citizenry by 3:00 p.m. today, September 20. Artillery action by the C.S.A. will begin promptly at 3:05 p.m.

Respectfully,
Robert E. Lee
General, Army of Northern Virginia, C.S.A.

44

Tad sat with Red and Bert. They said nothing to each other. Twenty, then thirty minutes went by. Every once in a while the three men heard loud, angry voices emanating from the mayor's chambers. Tad guessed at the content of the letter. Lee was probably giving the Yanks a chance to surrender with dignity. Of course, the locals wouldn't see it that way. Tad again heard the name Burnside. This was the third time he'd heard Burnside's name mentioned. Tad wondered how and where Burnside fitted into the scheme of things.

Suddenly the door to the waiting room opened.

"Lieutenant Dwyer."

"Yes, sir," replied Tad, rising to stand at attention with Weatherly and Dawkin.

"We've drafted a reply to the letter from your commanding general," Blackledge said in a kindly tone of voice.

"In order to ensure your safety as you return to your lines, we will triple the number of escorting cavalry to the south side of the bridge. Please don't display your white flag until our cavalry cease to accompany you. Understand, this is for your protection."

"Yes, sir. Thank you, sir." Tad realized more than ever the necessity to keep his mouth shut, to say nothing, and to refrain from any word or gesture that might provoke or lead to rash action. Tad made sure his eyes met Red's and Bert's. A stern look at both of them proved sufficient.

As they left City Hall Tad noticed one of the civilians staring at him. He was a man of medium height, strong blue eyes with sagging eyebrows and a rather weak cut of jaw. His mustache was sizeable and sharply trimmed. His posture was erect. Overall he gave the appearance of reflective composure, yet Tad felt something about him to be menacing. Tad could almost feel the man's scorn. He knew he'd never seen or met this man before, yet he felt that if he were ever to meet him again, he'd know him immediately and tie him to this time and place.

Much to Tad's great relief the return was uneventful. Except for the sneers and insults nothing untoward happened. Their escort stopped at the south end of the bridge. Tad nodded a non-verbal 'thank you' together with a perfunctory salute to the lead officer and ordered Red to hoist the white flag of truce. Tad set a brisk pace but quickly went into a gallop.

Mumbling to himself while still on the gallop, Tad considered the fact that this war was getting to him. "Can't fathom the idea of Americans killing Americans. This is the first time since the war began I've had any contact with Northerners. We've invaded their territory. No wonder they look at us the way they do. If only they'd let us leave the Union in peace. If only they'd let us go and be our own country there'd be no more bloodshed and killin'. The idea of war isn't only absurd, it's patently stupid."

Upon arrival Tad confessed to Bert and Red: "Must admit I was far more anxious than I thought I'd be." At this, Talker admitted he had found it surprisingly easy to keep his mouth shut.

Lee greeted the couriers and without missing a beat he opened the sealed envelope from the Mayor of Harrisburg.

Saturday, September 20, 1862
General Robert E. Lee

The Army of Northern Virginia is an alien belligerent that the militia and citizenry of Pennsylvania are duty bound to resist. There will be no evacuation of citizenry and all bloodshed will be forever on your shoulders.

Lee remained silent for a moment and then said to Tad: "What was your impression, Dwyer?"

"Sir, the mission went well, but there is one detail I think might be important. On three different occasions I heard Yankee hecklers or onlookers mention the name of 'Burnside' or 'General Burnside.' I can't make sense of it."

Upon hearing it, Lee slapped himself on his forehead as a gesture of self-castigation. "How blind could I be! I should've sent Wade Hampton for a newspaper instead of a scouting expedition. Thank you, lieutenant. That will be all."

Lee immediately dispatched a small squad of cavalry to secure newspapers in Carlisle. After hearing Dwyer's comments about Burnside, Lee surmised that Burnside had replaced McClellan.

It wasn't long before Lee had two newspapers, one from Harrisburg and one from Carlisle. And his answer. Burnside hadn't replaced McClellan, but Burnside had been given command of the III Corps, which was now pursuing the Army of Northern Virginia on the route of the Cumberland Valley Railroad. Generals Hooker and Meade, under McClellan's overall command, had been given command of the V and VI Corps respectively. Burnside, according to the news dispatch, was now under the direct command of U. S. General-in-Chief Henry Halleck.

"With newspaper accounts like this who needs scouts and spies?" Lee muttered to Chilton, "Sure wish I'd thought of newspapers twenty-four hours ago. That Dwyer was really alert. Must remember his name."

Major General Ambrose E. Burnside was a very familiar name to Lee. Burnside was a manufacturer of firearms before the war, and had invented a type of breech-loading rifle. Service at First Manassas and attacks on North Carolina coastal installations had contributed to Burnside's reputation as a fighter worthy of independent command. Burnside wasn't the organizer that McClellan was, but Lee knew immediately that he'd have a huge fight on his hands, perhaps the telling battle of the war. Lee turned to Major Wilson. "Burnside'll be tougher than McClellan. If we fail to defeat Burnside our whole northern invasion will have been a waste."

Lee was anxious for Hampton to return with information regarding the estimated size of Burnside's forces. Turning again to Wilson, Lee amplified his thoughts. "We can defeat an army of approximately equal strength and hold our own against an army one and one half times ours. But I doubt we can be successful in facing an army twice as strong. On defense, yes. But not on offense. And it's imperative that we carry the field. A stand-off just won't do."

At precisely 3:05 p.m. one could feel the earth shake. The bombardment of Harrisburg was deafening. For almost three hours, from all positions on the south side of the river, the Confederate cannon spewed forth an angry deluge of noise, fire, and smoke. One by one the targets changed—from factory to factory, from distribution center to loading dock, to warehouse, to lumber yard. The bombardment seemed to be endless. Harrisburg was an inferno of fire and smoke. By 6:10 p.m. all the prime targets had been leveled except for two munitions factories which were too far to the north. Lee would have to come up with an alternative plan for them.

All Lee's energy and attention would now be focused upon Burnside's army. Burnside would follow the same route that Lee's Confederates had taken three days earlier, except Burnside would not be able to use the railroad that Hill's men had devastated.

Lee knew that he had the advantage of choosing the ground for this confrontation with Burnside. "I want a field," Lee barked to Wilson, "where there's sufficient terrain for advancement without giving the foe a natural haven for redeployment or retreat. But we must also safeguard our own retreat."

With this in mind, Lee chose the vicinity of Carlisle with

special attention to the area east of the town. Lee conferred with Longstreet: "The rolling terrain is to our advantage. The slopes of the fields are generally downward to the west. Must guard against the possibility of those people attempting to flank either end of our line."

"And if we have to retreat?" Longstreet responded.

"Well, I hate the thought, but if it comes to that we have this great rolling valley to our rear. I think we could bring it off," Lee said pointing to the southeast.

Lee decided that Jackson would command the center, Longstreet the left, and Walker the right. D.H. Hill and McLaws, recently arrived from the duty of destroying the Cumberland Valley Railroad, would be held in reserve, Hill behind Longstreet and McLaws behind Walker. Both reserve divisions would be especially attuned to the possible danger of attempted flanking movements.

With this alignment, the weakest part of the Confederate line would be the center because it would be without immediate back up. That's doubtless why Lee positioned Jackson in the center. The man would stand firm.

Wade Hampton and his cavalry arrived about 1:00 a.m. on Sunday, the twenty-first. Following instructions, he awakened Lee and gave him a thorough briefing after which Lee summoned the couriers to report for duty immediately. Lee instructed the couriers to rouse the generals and return *with them* to headquarters. There were to be no exceptions. The meeting was to commence at 2:00 a.m.

After outlining the placement of divisions, Lee was to the point.

"This may well be the turning point of the war. We need maximum effort, with no slip-ups in logistics or communication. We'll begin by taking the defensive. We're in federal territory and they wish to dislodge us. The positions I assigned you will enable us to assume the offensive once we repel their initial attack. It's imperative they be given no opportunity to turn our flanks. This will be up to D. H. Hill on the left flank behind Longstreet, and McLaws on the right flank behind Walker. If they attack our center, and should it give way, then we will need to bring part of the Hill and McLaws divisions into the center.

"The key is to withstand their initial attack and not yield our position. If we're successful in holding, we'll immediately press onto the offensive. We'll begin with an artillery bombardment of approximately seven minutes. The order to attack will be given by me, and *only* by me. When this order comes it will be do or die. If we can catch them in retreat, they'll be at their most vulnerable point. We don't want to give them breathing room. We'll pursue and pursue. Remember, real estate means nothing. We want to vanquish their army, cripple it so that it ceases to be a threat in our movement toward Baltimore."

On this last point, nobody could have been more in agreement with Lee's tactics than Abraham Lincoln himself. The conquering, occupation, and destruction of cities and territories might indeed be helpful, but victory would go to the side that first reduced the ability of the opposing army to wage war.

Until this point in time, the Union forces had failed to capture or reduce the effectiveness of the Confederate armies. Both armies claimed victory of sorts at Shiloh, and the Union had won significant victories at Forts Henry and Donelson. The Confederacy had swept the enemy from the field at both battles of Manassas, and repelled McClellans' intended assault upon Richmond in the Peninsular Campaign, but neither army had yet been successful in severely reducing the ability of the opposing army to fight.

Lee continued: "I want your questions. Is everyone clear? Are each of you absolutely certain about what's expected of you?"

There were questions dealing with the care and provisioning of the wounded. There were also questions about supplies and availability of ordnance. Where would the ammunition reserves be located? Where would the commanders of artillery be located in relation to the three front-line divisions? Would communications primarily be through courier or would signal flags be better?

General Walker asked about the artillery barrage, "Why an artillery barrage of only seven minutes?"

Lee responded: "I think the worst damage is inflicted very early in a fusillade because it can cause the most disruption and panic. If it continues longer it will tend to lose its effectiveness. Also, I'm very anxious to guard our reserve of grape and canister."

The meeting was adjourned at 3:15 a.m. Since Stuart and part of his cavalry were scouting the movements of Union forces toward Baltimore, the immediate intelligence operations fell upon Nathan Bedford Forrest. Forrest's cavalry had the situation well in hand, and at 5:10 a.m. they reported that Burnside had moved through the night and now was within five miles of the Confederate vedettes and mounted sentries.

49

At dawn the five division commanders led their forces to their designated positions on the battle line. All was made ready for an immediate engagement. The Army of Northern Virginia waited for Burnside to make the first move.

The ensuing clash of two great armies, to be henceforth and forever known by both sides as the Battle of Carlisle, did not begin until one day later, Tuesday, the twenty-third of September. Burnside had decided to rest his army.

As per his plan, Lee would wait for Burnside to commence operations. If the battle had begun on Monday, the twenty-second, as Lee had anticipated, the Confederate forces likely could have done severe damage. Lee's defensive stance, however, was influenced by both the terrain and his plan of battle. This was one occasion when Lee wanted his adversary to attack first, even if it meant losing the element of surprise. He wanted Burnside to come to him. He could wait another day.

CHAPTER SIX

The day of the battle of Carlisle, Tuesday, September 23, broke with sunshine, but by 8:00 a.m. a bank of clouds had moved in creating an eerie gray overcast. Lee's forces were facing westward and the Union forces were facing due east. Union artillery opened fire shortly after daybreak. Burnside's goal was to create massive devastation along the Confederate lines. The cannonade lasted for over twenty minutes and amounted to little more than sound and fury. Most of the canister and grape fell far short of the forward Confederate positions. Yet some hit close to home.

"Kick me for ever thinking courier duty was safer than infantry," Tad shouted to Billy as shells were exploding all about him in erratic and seemingly random patterns. Tad had drawn duty riding back and forth between Lee's headquarters and the several divisional headquarters. There was no way he could intelligently choose to avoid or enter a given area. At one point the impact of an exploding canister was so great that it almost blew Tad from his mount. Although quite shaken up, neither he nor the horse was hurt.

Lee surveyed the damage. He rode along the lines and concluded that the Yankees were simply wasting ammunition. Lee was fairly positive the Union infantry would soon begin a charge on the Confederate line. At least that was the expected routine.

A silence fell over the area that was frightening for those waiting to make the inevitable charge and for those poised to receive it. The silence was made more powerful and foreboding by its sharp contrast to the noise of the bombardment that preceded it. During such a pause, a soldier's life may parade before his mind, much as a dream may encompass weeks, months, and even years in a few seconds of actual time. It's at this time that vows are sworn and

51

bargains are supposedly negotiated. "God, if you get me through this I'll never touch another drop. So help me." "Lord, if I survive this I promise my life will never be the same and I'll never again stray." "Just this one time, Lord, please."

Others were more fatalistic, believing either in a senseless fate, or in a divine Providence which assigned minie balls to specific persons. If your name were written on one of these, then there was nothing to be done. This belief gave those who held it a dose of courage because it relieved them—so they felt—of any need to try to control their destiny during the battle. If a minie were going to get you, it would get you. This type of pre-determination also proved comforting to those who wondered and worried about their own ability to face the foe without skedaddling.

The first wave of Union infantry was advancing on the double quick, heading toward the center of Jackson's division. At a given signal, when they were at a distance of about 1000 yards, they all went stomach flat. Then another wave behind them, and another backed up by still others. To the watching eyes of the Confederate infantryman it appeared ominous. Was there no end to the advancing Yankee waves? Then there was a silence more deadly than ever.

Confederate soldiers liked to believe the myth that Union soldiers were chicken shit in battle and would turn and run at the slightest provocation. Even if the Yank wanted to turn tail and run, he did not dare for he would surely be killed anyway or shot to death as a deserter. No, these Yanks weren't cowardly. On this day they didn't have the protection of woods, shrubs, or even cornfields. Lee had chosen his ground well. The open meadows afforded Yank no place to hide, unless one fell down and played possum and even that was no guarantee.

Confederate infantry cut them down like a scythe cuts through the hay field, yet the advance continued, especially upon the Confederate middle. More and more men pressed forward, and the rebels could scarcely stop them all. Their sheer numbers became overpowering and the advancing Union tide now walked upon their own dead and wounded. There was hardly any soil not covered with bodies. Most were silent forever, hundreds writhing in pain, some mercifully unconscious.

Lee had summoned Tad to deliver an urgent message to D. H. Hill: "Tell Hill to detach two regiments and send 'em to back up Jackson soon as possible. Report here soon as you get back." Hill was far over on the left flank behind Longstreet. Riding swiftly, within eight minutes Tad was in the presence of D. H. Hill. Tad awaited Hill's response.

"Tell General Lee I'll see to it," Hill said.

"If I may, sir?" Tad said, even surprising himself by having the temerity to speak his own mind to General Hill.

"Yes, what is it, lieutenant? . . . Ah, . . . I know your face, but I've forgotten your name. Oh yes, you're that courier who . . ."

"Dwyer, sir," Tad said, thinking back to his previous meeting with General Hill. "As I came over here things appeared to be getting much worse on Jackson's left. Begging the general's pardon, sir, but I believe that haste is most vital, sir."

"Yes, Dwyer, 'preciate your report," Hill replied and turned away.

During the brief period of time that it had taken Tad to deliver the message, the situation had grown more desperate. The center of Jackson's line had broken. The Union pushed Jackson so far back there was a deep Union salient forming between the left and right of the Confederate lines. Confederate infantry on the left of the salient were firing into the Union lines toward fellow Confederates on the right and those on the right were firing into the Union lines toward Confederate forces on the left, a situation which Lee had feared. Though Union troops were thus exposed to a deadly crossfire, Confederates were in constant danger of wounding and killing each other. Within minutes after departing from D. H. Hill, Tad was astride his mount, just behind the front lines when a canister exploded in front of him. The shot exploded just under the animal's forelegs, sending horse and rider to the ground. The horse whinnied violently just before death mercifully claimed him. Tad was thrown a hefty distance, hitting his head against a giant oak tree. He lost consciousness for about two or three minutes, and slowly awoke to the sound of increased infantry action. His felt as if someone had clubbed him in the head with the butt of a rifle. Despite a number of bruises, he still had the use of his arms and legs. Nevertheless, the slightest movement brought excruciating pain. Tad started crawling toward the nearest pod of three gray-uniformed secesh, lying prone as they loaded and fired, then rolled over and reloaded, and then fired again.

Tad worked his way over to this small enclave of Confederates. Being a foot soldier was a new experience for him. He had no rifle, only his trusty Colt. He wanted to get back to headquarters, but now there was no choice. All about him men of Jackson's left flank were retreating.

A wild-eyed, scraggly bearded private saw Tad get thrown. The reb happened to glance rearward as he was ramming home his charge of powder when he caught a glimpse of a human form flying through the air. A few minutes later he realized the flying form was the courier crawling up next to him on the firing line. The bearded Confederate tossed him an ownerless rifle along with some minies and powder. "Here yaller dog. Welcome back to the living. Use this if'n you know how!"

"Damn right I know how," Tad snapped, his pride wounded by the insinuation that he wasn't capable of being a fighting man. He took the rifle, loaded it, and set about getting as many shots off as he could.

For a full seven or eight minutes Tad was a private in the infantry, lying prone, taking the shot and feeling the whizzes, the whistles, the swishes, and the zing of minies brushing past his ears. The smoke about him was blinding and suffocating. Tad could scarcely open his eyes from the sting. He thought he was going either to puke or suffocate—or maybe both at once. He started coughing something fierce.

The reb next to him, who'd given Tad the rifle, was loading and firing and reloading with a speed and determination that Tad couldn't help but admire. Even though he was still smarting from the insulting remark about being "a yaller dog," Tad shouted an honest compliment to him in the midst of the din, "Gees man, y'er *really* fast!"

Just as Tad spoke these words, warm blood from a severed artery spurted onto Tad and he fought against the nausea that suddenly overcame him. It was not Tad's blood. It was the man next to him who had called Tad "a yaller dog." A minie ball partially severed the man's head from his neck. Tad swallowed hard as he tried to create a makeshift tourniquet. Lying almost on top of the wounded man, Tad attempted to place the tourniquet just above the huge gash. It was useless. Blood spurted like water from a geyser—a bright red sign of impending death. Each spurt seemed to weaken until a slow oozing indicated the emptiness of the artery. This brave and arrogant man who'd insulted him would never speak again. Tad waited for the retching, which he felt certain would come, but all that came were shells and the screaming reports of more minies.

There was no time to tend to the wounded or mourn the dead.

If the Union was to be repelled it would have to begin right here and now with no further retreat. On either side of Tad more men were piling into line, lying prone, shoulder-to-shoulder. To kneel or stand up would be almost certain death. On came the enemy, pressing their advantage, determined to drive at Jackson with all they had.

The next thirty minutes would tell the tale. When Hill's regiments arrived, they'd be pressed into a second line of defense. Yet there was still no sight or sound of them. Reinforcements from McLaws' division were pouring into the right flank of Jackson's forces and putting pressure on the Union left. Tad began to wonder about Hill: Why weren't his reinforcements coming into line? Where were they? Certainly there could be no misunderstanding about the order.

From his forward observation post nestled in a grove of evergreens, Lee could see that his army was in grave danger if Hill's reinforcements didn't arrive soon. If the middle of the Confederate line broke there would be no tomorrow. It was only mid-morning. Neither darkness nor foul weather could come to Lee's rescue. Lee was concerned that perhaps Dwyer hadn't made it through to Hill. He was already upset with himself for not having sent more than one courier. Henceforth, he vowed, I'll send two couriers five minutes apart, and by slightly different routes.

Tad decided that since the line had stabilized for the moment, he'd attempt to work his way back to the rear and resume his trek to headquarters. He'd often wondered how he'd hold up under fire. He wasn't out of danger by any stretch of the imagination, but he was buoyed by a sense of pride in knowing he'd given a good account of himself. He wriggled backwards. It was slow and arduous work, as he dared not raise his head or his butt. He could only use his elbows to propel himself backwards. The prickles of the bull thorns jabbed him pitilessly, and he began to feel nauseated from the pain. His head continued to feel like it had been bashed in by the butt of someone's rifle. After covering about twenty yards, Tad reached a pile of rocks that afforded him an opportunity to rest a few seconds before making a run for it. In an effort to keep low to the ground, he ran in somewhat of a crouch, with his head extending as far forward as possible. He imagined he must look like some kind of crane making a dive for a fish. "Gawdalmighty," he thought, "if I get shot now not only will I look like a coward, I'll not be able to sit down for the rest of my life. If some secesh fixes his mind that I'm a deserter it'll just have to be. Long as he doesn't shoot. Just have to take my chances. Long as they ask questions before they shoot it's all right. But if they shoot first, well, . . . what the hell. Can't worry about that now."

Locating a mount proved to be no problem. Riderless horses were easy to find. Many a man had been shot from his horse. Tad had covered but a short distance when he saw Hill's regiments advancing on the double, late—but hopefully in time to turn the tide. Although it seemed like an eternity since he'd spoken to Hill, it had only been about twenty or so minutes. Hard to judge. He resisted the temptation to ride over and urge the colonel of the lead regiment to make haste, realizing that his first responsibility was to report back to Lee as quickly as possible.

Lee was greatly relieved to see Tad and hear his report.

"Delivered the message almost a half hour ago. General Hill said he'd be right on it. I took the liberty of stressing that haste was necessary as I observed the lines giving way." Tad sounded calm and efficient.

"Thank you, 'tenant. I was worried you didn't get through. What took you so long? I was beside myself because I had no way of knowing whether you got my orders to Hill." Lee was unable to mask both his relief and his irritation.

"Sorry, sir. On my way back, just after I left General Hill, a shell exploded right in front of my mount and I was thrown. Horse killed. When I came to I found myself caught up in a small group of clustered infantry. I had no choice but to dig in and fight. Once the line stabilized I moved out and found another mount."

"Oh, I see you drew blood? Better attend to it."

"No, sir. This here blood's not mine! Man next to me was struck with a minie and was practically decapitated. A good man too, sir, fast as blazes on the reload," Tad replied.

"They're all good men, Dwyer, each and every one of 'em. That'll be all."

Lee was facing the biggest and most important battle of his life, and things weren't going well. In fact, until Tad brought news of Hill's reinforcements, Lee was deeply absorbed in the gloomy thought of potential defeat. After Tad departed, Lee commented to Major Wilson, "Burnside's giving us everything he's got and we're barely hangin' on. If he comes at us with another regiment or two I'm afraid we're done for." Major Wilson just nodded in response.

By late morning the situation had stabilized. The Confederate right and left flanks were in the same position as at the beginning of the day. The Union salient was wiped out. Reinforcements from McLaws and Hill had successfully ended the forward progress of Burnside's forces. There was a brief lull before Pelham's artillery opened up the seven-minute barrage that would be followed by an infantry drive second to none.

The fighting continued unabated until about 2:00 p.m., at which time Jackson's division spearheaded the rebel counterattack, doing what he always did best—seizing the initiative. This is what the entire Confederate army did best. Jackson gave the order for the infantry to charge head-on.

Union troops were caught in utter confusion. Hundreds were trapped and so surrendered. Hundreds more abandoned their forward position and ran like blazes to the supposed safety of their lines. The moments that followed were perhaps the finest moments in the history of the Army of Northern Virginia. Thousands upon thousands of infantry poured forth from Walker on the right and Longstreet on the left. Like a volcano spewing its deadly lava, the crucible containing the Confederate infantry opened wide. It let out row after row of tattered Confederate soldiers voicing the shrill tones of the rebel yell.

The Army of the Potomac was thrown into confusion. The retreat seemed to resemble a swath of blue uniforms running for dear life. Like most retreats, this massive rush to the rear was contagious. Begun by a few, it became like a rolling stone, gathering a momentum that gave heed only to self-preservation. It was nothing short of panic and utter mayhem.

Although Lee's army was now successfully sweeping the foe from the field and could easily justify stopping its pursuit once the battle had been won, it wasn't permitted to do so.

Lee was relentless. Riding to each of his divisional commanders he made sure they understood that this was the moment for which they'd been waiting. "No matter how far you advance or how exhausted your troops become you're to drive those people as far as you possibly can. Can't worry about the cost."

This was the greatest opportunity ever afforded any army of the Confederacy. Lee held nothing in reserve. It was all or nothing. He wouldn't lose this moment, even if it cost him his career, or his life.

Nightfall was the only thing that saved the Union army from total ruin. Jackson had pursued them for a distance of almost three miles. The Union lost well over twelve hundred pieces of artillery, over three hundred wagons of supplies and ammunition, over thirty commissary units, and close to six hundred captured troops. Burnside's III Corps would survive to fight again, but not for a long, long time. On this day Lee had come closer than any other general to achieving the primary military objective of this war.

And yet in this moment of the greatest rebel triumph of the war, a malignant force now visited the Army of Northern Virginia. To the *cause* of the Confederacy there came a mortal blow, the likes of which even the enemy could not deliver. It happened well after the battle was over. The light of evening twilight was passing to darkness. Jackson and his aides, and several colonels, had reconnoitered and were returning from the forward lines when several rifle shots pierced the quiet of the evening. Jackson fell from his horse, his left arm severely wounded.

"Hold your fire! General Jackson here! Cease firing, you fools!" shouted Jackson's adjutant.

It all happened so fast—a tragic case of frontline panic and failure to ascertain identity before firing. Luckily, it wasn't a mortal blow.

"Thank the Almighty for that," was the only remark Lee made when he was informed.

Deep penetration of Northern soil ruled out any possibility of returning General Jackson to the safety of the South for his recovery, and he would have refused to leave the field even if it had been possible. It was determined he would remain with the medical detachment throughout the coming weeks. It might become necessary to amputate his arm, although this decision would be postponed as long as possible.

Nevertheless, after two days the surgeons determined it would be risky to put off amputation any longer because the healing was going badly. The decision to amputate was made. The surgery was successful and it appeared that Jackson would be restored to his rightful place of honor and command. But in his weakened condition he caught a severe chest cold that soon developed into pneumonia, although later some said it was blood poisoning. In another six days Lieutenant General Thomas Jonathan Jackson was dead.

The elation of victory was tempered by the sobering fact that Lee's greatest and most capable general was dead. A more lethal blow to the Confederacy could hardly be imagined.

Another serious blow, this time a very personal one, came upon one of Tad's closest friends. Tad came across Red Dawkin and was surprised to see tears running down his dust-covered cheeks. "What's the matter, Red?" Tad asked. "What's happened?"

"Just got word my brother-in-law's been killed. He was in Jackson's center. Ben Hatcher. Don't recall if I ever told you I had kin in Jackson's division. Seems like I did. He was captain of Company D, Third Regiment. We weren't close, like buddy-buddy, but we kept check on each other. Caught right in the middle of the breakthrough of Jackson's center. I feel terrible. My poor sister. What can I possibly tell her?"

Tad did his best to comfort him, but what could he say or do? There was mass slaughter all around them. Only the very fortunate lived through this day.

"Please, Red, be extra careful about what you do and where you go till this battle's over. Worst thing can happen to your sister is for her to lose both her husband and her brother. Hear?" Tad took the part of a caring older brother. He was quite protective of Red and anxious to keep him out of unnecessary risk. "And don't you be tryin' to find his body. There'll be time enough tomorrow, and I will go with you."

CHAPTER SEVEN

William H. Seward
Secretary of State
United States of America
January 1, 1862
The Commandant, Boston Naval Yard
Boston, Massachusetts

Upon receipt of this message and your procedural confirmation of its authenticity, you are authorized and directed to release Mssrs. James Mason and John Slidell who have been in your keeping since mid-November, 1861.

Upon their release you are instructed to give the following account to the press with no further comment or explanation.

The President of the United States of America has released from confinement Mssrs. James Mason and John Slidell and their secretaries. All allegations and charges proffered against Mason and Slidell have been dropped.

Mason and Slidell were wrongly removed as contraband of war from the HMS mail streamer Trent on November 8, 1861 by Captain Charles Wilkes of the USS San Jacinto, outside the port of Havana.

The President of the United States hereby apologizes to the government of England for this action against the passengers of the Trent, which resulted from an error in judgement on the part of Captain Charles Wilkes of the USS San Jacinto.

By order of the Secretary of State, United States of America
William H. Seward

*T*he *Trent Affair*, as it became known, could have proved disastrous for the Union. Fortunately, Lincoln and Seward privately concluded that the error in judgement by Captain Wilkes was in failing to take the Trent under tow to an American port. Mason had a diplomatic commission in London and Slidell in Paris. Their mission was to win support for the Confederacy. The fact that a Union vessel, the *San Jacinto*, commandeered and then boarded the *Trent* and forcibly removed Mason and Slidell was a breach of maritime law.

When the *Trent* arrived in England news of the seizure spread quickly throughout both England and France causing a swelling of animosity toward the Union with its high-handed tactics along with a wave of sympathy and support for the Confederacy.

England, threatening war, dispatched 14,000 troops to Canada. Prime Minister Palmerston demanded the release of Mason and Slidell along with an official apology. Lincoln knew that war with England was unthinkable. Upon the release of Mason and Slidell the crisis abated, although for a brief time there was a great uproar throughout Great Britain.

Nine months after the release of Mason and Slidell the incident was still fresh in the minds of members of the English Parliament. Feelings were running high against the United States. The *Trent Affair* gave the English people, Parliament, and the cabinet an acceptable opportunity to vent anger toward the United States. This anger had been smoldering for a long period of time, back to the American Revolution. In the eyes of the English, the Yankees were an uncouth and unattractive people, unlearned in the manners and skills of genteel society. They were abrasive and ill deserving of the finer points of aesthetic refinement. In truth, English support for the Confederacy was less a pro-Confederate States position than an anti-United States position.

Now, on November 10, 1862, the day after news arrived of Lee's victory over Burnside on October 23, Lord Palmerston addressed his cabinet.

"Gentlemen, the single item of business on today's agenda is this: Shall we or shall we not recommend to the House of Commons that Her Majesty's government extend formal diplomatic recognition of sovereignty to the Confederate States of America?"

Most members of the British cabinet, including Lords Palmerston, Russell and Gladstone, were in favor of recognition of the Confederacy. Palmerston had simply been waiting for the right moment. News of the last major Confederate victory, Second Manassas on August 29 and 30, didn't reach England until mid-September. When news of Lee's advance upon Harrisburg and the overwhelming defeat of Burnside at Carlisle reached Palmerston, he considered the time ripe for placing the matter before the cabinet.

Opposition was immediately forthcoming from a man by the name of George Galbraith, a staunch moralist and the self-appointed moral conscience of the cabinet. Galbraith insisted on placing the question of recognition within the context of the larger issue, the morality of slavery.

"I do not see how we can say that this war is not about slavery. Oh yes, I know what Lincoln said in his inaugural address, but if it were not for the issue of slavery there would be no cause for the Southern states to secede from the Union. Therefore, the ultimate cause, the underlying first cause of this war, is slavery.

"Make no mistake about it, gentlemen, slavery is an affront to human dignity. When one human being can own another human being without his consent, and further, when this enslaved person can be sold or traded regardless of the fact that he or she may be married and the father or mother of children, then this practice should be an affront to every subject of the Crown. The only right thing for England to do is to support abolition. I say to you that for England to recognize the Confederacy as a sovereign power is akin to enshrining Lucifer as Christ's Vicar on earth."

"Hear! Hear!" came the collective echo of members of the cabinet.

"Galbraith, who gave you the right to presume to talk with such moral authority? Lucifer indeed! You speak blasphemy," sounded the voice of Albert Chenoweth.

Palmerston knew he was better off not to enter directly into the ensuing debate, so he let Chenoweth carry forth the rebuttal to Galbraith. Now rising to his feet, Chenoweth continued:

"Galbraith, do you have any idea of the implications of abolition? The Negro in America cannot survive or even support himself. They cannot read or write. They're neither able to think as we do nor apply their minds to matters of business and finance, trade and barter. I tell you the American Negro is far better off being cared for by his master and mistress with three square meals a day, a place to live and clothes for his back. I agree with you, Galbraith, that the families should not be split apart, but except for that, I say the only civilized and Christian thing to do is to treat them as persons who would otherwise not be capable of surviving. It is our duty to feed, clothe, and protect them much as we do our horses, our pets, and our livestock.

"Besides Galbraith, you're dead wrong when you say that slavery is what this war is all about. Lincoln says it's about the survival of democracy, not slavery. But Lincoln is a fanatical reactionary who thinks the only kind of democracy is his kind of democracy. We English value and treasure democracy just as much as Lincoln, but we don't pretend to think that all men are qualified or entitled to vote.

"Galbraith, I'll tell you what this war is really all about. It's about preserving that part of the United States that still prefers our English way of life. It's about preserving the aristocratic ideals we Brits have always valued and treasured. Don't you see, Galbraith, that the Southern states are still pro-British and still our true kin? Don't you see that the Southern states never really were in rebellion against the Crown? Don't you see that the Confederacy is our greatest opportunity to preserve the British Empire in America?"

Chenoweth finally sat down.

"I'll tell you something else, Galbraith," added Sir Louis North. "If we don't recognize the Confederacy in the very near future, France will."

At this statement there was murmuring and mumbling amongst the cabinet. France? That despised rival across the channel. That sovereign power that too often found ways and means of embarrassing England. That nation of rogues and wags with loose morals and only the pretense of justice!

Now the voices did not wait for recognition by the chair.

"France is on the brink of recognition, and if they beat us to the punch on this thing we'll forever lose our edge in Confederate policy."

"Yes. And if we recognize first, and France follows our lead, what then?"

"The point is that whoever recognizes the Confederacy first has the key position and the seat of greatest future influence."

After much further repetition and a good amount of rancor, the debate was finally concluded. Palmerston held his breath, as he was not certain of victory. But Palmerston was surprised! Except for the negative vote of George Galbraith and one abstention, the vote was one-sided in favor of immediate recognition. The matter would

John F. Crosby

now be brought to Parliament.

The newspapers were filled with the news. Among that portion of the population that cared to follow the doings of Parliament there was talk of little else. The upper classes and the well-to-do seemed to be overwhelmingly in favor of full sovereignty for the Confederacy. The middle classes seemed not so unanimous about the matter and the lower classes paid no heed, for most of them were disenfranchised and their lot was mostly a continuous state of alienation.

Word spread quickly, and for this reason it was important to place the issue before Parliament at the earliest opportunity. London was at a fever pitch. The streets and public places were alive with talk and frenzied discussion. Even the pubs were full of spirited debate.

Not surprisingly, there was formidable opposition to the resolution that England recognize the sovereignty of the Confederacy. There were numerous members of Parliament who spoke against recognition. Thomas Grosvenor Cooke drew attention to the sad plight of many Americans whose families had become bitterly divided.

"Members of Parliament, I stand here as a second cousin to a Union brigadier general by the name of Philip St. George Cooke. General Cooke is a commander of a brigade of U. S. Cavalry. Philip's son, John R. Cooke, a Confederate, is Colonel, 27th North Carolina artillery. Philip's daughter is married to Confederate Major General James Ewell Brown Stuart, commander of cavalry in the Army of Northern Virginia. James is better known as Jeb Stuart. Philip's nephew, John Esten Cooke, Confederate, is an ordnance officer serving under Jeb Stuart.

"I tell you all this in order to make a simple point. There are thousands of divided families in America. This war has torn that country apart in ways that few of us here today can really understand or comprehend. Think of a mother bidding her sons farewell, one to go with the Union, and one with the Confederacy. Think of a father, such as my cousin Philip, perhaps being asked to fight against his own son and son-in-law.

"Friends, we in England have no business taking sides. Neither side is entirely right or entirely wrong. More importantly, this is not our fight. This is not our concern. We have gone far enough in granting the Confederacy the status of a belligerent. We need go no further. Our economy will withstand the loss of cotton. And who are we to pronounce on the rights and wrongs of slavery?

64

Is our history unblemished?

"This war between the American states is not our war, and it is not for us to judge. We do ourselves dishonor to recognize the sovereignty of those eleven states in rebellion against all the others. We'll do ourselves even greater dishonor if we attempt to intervene or support either side."

Cooke received a fair hearing with no interruptions or the taunting of the familiar *Hear! Hear!* When he finished, there was a loud round of applause. One could hardly infer that the impact of his speech would sway the voting, yet it did seem to have a sobering effect on how Parliament viewed the American struggle. Cooke certainly personalized the struggle by shifting it from the realm of the political to the realm of the family.

Harold Seymour was probably more persuasive with his emphasis on the implications for England if the Confederacy was to lose the war:

"Mark my words gentlemen, if we recognize the sovereignty of the Confederacy, we must be ready to come to her aid with food, military supplies, ordnance, naval support, and thousands of troops. I say this because if we recognize sovereignty without coming to the aid of the Confederacy, and if by some twist of fate the Confederacy should lose, we would be in an embarrassing and vulnerable position in our relations with the United States. We cannot recognize the Confederacy and then just let it go at that. Let us be very clear about this. If we vote to recognize the sovereignty of the Confederacy, we are also declaring war on the United States."

There was no applause or cries of derision at Seymour's remarks, which was all the more reason to think that his thoughts hit home, at least with some. Charles Imboden then made some telling remarks about the state of things to come, assuming that the Confederacy was victorious.

"Gentlemen: Let us assume for a moment that here today we recognize the sovereignty of the Confederacy and, in keeping with the remarks of Mr. Seymour, commit our resources, both material and human, to the cause of establishing that nation's freedom and independence. Let us also assume that France will follow our lead. Then let us further assume that our efforts will be successful.

"Now let us ask, what will the future look like with two nations across the seas, a United States of America and a Confederate States of America? My best guess is we will enjoy excellent relations with the Confederate States but not with the United States. We can expect that the people of the Union will be our adversaries in almost everything. We can expect a reduction in trade and scarcity in almost everything they export, from raw materials to all sorts of manufactured products.

"Even though many of us feel animosity toward the Union for past grievances, it may behoove us to think twice before we commit so blatant an act such as backing the Southern states in their rebellion.

"And let me ask you this: How do we continue to feel about France, our nemesis across the channel, who sealed the war of American independence against us, especially Rochambeau and de Grasse at Yorktown? Is it not true that we have been enemies of France for generations and would, if we were not a civilized and enlightened people, find cause to go to war with France?"

At this last point the floor and the galleries burst forth in cheers and applause. Imboden had struck a chord when he mentioned the position of England with regard to France. With the mention of France's role in helping the Americans during the revolution, Imboden was able to capture the attention and agreement of many in his hearing who otherwise might not have given his argument credence.

"Just so, gentleman, the way we feel about France meddling in our internal affairs back in the decades of the 1770s and '80s is probably the way the Americans will feel about us if we throw our considerable support to the Confederacy. I don't think it's either prudent or wise for us to risk the considerable benefits of so great a potential ally as the United States by backing those eleven states."

Just as a crowd can one minute applaud the hero, and at the next, laugh him out of court with cynical and derogatory statements, the floor and the galleries greeted Imboden's latest sentences with nay saying and murmuring.

Sir Horatio Nelson Montgomery stood to be recognized.

"May it please this august gathering, I would like to point out that the Southern states do not really need Her Majesty's recognition or support. In fact, with recent victories at Second Manassas and Carlisle, we have every reason to expect that General Robert E. Lee has the situation well in hand. Lee has driven McClellan out of the Peninsula. He has swept to distinguished victories at Manassas and Carlisle. Our latest dispatches put him on the cusp of victory at Harrisburg. He will obviously head toward either Philadelphia or Baltimore. Mr. Lincoln has not a single general who can stand up to

General Lee. Besides, Mr. Lincoln has little support from his own party, his cabinet, the House of Representatives, or the Senate. The people of the United States are divided on the issue of slavery. Some want freedom for the Negro without the franchise. Others would ship them back to Africa. Many simply don't care. Don't we all see, gentlemen, that the United States and President Lincoln are fighting a losing cause? The only thing the Northern soldier is committed to is fighting to keep the Union intact. Toward this end he is failing miserably. Therefore, why should we intervene? Given the situation as I've described it, we have little to gain by extending recognition.

"Gentlemen, please, in the name of God, let us prepare to extend diplomatic recognition the instant we hear that the Union is defeated, and not one minute sooner."

Montgomery's remarks were well received. There was an emphatic chorus of *Hear! Hear!* resounding through the gallery. After Montgomery sat down the speeches started to become very repetitious. People were making the same points over and over. The hours dragged on. Finally, a relatively unknown member of Parliament stood up and seemed to say something new. Matthew Stewart was a man of few words:

"Gentlemen of Parliament, I would like to venture a thought that may, for the moment, seem to be so far-fetched that it borders on the ridiculous. It is this: The system of government of the Confederacy is untenable. The idea of states' rights sounds good on paper, but in practical matters it breeds envy, jealousy, competition, and alienation. I predict that if the Confederacy wins the war they'll lose the peace, and become a fragmented collection of autonomous and quarrelsome states. My dream, rather my hope, is that some of these states, especially those bordering the Atlantic, will then be amenable to return to mother England from whence they came and with whom they have always had the affinity of birthright. I think we should do everything in our power to bring this possibility into reality. By supporting the Southern states we take a long step toward restoring the Atlantic coast states to England."

Stewart's short speech, coming as it did after a seemingly endless array of repetitive statements by members on both sides of the issue, seemed to bring closure, at least for those favoring recognition. Immediately there came a round of shouts.

"Call for the question!"

"Question!"

"Call the Question!"

But the Chair did not recognize the calls for question.

Still others, pro and con, demanded to speak. Feelings were running high. The outcome was by no means clear. Finally, Palmerston allowed the question to be called, which led immediately to the ensuing division of the House of Commons. It was decision time.

For a brief moment history was suspended. Time stood still. The future was to be forever determined by the vote that was about to take place. If the motion for recognition of sovereignty were to be defeated perhaps history would not be greatly affected, but if the motion for recognition were to carry, history would be forever altered.

"The clark will count the ayes," Palmerston's voice rang out. "Now the nays."

In a moment it was done. The motion carried. Her Majesty's government recognized the sovereignty of the Confederate States of America. By a margin of three to two, the future direction of international relations in the Western Hemisphere had changed. Now there would truly be a *New* England, an aristocracy of English who had never really been comfortable with the American experiment of government by the common people, with its emphasis on equality. The American Revolution had now come full circle with the great grandchildren of the rebelling parents returning, so the English liked to think, to their rightful home.

It would be two weeks before the news would reach the American shores, and then the shock waves would reverberate. Both the U.S.A. and the C.S.A. would receive the news on or about November 25. Diplomatic ties would be established as soon as logistics would permit.

CHAPTER EIGHT

On Wednesday, September 24, the Army of Northern Virginia was faced with the momentous tasks of caring for the wounded, attempting to track the missing, and accounting for and burying the dead. Tad was assigned to oversee one of the burial details, a gruesome task everyone hated. Dead bodies were quick to decompose in the early autumn heat, and the odor rapidly became a stench causing many to retch. The beasts of the field and the scavengers of the air had already begun their instinctive feeding on the fallen flesh.

Earlier in the morning Tad helped Red bury his brother-in-law, Ben Hatcher. "Sure feel bad for you, Red, I'm terribly sorry."

"Can't be helped. But I tell you, Tad, I'm gettin' mighty fed up with this killin'. Don't care if we are winnin'! I'm getin' to the point I just don't give a damn anymore. War is such a waste."

The battleground was an avatar of the seemingly endless struggle between Reb and Yank, a struggle that had lost much of its original meaning and purpose, and was now perpetuated by the growing hatred and quest for revenge and retribution that flows inevitably from the loss of comrades. Many a man would vow never to fight again after serving on burial detail, while many others would vow to fight on with an increased ferocity that would mask their deep grief and anger. Thus, the act of killing fed on itself with the rank and file of each side engaged in a personal vendetta.

Bert Weatherly was moving slowly through a dense grid of bodies when he heard a loud shrieking cry, much like the shrill of a man whose leg or arm was being sawed off. Turning toward the sound, Bert noticed several men surrounding a private who was supporting in his arms the upper body of a Union soldier. The cry

69

was unmistakable. It was a constant shrieking of two words, "My brother! My brother! My brother!"

Bert went over to the soldier and tried his best to console the man. Minutes passed. The private was clutching the left hand of his dead brother. "How'd you come upon him?" Bert asked, daring to hope that talking about it would help.

"I approached this pile of bodies near where one of our batteries had been operating. Everyone knows the first rule of death detail is to avoid eye contact. So I reached to secure a grip on his hand to drag him from the pile." John Short was regaining his composure as he continued.

"When I grabbed his hand and pulled on it I felt a stiff and gnarled finger. At first I thought nothing of it, but then this terrible vision darted through my mind. I remembered clear as anything one day when I was young my brother Andrew came runnin' and screamin' into the house holdin' his left hand like it was some sort of small critter he'd found. He'd caught his baby finger in a sprocket on a piece of farm equipment. Far as I could tell it looked like his baby finger would need to be cut off. It was dangling from the middle joint."

"Well, the finger never was amputated. My folks had no money to speak of. Don't remember 'xactly what happened 'cept my Mom bandaged it all up. All I know is when it healed it was turned downward with the tip of his finger touchin' the base, making it gnarled and sort of grotesque. That's what I felt when I reached into the pile of dead men, his gnarled pinky."

John clutched harder at the withered hand in his grasp and began to cry and sob once again. "After I felt his finger I forced myself to look at his face, and . . . it was . . . it was Andy."

Tad detailed Bert to remain with John to bury his brother. John went about the unpleasant task of removing personal items from Andrew's body—military appointment papers, a ring, and a few odd tokens of sentimental value. While John went about this task, Bert and several others finished digging the grave. In a few minutes they placed Andrew into it. Bert put his arm around John and said a prayer. John knelt by the covered grave, apparently in a daze, seemingly disconnected from the world about him. He kept saying, "What will I tell ma and pa? What can I say to them?"

The Army of Northern Virginia could hardly afford to join John Short in his grief. Wagons by the hundreds were waiting to be packed, ordnance repaired, commissary replenished, and plans carefully laid for the eastern movement to Harrisburg and beyond.

On September 25, 26, and 27, the entire Army of Northern Virginia joined Longstreet on the south bank of the Susquehanna, spread along a front of approximately twelve miles, with concentrations of wagons and troops clustered near the three bridges spanning the river.

At headquarters Lee was instructing Longstreet: "Pete, take Pelham and all of his artillery and knock out those two munitions factories on the north side of the city." Lee used a pointer to indicate on the map the exact spot where the factories were. "Situate Pelham's batteries as close to this side of the river as possible. After it appears we've done sufficient damage I want you to send one regiment over each of the three bridges. If more regiments are needed we'll send them over. I want to confirm the city's surrendered so's we can move on. Don't really want to invade."

Upon signal from Longstreet, the artillery fusillade began. Pelham employed his Napoleons and Parrotts in a two-hour barrage that leveled the factories. Whenever a shell would hit one of the storage areas a chain of explosions would send streams of dark smoke billowing into the blue fall sky. Fires burned fiercely all around the area. Within the first half-hour all of Harrisburg appeared to be under a dense, dark cloud.

By 2:00 p.m. on September 27, a full week after Tad, Red, and Bert had sojourned into Harrisburg to meet with the mayor, white flags appeared at the Harrisburg side of each of the three bridges. Longstreet and a contingent of three companies crossed the center bridge and took possession of the city. By 4:00 p.m., the city hall and courthouse were flying the Southern Cross.

Lee's northern campaign was successful. In the view of some, Harrisburg was the most important of all Northern cities because of its strategic rail facilities. The people of the North were now threatened in a manner few had thought possible. Baltimore was a mere seventy miles away, and Washington an additional thirty-eight. Wilmington was only seventy-two and Philadelphia ninety.

Of greater importance, Burnside's III Corps had been severely crippled and its ability to pursue Lee was out of the question. Lee's army took possession of huge supplies of Union ordnance and abandoned artillery. Lee was hopeful the captured ordnance would make the difference in the siege of Baltimore.

The last hope of the Union was McClellan's army: The

divisions of Reno, Heintzelman, Couch, and Mansfield formed the V Corps under Joe Hooker, and the divisions of Humphreys, Hitchcock, Sedgwick, and Sykes comprising the VI Corps under George Meade. Altogether, the V and VI Corps totaled 70,000.

The lead editorial in *The Washington Times* suggested that if McClellan moved swiftly to head off any approach of Lee against Baltimore there was every possibility that the Union could still win the war quickly and decisively. The editorial proclaimed that while Lee was victorious over Burnside at Carlisle, he was also extremely vulnerable. He had taken a terrible risk and was really not strong enough to win an all-out battle. Best estimates indicated Lee's forces numbered only 45,000, including the cavalries of Stuart, Forrest, Hampton, and Morgan.

In Lincoln's mind, the Union had the men, the equipment, the supplies, and the transportation necessary for victory on the battlefield. If only McClellan would provide the leadership.

But neither the government nor the populace shared Lincoln's views. The Congress was skeptical, and every rebel triumph brought out the Peace Democrats calling for an end to hostilities. The cabinet, as usual, was divided with most members now convinced that the war should cease by negotiated settlement. Only Stanton and Welles stood with Lincoln.

Lincoln not only felt alone, he was alone. He couldn't understand Seward, Blair, or Chase. They were of the same cloth, afraid to press ahead and absorb the necessary losses in order to gain a complete victory. Things were the same with the Senators and Congressman. It seemed to Lincoln that everyone had one ear glued to the message of the Peace Democrats and the other ear fixed on the wishes of his home constituency. The abolitionists were the only group left who appeared to want to continue the war, and yet they too were complaining about the mounting casualties.

Upon hearing of the surrender of Harrisburg, the president was again faced with McClellan's slow-poke attitude. McClellan was now being tested. Would he, or would he not, rise to the challenge and take immediate action to engage the secesh in a critical confrontation. Lincoln now put a time limit on the test.

General George McClellan, Commander, Army of the Potomac, USA
September 28, 1862

> *You will proceed with the V and VI Corps in your command*
> *and take every possible action to engage and utterly defeat the approaching*
> *forces of the Confederacy presently in route from Harrisburg to Baltimore.*
> *The time is past for reinforcements. Ask for none. None are available.*
> *Your armies are well provisioned and well supplied, and there can be no*
> *more time spent waiting for further supplies.*
> > *You are to be situated and ready for battle west and northwest*
> *of Baltimore by no later than Sunday, October 5. When you cripple the*
> *enemy army do not hesitate to proceed against him as he retreats. Only*
> *in determined pursuit will you be able to destroy him. It is imperative*
> *that you grasp the extreme importance of pursuit to the death.*

Abraham Lincoln,
Commander-in-Chief, United States of America

But of course, McClellan being McClellan, there could be no meeting of the minds with Lincoln. Lincoln was waiting at the telegraph office when he received McClellan's reply. Unfolding the telegram, Lincoln drew in his breath as he read.

"Your orders received. Will attempt to carry out although against my better judgment. The V and VI Corps are not quite ready. If disaster overtakes this army, the final responsibility will *not* be on my shoulders."

Lincoln threw up his hands and sputtered a few unintelligible words. While outraged, he was not surprised. How could he be? This was McClellan. This was McClellan in the Peninsula campaign all over again. This was McClellan at Frederick, Maryland and at South Mountain. "Prove me wrong, Little Mac," Lincoln muttered to himself. "For God's sake, man, prove me wrong!"

Thank God for Hooker and Meade, thought Lincoln, especially Meade. When I remove McClellan, I'll replace him with Meade. Meade strikes me as quite the opposite of Little Mac.

Opposite he certainly was. John Gordon Meade was a dour and irascible sort of a person. He had a terrible temper and was sometimes a difficult person with whom to communicate. But he would fight. And right now that was all Lincoln could think about. He desperately needed a commander who'd take the necessary risks. He needed someone to match wits with Lee.

73

John F. Crosby

Lincoln determined not to share his thoughts with anyone except Stanton. To Lincoln's way of thinking, Halleck seemed almost as slow as McClellan to grasp the necessity for quick and decisive action.

Lincoln took Stanton into his confidence. "When I sack McClellan I'm going to give the command to Meade. I know Sheridan, Wright, Baldy Smith, and Warren have each feuded with Meade. So what? Meade proved himself as commander of a brigade during the Peninsula campaign and at Second Bull Run. He'll fight! That's all I ask."

"McClellan might still come through," Stanton replied. "Seems to me he's taken long enough to get his house in order. But if he stays with the slows, wants more of this or more of that, then I agree with you about sacking him and giving the command to Meade. Seems to be the best choice."

October 5 was eight days away. Maybe McClellan would still meet the challenge.

In the meantime, Lee was wasting no time. The cavalry commands of Hampton and Morgan were dispatched toward Philadelphia while Stuart and Forrest were busy seizing the facilities of the Northern Central Railroad from Harrisburg to Baltimore. Forrest was working the northernmost parts of the line, while Stuart's forces were dispatched to the thirty-five miles immediately north of Baltimore.

The cavalries were a motley crew of equestrians, scions of wealthy families from the upper and middle echelons of Southern society. These young men were usually brought up on cotton plantations and larger farms. Craftsmen, merchants, and other tradesmen were seldom candidates for the cavalry.

The cavalry thrived on the bravado of young men who liked to think of themselves as dashing and resplendent warriors. Some were. Most were not. They were fueled by feats of daring which often amounted to nothing more than shouting the rebel yell as they devastated defenseless homesteads and then trashed most of the booty.

Even so, the Confederate infantry envied the cavalry. No doubt this was because the Southern public romanticized the cavaliers. In their eyes the cavalry represented the dash that was the mark of Confederate valor. Jeb Stuart's legendary feats epitomized the cavalry. Most everyone in the South believed *If you wanta have fun . . . if you wanta spell hell . . . jine the cavalry.*

74

That's exactly what James Ruther Donley did at the age of fifteen, in Nashville, Tennessee. For as long as he could remember, he and his father were in constant conflict. The old man was always taking him to task for real or imaginary offenses, and many times Ruther felt the sting of the whip. After his mother's death things became impossible. After one such beating Ruther went packing and *jined* the cavalry.

Of course he lied about his age, as did hundreds and hundreds of other adventurous young boys. Ruther found his way to the cavalry of Nathan Bedford Forrest when it was diverted to middle Tennessee in the summer of 1861. Ruther passed himself off as being seventeen years old. He was quite capable on his mount, which he'd brought with him when he enlisted.

Ruther was quite the lively lad in his outfit, Third CSA Cavalry, Company C. He seemed to be everybody's mascot, much like a drummer boy. He took a lot of good-natured teasing, especially about not needing to shave and not having any apparent body hair. Actually, he did have some body hair, but it was all down below. His voice was changing slowly, and no one believed for one minute that Ruther was as old as he claimed to be.

"Hey, Ruther. Get any hair on your balls today?"

"Hell, don't embarrass the kid. He probably don't even have balls yet."

One night one of the most vocal of Ruther's tormenters, Corporal Jason Harding, along with several others, decided to pull a caper on the youngster. While Ruther was sleeping, they tied his hands and his feet to the side of his cot. They did this so quickly that Ruther, once awakened, had little chance to pull away. Harding commanded, "Put him on his back. Pull his pants down and his drawers too."

Whipping up a mug of shaving cream, Jason Harding took his razor in one hand and his shaving brush in the other and made like he was going to shave all of Ruther's pubic hair. Jason painted a thorough dose of lather all over Ruther's manhood and surrounding areas. Deftly turning the razor so the sharp blade side was pointing upward, Jason used the dull side to scrape against Ruther's flesh. At this Ruther started to yell and curse in his high-pitched voice, lashing out at his tormentor. "You sonovabitch. I'll get you for this if'n it's the last thing I do."

Finally, after Ruther carried on for what seemed like a good two or three minutes attracting about twenty onlookers, Jason instructed his men to untie Ruther. Even though Jason Harding was much bigger than Ruther, Ruther sailed into him, arms flailing wildly, and it took three men to subdue him and explain it was only a joke.

"We're only funnin' you, Ruther." By now everyone was laughing so hard no one could hear Ruther's ongoing diatribe.

Jason finally convinced Ruther that they'd only been testing him. "See here, Ruther, I turned the blade upward so what actually touched you was this here dull side. None of us woulda' ever hurt you. Truth be told, we like you, Ruther. We've seen you on your mount. Even seen you cut down some Yankees, but we had to find out if you could take a joke. You're all right, Ruther. You're in the right company buddy."

Soon, the men were slapping Ruther on the back and shaking his hand. Slowly, a smile swept across his face and he seemed to accept Jason's explanation that they only picked on him because they liked him.

Life hadn't been kind to Ruther. His mother was killed when he was twelve years old. His father had caught his mother in bed with a lover and in the ensuing struggle Ruther's mother was accidentally shot. The lover escaped and was never found. There was still a warrant out for him in Nashville.

*****

Tad's agitated state of mind didn't allow him to sleep well. Doing burial detail and finding John Short's Union brother among the pile of dead affected him. He also worried about Red. Red seemed subdued and depressed, not at all like the fun-loving Talker, the Red that Tad knew.

Aroused from sleep by an urgent need to relieve himself, Tad felt restless as he stood amongst the trees. What a beautiful night, he thought as he wandered into the clearing and observed the clouds scudding across the face of the full moon. The world seems so peaceful and serene, it's hard to believe in a matter of days, hours even, the shootin' and killin'll start again. Are the differences between North and South really enough to warrant all this bloodshed and destruction? Even if I come through this war alive, nothin'll be the same. The world'll be changed. I'll be changed.

Realizing that he was too wide awake to bother trying to get back to sleep he found a grassy mound on which to sit, leaned back against a tree trunk, and continued his thoughts. Life seemed to be racing past him. He recalled the psalmist's lament, *What is man that Thou art mindful of him?* At such times, Tad felt insignificant. He sensed he did most of the crazy things he did so's he wouldn't have to deal with himself. Playing cards, shooting craps, drinking with the guys. As much as he enjoyed these things they became boring after a while, and he was eager to move on. Tad wondered, What's it all about? Life, death, pain, sufferin' the war?

Tad buried his face in his hands for a period of time, almost welcoming the self-pity that engulfed him. He began to think of all the times he'd let people down. He'd never lived up to his father's expectations. He didn't have his father's work ethic or self-discipline. He was too much of a free spirit. Couldn't go along with the traditional religious beliefs of his father. Church, Jesus, God, a day of judgment, the afterlife.

Most of all he'd failed in his professional duty as an officer. He'd lost those damn orders. And, as if that wasn't bad enough, he'd lied to General Hill.

It was nearly dawn and he made his way toward a nearby stream. Perhaps the cool refreshing water would wash away his feelings of guilt and failure. At least the water would feel good.

He was just struggling back into his clothes when a voice startled him. "You been cleanin' body or soul?" He saw Billy Dean smiling at him. Tad returned the greeting. "Both."

"Up pretty early, aren't you?"

"Had to do some house cleanin', Billy. Amazin' how much dirt you collect in thirty-three years."

"Huh," Billy grunted. "Someday I'll show you what dirt really looks like." He stripped off his clothes and headed for the water.

Puzzled by his friend's response, but knowing that Billy Dean didn't intend to say more, Tad headed back to his tent. Even though he'd not solved anything, he felt better.

*****

At 9:00 a.m. on November 2, the men of the 3rd C.S.A. Cavalry, commanded by Nathan Bedford Forrest, were called together to witness an execution. A spy had been uncovered from the ranks of Company C. The man, whose code name was Ruff, was accused of passing information to the enemy regarding the operations of the 3rd Cavalry. Of course it didn't matter if the information was scanty or voluminous, false or accurate. A spy was a spy. The mandatory sentence of death by hanging was handed down by Forrest himself.

Ruff and his guards walked slowly through the ranks to the ominous sound of the snare drum, the beat of death being intoned to every listening ear. Heads craned and eyes strained to catch a glimpse of the disgraced prisoner. The men were shocked to see how young this Yankee spy appeared, this despicable piece of human vermin. He couldn't be but fifteen or sixteen at best. Up to the platform he was marched. As the drum ceased its funereal intonation, the officer read the charges. Certain words seemed to stand out: "Treason—passing information to the enemy—conspiracy to betray the Confederacy." Then came the name. The name no one in Company C could believe. The name many had come to respect. The one many had befriended like a father accepting a son!

James Ruther Donley.

During his interrogation the officers had attempted to get Ruther to open up and give them answers. Who was his contact person? How did he pass on the information? To whom was he responsible? Who recruited him? Who else was spying for the Union? But Ruther would have none of it. He maintained his silence except to protest his innocence. He was placed in solitary confinement under heavy guard while awaiting trial.

Ruther considered the options that were open to him. He could plead not guilty and protest that he'd been falsely accused, that he loved the Confederacy, and that this whole thing was a miscarriage of justice.

He could repent and claim that he was coerced and pressured into a false life. He could claim he'd only passed on false and misleading pieces of information.

He could plead guilty and show pride in his allegiance to the Union, proclaiming to one and all the righteous position of the Union. He could march proudly to his death like a man and a martyr.

Or he could beg for mercy.

Early on Ruther decided he wouldn't give his accusers the satisfaction of knowing for certain they'd executed a Union spy. Let them suffer twinges of guilt that maybe they had in fact executed an innocent man.

After the sentence was pronounced Ruther shouted for all to

hear. "I'm innocent. You've the wrong man. I love the Confederacy. I'd never betray my country or my comrades. Ask my friends in Company C. They'll tell you I'm no goddamned spy."

Now the assembled soldiers were silent. It was a sickening sight to see a mere boy being readied for the gallows. Was he really a spy? Was he really guilty of doing all those things? How could one so young be so clever and so connected with a Yankee spy network?

Chaplain Whitfield asked the lad if he had any last words.

Ruther responded in a loud voice, "I'm innocent. I've been set up to take the blame for someone else. I'm no traitor."

Then Ruther added some words of Jesus he'd heard a preacher quote at a Good Friday service:

"Father forgive them for they know not what they do."

He stood before them with bowed head. He spoke no more.

The Chaplain began reciting the 23rd Psalm.

The Lord is my Shepherd. I shall not want. He maketh me to lie down in green pastures. He leadeth me beside the still waters. He restoreth my soul.

The prisoner was blindfolded and a noose placed around his neck, drawn up enough so there was just a bit of slack.

He leadeth me in the paths of righteousness for his name's sake.

The order was sounded forth: "Death to traitors."

Yea, though I walk through the valley of the shadow of death,

The platform beneath Ruther's feet suddenly gave way and his descent was abruptly stopped by the noose cutting under his chin. There was a sickening sound as his neck snapped sharply.

I will fear no evil for Thou art with me.

The body swayed gently after absorbing the terrible jolt.

Thy rod and thy staff, they comfort me.

The crowd gazed in stunned silence.

Thou preparest a table before me in the presence of mine enemies.

Ruther dangled at the end of the rope, slowly twisting first one way and then the other.

Thou annointest my head with oil.

Near the front of the gallows, two men appeared to sicken, slowly crumpling and falling to the ground.

My cup runneth over.

A private doubled over, retching.

Surely, goodness and mercy shall follow me all the days of my life.

Jason Harding, the tormentor who had led the shaving prank with Ruther, dropped to his knees exclaiming, "His blood be upon us."

And I will dwell in the house of the Lord forever. Amen.

Ruther was cut loose from the gallows. His body fell straightaway into the pine box coffin beneath.

The commanding officer's booming voice broke the silence of that fateful morning, "Company dissssmissed."

CHAPTER NINE

Corporal Gabriel de Grasse rode with a sense of urgency. General Hampton instructed him to make haste to deliver the report to General Lee.

The October day was foreboding. The skies appeared ready to unleash their stored up treasure, be it rain or sleet or snow. It had turned unusually cold for early October and de Grasse felt the sting of the wind against his face. Seeing three mounted Yankees approaching, still at some distance, de Grasse quickly guided his horse into a clump of trees. He dismounted and pushed aside branches, leading his mount further into the cover of trees and brush. He pushed back a branch a bit too far and lost his grip. The branch suddenly swished back at him with a whiplash sting, striking him across the right side of his face. His right eye was bloodied and he couldn't open it. In spite of excruciating pain he waited in silence as the Yanks rode past. He tried to read the insignia, but with only one eye everything seemed blurred and out of focus. He was now fighting nausea and dizziness.

Even though he could not see, he could hear their conversation quite clearly. One of the men was giving directions to one of the others: "You have to act like a frightened prisoner or your responses won't be believable. Don't volunteer anything. Let 'em think they've got a tough nut to crack."

"Yeah," the third Yank interjected, "so's when you do spill some beans they'll go for it."

After about half an hour de Grasse saw two of the Yanks returning. He made himself wait another fifteen minutes before resuming his journey. If de Grasse's hunch was correct, the third Yank was soon going to set out alone as a deliberate plant. He would accidentally-on-purpose allow himself to become a prisoner of war. Then, under interrogation, he would slowly give misleading information regarding Yankee movement and strength.

Covering his right eye and ignoring the pain as best he could, de Grasse set out to catch up with the would-be prisoner and oblige him.

Riding at a fast gallop, de Grasse soon caught up with the Yankee guinea pig. He figured if his hunch was correct he didn't have to worry about a deadly encounter. The Yank would feign resistance and then allow himself to be taken prisoner.

As de Grasse approached he fired a shot well over the Yank's head. The Yank headed instantly for the shelter of trees. De Grasse elected to fire two more shots in the direction of the trees. The Yank returned fire, the shot passing far to de Grasse's left.

"Surrender, Yank! I've got a patrol right behind me and you don't have a chance in hell," de Grasse yelled out.

The Yank feigned surprise: "Don't shoot, reb. Don't shoot."

Next thing he knew, de Grasse was following the disarmed Yankee prisoner, keeping his Colt .44 pointed at the Yank's backside. This could turn out to be fun, mused de Grasse as he rode on to Lee's headquarters, knowing full well the Yank's secret was already compromised.

An hour later the prisoner was under interrogation and Lee had Hampton's message in hand.

October 6, 1862, 8:00 a.m.
Army of the Potomac, 2ⁿᵈ CSA Cavalry
B.G. Wade Hampton, Commander
To: General Robert E. Lee, Army of Northern Virginia,
CSA

As of this date operations of the Second CSA Cavalry under my command and the Seventh CSA Cavalry under the command of John Hunt Morgan are complete in regard to the semi-encirclement of Wilmington. Morgan took his forces to the north of Wilmington, and I took mine to the south. The two cavalries formed a crescent, pushing into the city toward the Port of Wilmington.

Both cavalries destroyed every rail facility in sight. Complete annihilation was impossible, but the destruction is impressive. There was no opposition except the Pennsylvania and Delaware militias. Morgan reports his men pushed most of the Pennsylvania militia

*southward into Delaware. My men pushed the Delaware militia in
toward the port of Wilmington. There were numerous chevaux-de-frise
around Wilmington but we easily maneuvered around them.*

*After tying hundreds of neckties and torching several hundred
rail cars, I believe the Wilmington area to be secure. By last evening no
through traffic from anywhere in the north could get much further south
than the Pennsylvania-Delaware border. As a result only the Delaware
River can sustain Wilmington. I await further orders.*

B. G. Wade Hampton, Commander

Lee asked De Grasse to tell him the full story about the Yank.
"Thank you, corporal. Did a good job. Yeah, the Yank's
probably a plant. That eye of yours looks bad. I've instructed Major
Wilson to get you to the medical people."

Between October 6 and 9, Lee's entire army moved south to
Baltimore. However, just prior to leaving there was a hanging. De
Grasse's Yank was quickly found guilty of being a planted spy and
sentenced to immediate death. On hearing about the Yank's fate,
de Grasse couldn't help think that the bargain wasn't too bad. De
Grasse commented to his buddy, "The Yank's life for my right eye."

Company after company was placed on the cars. The
Northern Central was the key. If the cavalry of Stuart and Forrest
could maintain control of the right of way and protect against
sabotage there was little reason why artillery, ordnance, livestock,
and commissary, could not proceed quickly.

Within three days the Army of Northern Virginia was well
along in forming the planned crescent. By October 10, Baltimore
was surrounded on three sides, following a line from the Chesapeake
on the north, extending west and then south, and finally east toward
the Chesapeake again.

There were miles and miles of chevaux-de-frise erected by
Northern sympathizers, but this meant nothing to the Confederate
Army as there was no need to actually invade and occupy Baltimore.
Similar to Wilmington, all that was necessary was to surround the
city and cut if off from all land supply, as well as prevent escape and
exodus by land.

By the fifteenth of October the artillery was positioned in
such a manner that the entire city of Baltimore was vulnerable.
Lee commented to Wilson and Chilton, "I intend to maintain this
position as long as we possibly can. This'll be determined by how

long it takes McClellan to bring his army north. I'm more certain than ever that this battle'll determine the final outcome of the war."

"How is our fire power holding out? Will we have enough to maintain a prolonged siege?" asked Wilson.

"Worries me. Just have to pace ourselves and take the risk. Thank heaven for the ordnance we captured at Carlisle."

"What about provisions?" Wilson meant no disrespect, but he saw his role as sort of a shadow to Lee's thoughts.

"Should be able to resupply ourselves through Frederick and then south across the Potomac."

*****

Late one evening Tad was heading back to his tent using a path only he and the other couriers frequented. They were encamped about fifteen miles east of Harrisburg.

Something, or someone, suddenly wrapped itself around his legs just as someone else lunged at him from behind, striking him with such force that he fell face down. He felt the jerk of rope around his neck and another around his ankles. His arms were pulled behind his back and his wrists securely tied, a gag stuffed into his mouth. His legs were doubled up and a rope was tied between the bonds securing both his wrists and his ankles. Tad's attackers pulled a large gunnysack over him. The smell of burlap was strong as Tad struggled to breathe through his nose, the gag pushing against his nostrils. He was livid. It all happened so fast that he hadn't had a chance to defend himself. At no time in his life had he felt so completely and utterly helpless.

He felt himself being lifted and placed on the shoulder of a very large man, with at least two others helping to hold him in place. He could hear his bearer grunting and swearing as he carried him off into the darkness.

Tad bounced along on the man's shoulder for what seemed like an hour but was probably no more than twelve or fifteen minutes. The men obviously knew where they were headed because there was no hesitation. At first, all Tad could hear was the heavy breathing of the man carrying him, but he soon began to hear other sounds at a distance. Gradually the sounds became voices, and soon he recognized familiar camp sounds. Tad felt relieved for he couldn't imagine that his captors would bring him into camp if they planned on killing him. He couldn't be sure, but he felt certain he was in the hands of fellow Confederates.

Eventually they stopped and he was lowered from the man's shoulder, carried into a candlelit tent, and placed on the ground.

"God almighty, I'd hate to carry him much further!" his bearer exclaimed, sounding completely exhausted and out of breath.

An authoritative voice spoke out crisply, "Get him out of the sack and tie him in that chair. Remove the gag, but make sure his hands and feet are still securely bound. I want some answers from this sonovabitch."

Tad began to piece things together. This must have something to do with Stoesser, General Hill's staff sergeant. Tad recalled that Hill suspected Stoesser of being the one who blundered. The day Tad was confronted by General Hill in the presence of Chilton, hadn't Hill said something about his staff being careless and sloppy in the way they did things? In fact, Hill specifically mentioned Stoesser by name.

After the gunnysack was removed, they lifted Tad on to a chair. A quick glance around assured him that he was in a headquarters tent. Two lighted candles revealed boxes and other paraphernalia connected with recordkeeping. His abductors were three Confederates: a sergeant, a corporal, and a private. Two of the men had beards that were neatly trimmed, and although all three looked formidable, they did not appear to be violent men. The private was a huge man, at least six feet tall, maybe six and a few inches, with a barreled chest and huge arms and hands. After they tied Tad securely to the chair, the corporal and the private stepped to one side. The man barking out orders was only about five feet tall, maybe five plus three or four inches. He didn't appear to be as muscular as the others, yet he had the look of one in firm control of the situation.

"I'm Staff Sergeant James Stoesser. Work for General D. H. Hill. These guys are also members of General Hill's staff. Thanks to you, I've been charged by Hill of failing to log an order sent by General Lee on the afternoon of September 9. According to General Hill, you were the courier who delivered a set of orders to us that afternoon."

Tad thought quickly. His hunch had been right. *Hill must've believed me and brought this guy up on charges. Stoesser knows damn well I never delivered those orders.*

"Dwyer, you're a lyin' son-of-a-bitch and you know it. You never set foot inside this headquarters tent that day. Why'd you tell

Hill that bullshit? Hell you up to?"

Stoesser grabbed the front of Tad's shirt and yelled into Tad's face: "You liar. You know goddamn well we wouldn't treat incoming orders that way. How can you sit there and lie with such a straight face?"

For a brief moment, Tad thought Stoesser was going to strike him. Even though he was trussed up and helpless, Tad's poker playing instincts told him he now held the winning hand in what he viewed as one of life's little poker games. If these men could prove he was lying, they would've dragged him straight to Hill. Even though he couldn't prove his accusation about their shoddy handling of the orders, neither could they prove that he hadn't delivered them.

Tad thought to himself, okay, Stoesser, I'll see your bet and raise you!

"Look, Sergeant Stoesser," Tad said confidently, "I don't know what you're trying to prove by ambushing me and dragging me here. If you can prove I didn't deliver those orders, then do it. Take me to Hill. Press your charges. Prove your case. But if you can't prove it, then you'd better untie me right now. I've had enough of your trying to pin your carelessness on me. I've a good mind to go directly to Hill myself and tell him exactly what you guys did to me tonight, how you tied and stuffed me into a gunny sack like some varmint."

Tad figured these men made a major blunder by abducting him. Their act would be seen as an attempt to intimidate Tad into changing his story out of fear for his own skin. By misplaying his cards, Stoesser was making Tad a winner.

Tad continued his verbal attack on Stoesser: "Look, I know you'd like to blame me for your mistake, but the truth is I delivered those orders and you somehow messed up. I remember that afternoon very well because I couldn't get a mount and had to walk the whole way."

Tad paused. "Back off and accept your responsibility, Stoesser. It's no big deal anyhow. Just admit you somehow misplaced the orders. Hill isn't gonna shoot you for that. Everybody loses something once in a while."

Even me, Tad thought as he continued.

"The worst thing you can do is blame me. You've no proof, just your word against mine. And I promise you this, Stoesser, if push comes to shove, I'll make you look so foolish you'll wish tonight never happened."

86

Tad spoke with such confidence that Stoesser had to think back to that afternoon and reassure himself that this bastard hadn't really delivered the orders. Damn, this Dwyer was certainly a convincing liar. He turned slowly to the burly private and in a subdued voice said, "Untie him."

Turning back to Tad, Stoesser's voice was once again filled with anger. "Dwyer, I don't believe one word of your goddamn story. You're a lyin' son-of-a-bitch."

Tad was now experiencing that same euphoria he always felt when raking in a large pot. It was even more exhilarating when you knew you'd won by bluffing. Again Tad mused, these men will testify they'd never seen me. So what? I'll counter by stating that Hill's staff was so preoccupied on the afternoon in question they wouldn't have recognized Robert E. Lee had he personally delivered those orders.

Tad continued deliberating with himself as he looked about the headquarters tent, taking in the arrangement of tables, files, and chairs, telling himself he might need to remember the way this place looked.

Stoesser made one final threat: "Go ahead, Dwyer, get the hell out of my sight. But remember, the three of us know you didn't deliver those orders, and so do you. One other thing, you better not say one word to anyone about what happened tonight. It never happened, understand?"

Tad continued to play his bluff by smiling confidently. "Oh, I can think of any number of people who might find this evening's events of considerable interest. Can't you? Better take care of those stripes, sergeant, they might just fall off one of these days."

While the distance wasn't all that far, it was a long walk home for Tad. Even though he was calm under fire and thought fast on his feet, now that he was alone and had time to think about all that had taken place he felt weak and sweaty. His legs felt like molasses. Tad felt they couldn't continue to bear his weight. He was disgusted with himself for digging his hole deeper and deeper, once again refusing to confess his dereliction of duty.

I'm as low as I can get, makin' Stoesser appear guilty for somethin' I did. But what am I to do? It's either me or Stoesser. It's my only way out. Stoesser will take the rap because he'll never be able to match wits with me.

You know, Tad chuckled to himself, when this war ends, I'll bet I could become a helluva politician. I could convince a jury that Stoesser got hit by a snowball in July. Tad smiled as he thought about becoming a politician. I could probably sell a lot of swampland too, if I put my mind to it. Dwyer, you're really slashing a trail straight to hell.

As soon as he got back to his own camp Tad immediately went in search of Billy Dean. He was anxious to tell Billy about this latest development and see what Billy had to say. Was there something he was overlooking? He knew better than to count his winnings before the game was over.

He looked everywhere, but there was no sign of Billy and nobody remembered seeing him recently. That got Tad to thinking that he hadn't seen him for quite a while. Was it yesterday? Or the day before? He scribbled out a note and left it on Billy Dean's bedroll: "Need to see you soon as possible." Billy would know it was from Tad.

Tad went back to his tent. He needed to rethink this whole thing. He tried sitting down, but he was too keyed up for that. I know what Billy would say, he thought. He'd tell me to keep a low profile and keep my wits about me. I wonder what Stoesser'll do next. Or Hill? According to Stoesser it's Hill puttin' the pressure on. Damn, all I can do is wait. Say nothin'. Do nothin'.

Tad did not dare talk to anyone or tell anybody about being ambushed. Luckily, his bruises weren't obvious. His shirtsleeves and pants covered the worst bruises. Only thing that showed were marks on each side of his mouth where the gag scraped his skin, but these were somewhat hidden by a couple days growth of stubble.

But then a thought hit Tad—a thought so powerful and condemning that it chilled him. Tad challenged his own thinking: Suppose Hill brings charges 'gainst Stoesser and he's found guilty? Much as I don't like Stoesser I couldn't let an innocent man take the rap for somethin' I did. It'll kill me to confess, but I couldn't look myself in the face if Stoesser was to be found guilty and the punishment was harsh.

Then Tad thought another second. Half out loud he said, "But what if he's found guilty and the punishment's light or even a suspended sentence?" Tad chuckled to himself. "That's different. I'd have to think about that."

CHAPTER TEN

O
ctober 5 had come and gone. President Lincoln, alone in the White House office, looked dour and downcast. His posture and deportment conveyed despair. He thought about his instructions to McClellan: *You are to be situated and ready for battle west and north of Baltimore by no later than October 5.* McClellan's V and VI Corps were still encamped just north of Washington and Burnside's battered III Corps had arrived back in Alexandria.

Today's cabinet meeting was about to begin. As Lincoln entered the cabinet room he observed several separate groups in conversation. Lately most of these conversations were an exercise in scapegoating. Everybody was blaming someone else for the terrible situation. Lincoln and Stanton blamed McClellan. Seward blamed Burnside. Bates blamed the cavalry. Everyone else blamed Lincoln.

The meeting was scheduled for 10:00 a.m. "Let's come to order, gentlemen." Lincoln's high-pitched voice rose over the din of noise. "As you recall, you didn't want me to dismiss McClellan. I abided by your wishes and placed him as commander of the V and VI Corps. I put Burnside in charge of the western army in hopes that he would fight Lee. He fought Lee all right, but at a terrible price and with horrible consequences. So now we're virtually reduced to the V and VI Corps while Lee is heading for Baltimore."

"Don't change a thing," said Seward with authority, though he was rudely interrupting. "We've a golden opportunity to stop Lee dead in his tracks. He's far from home. His supply chain is very thin. He's living off the land. He may be low on ammunition. His cavalries are spread all over creation, and McClellan's equal to the task. I say let things be."

"Yes," said Edward Bates.

John F. Crosby

"I agree," said Montgomery Blair. "McClellan's ready."

Lincoln would have none of it. "Gentlemen, I'm going to share with you the orders I sent McClellan on September 28." At this, Lincoln passed around several copies of the orders he'd sent to McClellan.

Note the last sentence: *You are to be situated and ready for battle west and north of Baltimore by no later than October 5.*

Lincoln was on his feet, his face turning red with the flush of anger. He labored to keep his voice in control so that it would not rise in pitch. It was obvious to everyone in the room that Lincoln was about to explode.

"Gentlemen," he said, making every effort to be cordial, "today is October 10. Think of it. The tenth! And just where is General George McClellan? Is he west and north of Baltimore? My latest reports indicate that the army began to move on the eighth and as of this morning the advanced division is only fifteen miles from where we sit right this minute. And to make matters worse, our scouts report that Lee has been moving toward Baltimore for four days now. Wilmington is lost. Nothing can get through from Philadelphia."

Lincoln drew in a deep breath. He wanted to be judicious in what he was about to say. Another deep breath. Then he just let it gush out: "I've replaced McClellan effective six o'clock this morning."

"Oh my god. You can't!" erupted Bates.

"It's suicide to replace him now," echoed Seward.

Steadying himself, Lincoln spoke in slow and measured words.

"I've taken this step because I refuse to allow this Union, this democracy, to die simply because the general of its greatest army refuses to hearken sharply to orders. No, sir. If we're to be defeated it will be because we've been whipped upon the field of battle and not because we sat by while some slowpoke general allowed Baltimore to be surrounded. I don't give a damn what General McClellan thinks of Abe Lincoln. Fact is he seems to delight in thumbing his nose at me. But I do care what McClellan or anyone else, for that matter, thinks of the office and authority of the president of the United States."

Lincoln was beside himself. "I find McClellan's brand of generalship absolutely unacceptable. He receives orders and then replies 'If I can' or 'I'll try.' He always builds in some lame disclaimer

90

or preemptory excuse for defeat by saying 'if we lose it won't be on my shoulders.'"

Lincoln again took a deep breath. He wanted to regain his composure before he explained to them who he'd chosen to replace McClellan.

"I've placed General George Meade in command of the Army of the Potomac. I take full responsibility for this decision. I do not ask you to like it or to agree with me, but I do ask you to support me. We are at a most crucial point in this conflict, and if we fail to stop Lee outside Baltimore our cause may well be lost.

"Make no mistake about it. For the secesh to succeed they need conquer nothing except the will of our people to fight. Once our people and the Congress lose the will to fight we lose our eleven sister states."

Lincoln's assessment was accurate. Although his words were intended to unify, they were divisive. Silence followed his blunt remarks. Lincoln was skilled at this: He'd listen to complaints and counterarguments and then, after due time, he'd take the floor and utterly silence the tongues of his opponents. The trouble was, even though he succeeded in silencing their vocal retorts, he wasn't successful in silencing their opposition, which simply became removed from his hearing and presence. Lincoln's tactics had the predictable effect of turning most of his cabinet against him.

George Gordon Meade now came under fire as the cabinet questioned Lincoln. "Meade's cantankerous and sour in disposition. He makes enemies everywhere he goes," Seward said, his face flushing and his voice cracking under the strain of anger.

Lincoln refused to defend Meade's personality and character. He only said: "Meade will fight."

"I believe that's what you said about Burnside and look how that turned out." Seward minced no words. Bates and Blair nodded in agreement with Seward.

Stanton, Welles, and even Chase stood with Lincoln. Stanton spoke in Meade's defense, "His enemies have never seen him retreat. He'll be equal to Lee. Mark my words."

After a few caustic side remarks, mostly inaudible to Lincoln, it was clear to all that there was no longer any purpose in continuing the meeting.

Upon adjournment, Lincoln walked the several blocks to the telegraph office. His habit was often to spend hours and hours waiting for news from the front. He would drive the telegraphers crazy with his stories and anecdotes, most of which were quite dull. On this day there would be little time for stories. The wires were full of bulletins. Morgan and Hampton around Wilmington, Stuart and Forrest wrecking havoc around Baltimore, and worst of all, Lee's entire army either on the rails or already forming a crescent around Baltimore.

Deep in his gut, Lincoln felt it was coming to an end. The Peace Democrats were down on Lincoln as much as the abolitionists. The Peace Democrats wanted peace at any price, while the abolitionists wanted a more aggressive anti-slavery policy that Lincoln feared would push the border states of Missouri, Kentucky, and Maryland into the Confederacy. Maybe even Delaware. The congressional elections were less than a month away and it appeared that the House would go strongly toward the Peace Democrats.

But Lincoln had made peace with himself. It was obvious that his own political career was over if the Union could not be preserved. Career, hell, he thought, my whole life would be an utter failure. What's there to lose?

Later that day, confiding in Stanton, Lincoln admitted his only chance of re-election in 1864 was the defeat or near defeat of the Confederacy. "The more I try to accommodate the Peace Democrats the more I weaken my own position. If I thought emancipation of the slaves in the rebellious states could help save the Union I'd draft a proclamation, but the way things are now I'm afraid emancipation would be seen as a show of desperation and weakness rather than strength."

Stanton remained silent, listening intently.

Lincoln continued, "I have no choice but to press General Meade for decisive and swift action. There's no other way open to me. I regret I waited so long to replace McClellan with Meade. I should've done it weeks ago. God Almighty, am I the only one who sees what a terrible loss it'll be if the secesh prevail?"

*****

At this very moment Lee was making final preparations for the siege of Baltimore. Lee's chief telegrapher Ernie MacIntosh rushed into Lee's headquarters tent. Pushing himself past Wilson and Chilton, he waved a single sheet of paper at Lee. "McClellan's been replaced. Word came just now. Meade's in charge."

Lee didn't know Meade well, but he knew what Lincoln knew—Meade would fight. Lee took the message from MacIntosh and scanned its brief text. "Could mean real trouble. Colonel Chilton, please see what you can find out about Meade? You know, his methods, his tactics, his favorite ploys. Anything you can find."

On October 17, after perfunctorily inviting the civil authorities of Baltimore to surrender, Lee gave Pelham orders for the artillery to commence bombardment of several industrial targets in and around the Maryland city. Lee planned for the artillery to continue indefinitely, although he knew full well that he might have to change his plans if Meade forced his hand.

After three days of shelling from north, west, and south, Baltimore was in shambles. Fires and smoke covered the landscape. In spite of Lee's avowed intentions to focus only on industrial targets and vital areas of the city, the civilian sections suffered immense damage. Entire blocks of houses were reduced to rubble. Civilian casualties mounted into the hundreds. News reached both Philadelphia and Washington by boat and by reporters who managed to slip through the Confederate lines.

The entire Union was suffering from a paralysis of nerve. Voices everywhere were demanding peace and proclaiming that the North would be far better off without the Confederate states. A majority of senators and representatives became aligned with the Peace Democrats.

And where was Meade? October 20, ten days since Meade took command and still no sign of movement. Lincoln began to second-guess his decision to place Meade in command. Meade had inherited a well-organized army, thanks to McClellan, but to Lincoln it still appeared to have the slows.

Nevertheless, Lincoln's choice of Meade ultimately proved to be correct. Although the great majority of Northerners still favored their Little Mac and were upset with Lincoln for relieving him, Meade's appointment brought results.

Meade's former VI Corps, now commanded by General Winfield Scott Hancock, combined with Hooker's V Corps numbered 70,000. Lee's forces concentrated southwest of Baltimore numbered only about 20,000, leaving another 25,000 spread around Baltimore and Wilmington, including the four cavalry commands of Hampton, Morgan, Stuart, and Forrest.

On October 21, Meade finally launched toward the enemy. Lincoln was elated. For the next several days the Confederacy and its sacred *cause* was on the brink of annihilation. Lee's forces were so spread out it was virtually impossible to do anything other than fight a defensive battle, something Lee hated to do. Almost in desperation, Lee decided he needed Hampton and Morgan. There was no further point in having cavalry operating around Wilmington now that Baltimore was under siege.

Lee summoned Tad Dwyer to his headquarters.

"Dwyer, get to Hampton and Morgan as quickly as possible. Here're your written orders. You may convey to them my concern for great haste. Check with Chilton for maps."

Officially, Tad still worked under Edward Groves Wilson, but most of his recent courier duty seemed to be at the behest of General Lee. Tad found himself considering this situation and wondered if Lee had taken a liking to him. The thought filled him with pride and made him more determined than ever to vindicate Lee's confidence in him.

Accompanied by Sergeant Malinski, Tad traveled at a pace to which he was unaccustomed. Sergeant Malinski was slightly younger than Tad and in better physical condition. He was lanky, and his arms dangled to his knees. Yet when he was in the saddle he seemed to become one with his mount. He was a likeable young man, with a warm smile and soft features, and had the reputation of being one of Lee's favorite staff sergeants. This was the first time that Tad had been paired with Malinski on any kind of assignment and they hit it off quite well.

"You holdin' up all right, 'tenant?" Malinski inquired at one point, sensing that Tad was struggling.

"Getting my second wind," Tad lied, smiling through his teeth.

They were about nine miles from Wilmington, moving at a gallop, with Tad about forty feet behind Malinski, when there was a sudden crack of gunfire. And then a second report. Tad saw Malinski slump over his mount. The mount continued on without the guiding hand of its rider.

Tad immediately reined in, dismounted, secured his horse to a tree, and worked his way into a thicket of trees. Acting on his gambling instincts, Tad assumed the sniper was alone. He had heard only two shots. Tad had no way of knowing if the sniper had seen or heard him. Common sense told Tad to assume he'd been seen. He worked his way slowly from tree to tree, his Colt .44 at the ready and his heart pounding. Coming upon a hedgerow of briar bushes Tad paused to shed the belt that held both his cap box and his cartridge box. The game he was playing allowed no room for error and the slightest noise could be his undoing.

Tad maneuvered out from behind the hedgerow of briar bushes and stealthily began to move toward the high trees shielding the sniper. In a matter of seconds Tad and the sniper froze stiff when they stumbled into each other. The sniper was in civilian clothes, disheveled and bearded, giving the appearance of an outlaw more than a Union soldier. He looked to be about five feet six. He was carrying two muskets. The larger musket looked like an old muzzle-loader, but the smaller one was a sidearm that looked to be of military issue.

They were both startled, so it was a question of who could fire first. With almost simultaneous cracks of fire, similar to what one might expect during a formal duel, the two men unloaded on each other. The sniper went down, gasping from a wound in his chest. Tad spun around, the blast biting into his left shoulder. He tried to right himself but fell to the ground.

Acting upon pure instinct and driven by the importance of his mission, Tad struggled to his feet and approached his assailant. Tad could see blood spurting from his chest. The clothing on his upper body soon became matted, but Tad was not certain the man was dead.

Tad felt dizzy and reached out to a nearby tree to steady himself, his gun still pointing at the sniper. Within another minute the sniper's blood stopped spewing and he appeared to have stopped breathing. Tad fought the briars as he managed to crawl to the man and relieve him of both his weapons. After assuring that the sniper had no pulse he started to make his way back to his mount. The last thing he remembered was stopping to pick up his belt with the cap and cartridge boxes. He lost all sense of balance and fell downward into a graceful faint. The last thing Tad remembered seeing was the approaching ground. A screeching noise penetrated his ears. His world went black.

Upon awaking Tad had no idea of where he was or what had happened. His head ached and his shoulder throbbed. His head was spinning and he felt like vomiting. He worked himself into a sitting position and sat perfectly still for about ten minutes. His memory now fully returned, he guessed he'd been out for quite a spell, perhaps as long as ten or fifteen minutes—maybe longer. He pulled himself up slowly and took the time to steady his every move as he made his way back to where he'd tethered his horse.

Mounting his horse was a matter of excruciating pain. Tad put his left foot in the stirrups but couldn't swing his body onto his mount. It seemed like every muscle in his body was on fire. Again, waiting a few seconds, he summoned every ounce of energy and swung himself onto his horse's back.

He rode less than a minute when he came upon Sergeant Malinski's lifeless body. Dismounting was easier and less painful, but as he put his feet on the ground he again felt dizzy and faint. After pausing to regain his equilibrium, he removed Malinski's belt and side arm. He rummaged through his pockets to retrieve any papers or other valuables. Expending every last bit of energy, Tad then dragged him into some nearby bushes. Malinski's haversack and saddlebags were attached to his horse but the horse was nowhere in sight. Time was still of the essence, so Tad simply bade his new friend farewell. "God rest your soul. Amen."

Another hour of agony and Tad made contact with Hampton. He delivered Lee's orders and explained the need for immediate movement of the two cavalry to Baltimore. Then Tad collapsed. He simply went limp and tumbled onto the ground. His shirt and coat were soaked with blood. Hampton called for an ambulance to get Tad to the surgeon's quarters.

The cleansing was painful but necessary. Tad started to come to but then blacked out again. The surgeon poured some whiskey over his open flesh and removed the minie ball. Fortunately, Tad remained unconscious. Later, upon awakening, he discovered he'd been left behind with one of Morgan's men.

"Long've I been out?" Tad asked in alarm.

"Couple hours. How do'ya feel?"

"Hurt like hell. Be all right once I get in the saddle. Name's Dwyer, Tad Dwyer."

"Ormsby. Paul Ormsby," the man replied, extending his calloused hand. "I've instructions to first make sure you're strong enough to ride and second to escort you to Lee's headquarters."

"Think we can catch the others?"

"Tain't likely, sir. They've more than an hour's lead-time on us," Ormsby replied.

"Let's get goin'. No sense in stayin' here."

"Are you sure we shouldn't hang back awhile longer?" Ormsby asked in a concerned tone of voice. "General Hampton gave me strict orders to get you back to Lee in one piece and in

sound mind. Lots of people impressed with what you did, bringin'
that message through."

Tad attempted to mount his horse. At first his body would
have none of it. Then, not wanting to show cowardice, he grimaced,
took a deep breath, and once again hoisted himself upon his mount.

"I'll be all right. But best you stay behind me just in case."

Once in motion, Tad reflected on Ormsby's words about
being impressed with what he'd done. Tad managed half a smile.

By the time Hampton and Morgan reached Lee's
headquarters, the future of the Confederacy looked very dim. Here,
to the northwest of Baltimore, Meade had struck blow after blow
and there was little time to regroup after each successive assault.
Lee hated being on the defensive but he had no choice. Even with
Meade's two-to-one superiority, Lee held fast to his belief he'd be
able to hold.

But still the enemy came at them. This assault by those
people, as Lee was fond of calling the enemy, was the most awesome
show of power by the Union since the war began. Wave after wave
of Union infantry pounded Lee's defenses. As quickly as one wave
commenced to recede, another wave swept forward, trampling
over the dead bodies of comrades who preceded them. There was a
panorama of flying bodies, arms, hands, legs, feet, headless torsos,
and decapitated heads. Yet, in spite of heavy rebel fire, the Yanks
kept coming. From the Yank point of view it was like charging into
the jaws of certain death. From the Reb point of view it was like an
endless stream of marauders coming directly at them, determined
to see them dead.

First, Lee covered his right and then his left. Now Meade
was testing Lee's center, and in so doing he was throwing every able-
bodied soldier he could find into the fray. This was the second day
of Armageddon, October 22, 1862. This was the day that General
George Gordon Meade was going to save Lincoln, save the Union,
and save democracy for posterity. "I can't worry about the losses,"
Meade confessed to his adjutant. "If I let myself dwell on the losses
I'll lose my nerve. I can't hold anything in reserve."

Meade knew it was not enough to focus on only one front. "I
want simultaneous attacks on the left, right, and middle. Give 'em
no opportunity to move troops from left to right or right to center."
Meade barked out his orders to Hooker and Hancock. Nothing
would dissuade him from the wholesale destruction of Lee's army.
Nothing could be left to luck. Meade was firm in his belief that we

create our own luck, be it good or bad.

By nightfall, the lifeblood of the Confederacy was perilously close to annihilation.

CHAPTER ELEVEN

Well behind the motionless bodies and the groaning of the half dead, behind the vedettes and the first line of entrenched infantry, Lee and his generals prepared for the morrow.

In line with Meade's belief that we create our own luck, Lee had created some of his own. The four separate cavalry corps arrived just in time to avert certain disaster. "I want Hampton and Morgan on our right in order to flank the Union left. Want Stuart and Forrest on our left to flank the Union right." Lee wasted few words during the afternoon of the twenty-third as the Confederate lines stabilized.

Early the next morning, the twenty-fourth, just before the 4:00 a.m. waking hour, the kind of luck that no man or army can create for himself or itself came to rest on the shoulders of the Confederacy. The heavens opened and the deluge began. Hour after hour the downpour continued. Both armies commenced maneuvers even as the roads became quagmires of mud. Soon, every soldier and every instrument of war came to a standstill. It rained all day and into the night. October 25 was little better, but the following day was a repeat of the twenty-fifth.

Late in the afternoon of the twenty-sixth, after three all-day downpours, while the graying skies threatened to unleash still more of their devastating armamenta, Lee gave order for his artillery to strike the Union center while his cavalries resumed their flanking movement. For two hours Pelham commanded an artillery fusillade that swept the field from flank to flank. By nightfall, just when Lee was feeling a bit better about his situation, Turner Ashby and several scouts returned and gave Lee some news that caught him completely by surprise.

"Meade pulled his troops back about half a mile. All the

canon shells and shots fell on unoccupied land. Looks like an earthen wasteland but no damage done. Leastaways not to our eyes." Apparently Meade guessed what Lee intended to do, and, in light of the three days rain, decided it was best to pull back and re-deploy.

Lee was down on himself and grumbled to Chilton, "I should've guessed it. Should've sent scouts out 'fore I used that precious ammo. Wasted a terrible lot of explosive on nothing. Meade's probably laughing."

*****

Tad awakened in a cold sweat. He grabbed his left arm to make certain it was still attached. His most recent nightmare found him being chased through woods and underbrush before he stumbled into a wetland bog with cold water up to his thighs. He didn't know who or what was chasing him but every nightmare ended with him being trapped, whether in a body of water, a deep forest, or in some sort of dilapidated building.

Even though he was in throbbing pain, he was determined not to ask for morphine. Best to remain alert, he thought, in the event an overstressed surgeon decided the arm should come off. He hoped it would never come to such a point, but there was no doubt in his mind that they would have to overpower and sedate him before they could take his arm. Then another thought crossed his mind— better to feel the pain than to lose control of my mind under the effect of sedation and blurt out a lot of loose talk about losing those damn orders.

Ormsby had taken Tad directly to one of the battlefield physicians who evaluated his injury and then sent him to a makeshift medical unit, an Episcopal Church just outside the town of Pikesville, to the west and north of Baltimore. The church cemetery, with all the gravestones pointing eastward, served as a holding area for separating the less serious cases from the more serious.

Tad didn't fully trust the surgeons. Being an officer, and hanging around headquarters staff, he'd heard stories about the incompetence of some of the medical people, especially overworked surgeons. Every regiment was supposed to have a surgeon and an assistant surgeon, but this system didn't work too well when there was intense fighting or massive retreat. At such times it was much better for the surgeons to come together from several regiments to work in a centralized facility so that, hopefully, there would be at least one competent surgeon on hand to oversee the more critical decisions.

"Your condition's critical but we might be able to avoid amputation. Least for a while. Healing's started. Lucky. Someone must've poured whiskey into your wound when they removed the minie ball. Best thing to ward off gangrene. Need to rest that shoulder. I mean complete rest. No movement! Understand?" The surgeon minced no words.

Tad thought about the irony that for once whiskey proved to be good for him. Can't remember them removing the minie ball. Had to've been when I passed out after deliverin' those orders to Hampton.

They placed Tad in the narthex, just inside the front door of the church. Here Tad had a commanding view of the main entrance as well as the inside of the sanctuary. Tad's thoughts turned to his mission with Malinski. Damn good man, that Malinski. Never knew what hit him. Lucky for me he was in front. Hope somebody gets his belongings to his family.

Tad saw many stretchers being carried the other way, from inside to outside. These were the fallen who'd been claimed by the angel of death. The dead always had a sheet or something covering their head. Tad didn't know whether to be glad or sad at their demise. Sad, of course, for all who suffer and die. Yet he was glad when he found out the deceased had been one of those writhing in pain and crying for deliverance.

The sights, sounds, and smells were appalling. Men with chest, head, and gut wounds were basically left alone. Perhaps they were given morphine. Tad was unsure. He assumed they were being left alone to die with dignity. Some sights he'd never be able to forget: a soldier with one eye shot out of its socket and another whose bowels had been torn asunder by a mortar explosion of grape or canister. One man was clutching a daguerreotype, probably of his wife or children, haunted by the realization that he'd never see them again. A soldier on the other side of the narthex was hallucinating about being with the Lord Jesus in a garden filled with reptiles and scorpions. Later Tad was taken back a bit when he heard a surgeon tell an aide to "leave the wound open and let the maggots do their job."

From his pallet, Tad saw the wounded as they were brought in through the front of the church, but even more disturbing was the growing pile of bloody and splintered limbs just outside the church door. The warm autumn sun beating down on the decaying flesh soon produced an unbearable stench. Tad focused his sight in the other direction and fought off the smell as long as he could, but before long he got the dry heaves. He cried out in pain as his violent retching aggravated his shoulder. A sanitation worker came over and offered him morphine. Tad held up his right hand, palm outward, in a gesture to indicate a negative response. "No morphine! But please, can you get somebody to move that pile of limbs so's we in here don't have to see and smell it?"

Within a half hour, the pile of limbs had been carted off and buried. As Tad began to feel better his eyes settled on the man across from him. He was lying on his right side and where his left ear was supposed to be was a tiny piece of skin, sort of like a flap covering a hole. Everything around the flap looked reddish brown. Tad noticed the man's head twitching as two flies danced around the flap, landing and then buzzing around and then landing again. Tad wondered why the man didn't swat or swish the flies. Perhaps he wasn't awake. Couldn't tell. Then, just as Tad was about to doze off, he noticed the man trying to turn onto his back. As he turned Tad could see only a stub of the man's left arm, dangling lifelessly midway down to almost where the elbow should be. No wonder he didn't swat the flies.

Tad took a deep breath and looked away, and said to himself half out loud: "Gawd, I couldn't take it. Let me die."

On the third morning he awakened with a feeling of lightness in spirit. Must be my fever's broke, he acknowledged, as he ate a huge breakfast, savoring every bite of the sausage, gravy, and grits. He was still in pain but it was not the constant throbbing he'd been experiencing. He wasn't surprised when the surgeon remarked that the wound appeared to be healing nicely. About noontime they moved him outdoors, right alongside several headstones. Tad played with the thought that this was not a great place to be, but as long as you're able to ponder the fact that you're *above* the ground rather than *in* it, it really wasn't half bad. The air was certainly fresher.

He looked up at the puffy fair weather clouds and noted a formation of Canada geese making its way southward. A couple of late season yellow jackets flitted nearby. Turning his head, he saw a squirrel working on an acorn. He wondered to what extent nature was affected at all by this damnable war. As grateful as he was that he was still alive, he was well aware that the world as he knew it would certainly never be the same.

What was this whole thing about, he asked himself for the millionth time. Was slavery this important? Why couldn't the Union just part company with the secesh? Just let them be? He'd been over these arguments time and time again with no resolution or answers that satisfied for more than a fleeting instant.

Tad drifted off to thoughts of the family homestead. It certainly wasn't a plantation, but it was much more than just a house on a village street. In truth, the Dwyer homestead was a small farm with a few cows, pigs, and beef cattle. Tad began to imagine his father working the land. Thank heaven Jane's there with him, he thought, cause he's not what he used to be and certainly Jane sees he gets fed proper like.

Most of the thirty-seven acres is in hay and corn for the livestock. The Dwyers did not own slaves, nor had Tad's grandparents owned slaves. Slaves were for the big plantation owners of Virginia, the Carolinas, Georgia, Alabama, and Mississippi. Tennessee was never like those other states. Eastern Tennessee was strong Union territory and the rest of the state simply had fewer plantations. Besides, slaves were expensive. They cost money to own and to keep. Seems like Tad never did hear a slave owner fail to complain about how expensive his darkies were.

Trouble is, Tad pondered, cotton is the major money crop in the South and you can't make money in cotton unless you've a huge acreage, and you can't afford to farm that acreage without slaves. When you get right down to it, this war is about economics. The North would take away the economy of the South. And the South isn't about to let it.

At least, that's what Tad believed. He didn't like slavery. He thought it was wrong for one person to own another. Yet, without slavery the South would be plunged into a depression that would eventually affect everyone—wholesalers, shippers, merchants, craftsman, and, of course, the banks. Even if slavery is wrong, without it the South faces depression and bankruptcy. If the war is lost, the South is lost. If the war is won, slavery continues.

Somehow Tad didn't like the direction or the logic of his reasoning. Why was everyone so sure the South couldn't exist without slaves? And why should thousands upon thousands of men die in order to protect the rights of the small number of plantation owners who had slaves? Tad considered the situation a few more minutes, and after a certain point let it go, fatigued by his own ruminations.

Another seven days and Tad was transferred to a recuperation facility just down the road, a livery stable near a beautiful grove of towering oaks and pines. Tad found himself with time hanging heavy on his hands. The better he felt the more restless he became. The thought of a drink and a poker game crossed his mind. A woman'd be even better.

His recovery was quite rapid, but he still wasn't released for return to active duty. He was free to wander and spend his time doing whatever he pleased during the day, returning to the recuperation center only for food and sleep. Medical furlough was out of the question as he was still fit and would be put back on active duty in several more days. No regular furloughs had been granted since the beginning of the Maryland campaign.

One afternoon, Tad made his way into Pikesville, a crossroads with several businesses. The entire area was in Confederate hands, but the townspeople acted as though nothing was different. Instead of Union militia milling around the streets there were secesh.

Being in a state of convalescence, Tad was unarmed. A sidearm drew attention and that kind of attention was the last thing Tad wanted. Tad opened the front door of the local watering hole, a tavern next to the Chesapeake Hotel, the only such facility in the vicinity. Although there were a number of customers seated at the bar, he chose a table toward the back. Even though he wished for someone to talk with, he didn't really feel like imposing on complete strangers. Be just my luck to tipple a few with a damn Union spy and end up saying somethin' I shouldn't, he mused as he downed his drink.

"Excuse us, lieutenant. We wondered if you'd care for some company."

Tad turned his head and saw two Confederate soldiers standing next to his table. One was a sergeant, the other a corporal. The thought vaguely crossed his mind that it was a little unusual for a non-commissioned officer to approach an officer, but those things never bothered him. Tad was never one to buy into formal military protocol.

"Sure, have a seat. Been talkin' to myself so long I know how all my stories turn out." He chuckled, and used his foot to push one of the chairs out toward them.

He was glad to have company because now he wouldn't be tempted to go in search of a woman. Even though the camp followers were discouraged from plying their trade near the hotel and the nicer parts of town, they were never far away. Prostitution presented a problem for the Army of Northern Virginia, but supposedly it was even worse for the Union armies. Louisville, Memphis, New Orleans, and even Nashville had reputations for being meccas for these women, primarily because of the large number of Union troops. Washington was notorious, and Baltimore wasn't far behind. Clap and pocks were common ailments among the troops of both armies. Tad considered himself worldly-wise about those things. On those infrequent occasions when he sought out their favors, he'd take care to wash thoroughly after his indulgence.

Better watch yourself, Dwyer. These guys could be spies. No tellin' by the uniform. Just guard your tongue, he admonished himself. Both the Union and the Confederacy had huge spy networks, and it wasn't unusual for both armies to utilize the ruse of the spy dressed in the uniform of the enemy. Or the pretended deserter who accidentally-on-purpose gets himself captured by the enemy in order to spy or to plant misleading information. Tad remembered hearing about Gabriel de Grass, and how he captured a Yankee spy. He thought about de Grasse . . . too bad about losing his eye.

"I'm Lee and this here's Andy."

"Pleased. I'm Tad," he replied as he nodded to both of them.

The two soldiers were friendly enough, but after downing another drink, Tad sensed that something wasn't quite right. Andy was only about five feet tall and was a bit on the heavy side. Lee was almost as tall as Tad, probably close to six feet, slim, and had distinct features. His chin was rather sharp and his face was clean-shaven and quite smooth. The thing that triggered Tad's uneasiness was that they'd chosen to sit on either side of him, with their chairs snuggled up quite close to his.

They chatted for several minutes and Tad told them he was recovering from a shoulder wound but was about ready to return to duty. Andy, who was sitting on his right, suddenly placed his left hand on the upper inside part of Tad's right thigh. At almost the same moment, Lee placed his right hand on Tad's upper left thigh. "We're sure glad to hear you only took a shoulder wound. Sure wouldn't want anything to happen down here would we?" Lee's voice softened. Tad damn near choked as each man began to gently rub his inner thighs.

"Son-of-a-bitch! Leave it to me to end up drinking with a couple of queers," Tad remarked, as he whisked their hands off him and pushed his chair back, ready to get up and leave.

They each grabbed one of his arms and a soft feminine voice

exclaimed, "Sit down, you fool!"

He looked first at one, and then at the other. One look at their knowing smiles and twinkling eyes and it sunk in. "Holy shit. You're . . . you're . . . you're women!" he gasped.

"Shhhhhhh! Not so loud! Just sit down and listen to me for a minute," the tall one said. After Tad sat back down, she continued. "Okay, I'm Leeanne and she's Mandy. If you want a romp that you'll never forget, you'll never get a better opportunity. Have you ever made it with two women at once, Tad?"

Tad felt flush and warm. He hadn't even talked with a woman in months. Now two at once!

"No, can't say I have. Guess that's somethin' every man dreams about doin'. You really serious 'bout this?"

Leeanne put her hand back on his inner thigh and began to stroke it lightly and lovingly. "Oh, we're quite serious. We just hope you're man enough to take care of both of us. You're a big man, Tad, I just hope that you don't disappoint us." Then, reaching for his manhood, she gave him a gentle squeeze. "Oh wow, I can tell this fellow's ready to get started."

Tad had no doubt he'd be able to make it with both of them. The very thought of a threesome emboldened him. Everything had happened so quickly. One minute he was laughing and drinking with two Confederate soldiers and the next he was being invited to make it with two horny women.

"So?"

"So here's the deal. Mandy and I'll go into the hotel. We'll be in room 206. You wait about ten minutes and then come tap on the door. Got that?" Leeanne was now strictly business. "And don't be tryin' to tell us you don't have any money."

Tad nodded his head. Andy, Mandy that is, leaned close to him and whispered, "Don't keep me waitin', darlin'. I've got a couple real nice surprises for you." She pushed her breasts into his upper arm.

Leeanne was already on her feet. "So long, Tad. Take care of that shoulder," she called out in her affected male voice as she headed toward the door. Mandy hurried along behind her.

"Yeah," Tad observed as he stared at Mandy's departing backside, "that's definitely a woman."

Many thoughts raced through his mind: How come they went to the trouble of dressing up as soldiers? No point in having them work in pairs. They could get twice as much information if they worked alone. Definitely not spies. They've got to be prostitutes. How come they didn't get specific on the price? Hell, how come I didn't ask? Plumb forgot. Damn. My brain's half scrambled.

Money. Damn it all, I've got too much on me. Gals like these've been known to roll their johns. Got to stash some of it.

Leaving his drink unfinished, he got up and went out back to the privy. Sitting on the seat, he removed his left boot. A short time ago, he'd taken some advice from another courier and placed a piece of folded cloth in the bottom of each boot to make them more comfortable. He removed the cloth from his boot and placed all of his Confederate bills, except for four five-dollar bills, inside the cloth. Twenty dollars should be more than enough, even with a tip if they were real good. This was money he'd been saving for months. He'd meant to send it home to Jane but somehow never did. He then slipped his boot back on and re-laced it. He hesitated once again as he tried to think of what could possibly go wrong. He didn't need another lost orders incident. Hadn't he had enough problems for one war?

Then it hit! Dwyer, don't you see what you're doin'? Sure as hell you're gonna regret this. If these two are prostitutes why are they working double? No way! I say they're spies and if you've an ounce of good sense in that head of yours you'll make tracks outta' here faster than Bedford Forrest can ride.

About ten minutes had passed since the two uniformed women left his table and now he found himself bolting out of the privy and beating a fast retreat down the road.

Am I runnin' cause I'm scared of them or am I runnin' cause I'm afraid I might change my mind? he wondered. I don't know but don't stop. The thought sounded like a self-directed command.

How many times had he told himself he needed to mend his ways? Someday, he thought, I must quit this. Come on Tad, you know damn well as long as you say *someday* you're safe, 'cause someday never comes. You'll always find an excuse to put it off. Talk of someday is your ploy to ease your conscience and make you feel better.

After another five minutes of brisk walking Tad stopped and gave answer to himself. *Someday is here. Someday is now. Dammit Dwyer! Now!*

*****

November 27 broke clear and sunny. With the arrival of a new day came the arrival of news that struck like a flash of lightning and spread quickly throughout both the South and the North.

"General Lee. General Lee. Sir!" Major Wilson called out in an uncharacteristically strong voice. "Sir, MacIntosh says the British have declared for us! It's on all the wires."

"How's that?" inquired the skeptical Lee. "Dare not believe it. Are you certain? Sure it's not some sort of hoax?" Lee headed to telegraphy to get first hand information from Ernie MacIntosh.

Several hours passed before the disbelieving Lee was convinced of the authenticity of the messages. Indeed, the English Parliament, on October 13, 1862, upon the recommendation of the Prime Minister and his cabinet, had passed an *Act of Recognition* wherein the Empire of Great Britain formally recognized the *Confederate States of America* as a sovereign nation. All that remained were the necessary steps creating an exchange of ambassadors and the establishment of a British embassy in Richmond.

Lee was too drained to show emotion. He knew more than anyone how close he had come to defeat and perhaps total loss of the Army of Northern Virginia. His only audible response was "We're delivered. We're vindicated. Thanks be."

CHAPTER TWELVE

The two armies were still encamped within a few miles of each other, like two fortresses stalemated, neither side probing beyond its forward vedettes. In spite of formal recognition nothing seems to have changed—the war drags on.

Red and Tad were looking for a game of cards when a familiar voice rang out: "Lieutenant Dwyer, here's a letter for you. General Hill no less. Marked *Urgent*. Must be you're in good with him or somethin'."

"Must be bad news, 'cause good news's never marked urgent."

Tad stared at the envelope for almost thirty seconds, wondering what its contents might be. It was addressed to Second Lieutenant Taylor Arvin Dwyer, Headquarters staff: Care of Major Edward Groves Wilson. The imprimatur on the envelope was simply, General D. H. Hill. He thought for a split second: Hill's comin' after me, sure as shootin'.

Tad took a deep breath as he opened the envelope.

Lieutenant Dwyer,

You are hereby subpoenaed to testify for the prosecution against Sergeant James Stoesser, defendant, in the matter of the lost Special Order 191, Army of Northern Virginia. (See attached Subpoena.)

For further instructions and information you are requested to report to the Judge Advocate, Captain Roland A. Watson, at the address noted on the subpoena.

Thanking you in advance for your cooperation in this matter.

Major General Daniel Harvey Hill, Plaintiff

109

The ambush incident seemed like a long time ago. The time spent recuperating from his shoulder injury gave Tad plenty of time to think things through, but he could never get beyond a certain point in his reasoning process. Tad had no intention of turning himself in. It was his word against the word of James Stoesser, and Tad figured he'd a better than even shot of embarrassing Stoesser if it ever came to litigation.

Reckon Stoesser tried to convince Hill the orders had never been delivered, Tad thought. Stands to reason, doesn't it, the most logical culprit in the chain of events is me?

So there it was. General Hill had evidently not been able to let the matter rest. Hill believed the culprit was Stoesser.

Tad's thoughts rambled on: I'll have to testify under oath that I delivered the order to Hill's staff. I'll be asked to describe exactly what happened. Then I'll be cross-examined. The defense'll attempt to break me down. Make no mistake about it, Stoesser will've primed his defense attorney, telling him absolutely everything, including the kidnapping episode. I'd best tell the prosecuting attorney about the kidnapping so he won't be surprised.

Tad was nervous. He'd bluffed his way past Stoesser at the time of the ambush. Now, could he bluff the jury of officers? Tad felt strongly there was really no way anybody could prove that Stoesser was guilty or innocent, just as no one could prove that he was guilty or innocent, unless Billy Dean Tanner were to betray him, but that was nonsense. Billy Dean would never do such a thing. But what about other surprises? Tad had heard about surprise witnesses and turns of events, but he couldn't imagine other possibilities. He drew a blank when it came to trying to imagine what tricks the defense might have up its sleeve. Of course, he couldn't be sure about Mandy and Leeanne.

Later that day Tad made his way to the office of Captain Roland A. Watson, Judge Advocate and Prosecuting Attorney. Watson was quite stiff and formal. He was about five foot eight inches tall with deep hazel eyes that seemed to penetrate into your insides. He had high cheekbones and was clean-shaven. He gave the appearance of being all business and in total control.

Captain Watson motioned to Tad to sit down. "Glad to meet you, lieutenant," and before Tad could reply, he continued: "Besides General Hill, you're my only witness. Unless you can come up with other people or ideas."

"Not sure I follow you, captain."

"Well, are there other witnesses? People who could testify they saw you deliver the orders to Hill's headquarters?"

"No, not that I can recollect," replied Tad. "I reckon everyone was so busy with their own duty that no one would've noticed me."

"Well then, what's your version of what took place that day?" Captain Watson asked crisply.

Tad knew he was being carefully scrutinized. He figured his best bet was simply to recount the events of that afternoon as best he could. Whatever you do, he thought to himself, don't embellish your lie. Just tell it plain and simple.

"Well sir, I was given the orders by someone in Lee's, excuse me sir, in General Lee's headquarters tent. Not sure who it was. Probably Major Wilson. Although it could have been Colonel Chilton. I went over to the livery to secure a mount. I have my own mount now, but I didn't then. We capture them from the Yanks as often as we can, you know. Anyhow, they were out of mounts.

"Told me to come back in an hour. I didn't like that idea so I set to walkin'. Walked almost an hour. I got confused once but finally found the right place. I remember entering the headquarters tent and asking specifically if it was the H.Q. of General D. H. Hill. Somebody said it was, and then I presented the orders. I don't remember what I said. Probably something like here was General Hill's copy of some special orders.

"At that point I remember one of the men—I think it was Sergeant Stoesser—saying to leave the orders on the desk. Stoesser seemed quite distracted. He appeared to be in conversation with two other men. I remember thinking that everything in Hill's headquarters seemed to be sort of easygoing."

"Then what'd you do?"

"Well, I set the orders down on the table. Stoesser pushed them to one side, near some other paper work."

"Then what?"

"I left."

"You didn't sign anything—or they didn't sign anything?" Watson asked in a surprised tone of voice.

"No, sir. We do now. General Lee tightened up on that shortly after this whole thing happened." Tad guarded his words. He didn't want to appear either too talkative or too withdrawn.

"Is there anything else I should know, Lieutenant Dwyer?" asked Captain Watson.

"Yes, sir. There is," Tad replied.

"On the night of October 17 I was walking a path through some woods at the encampment and out of nowhere I was jumped. You know, ambushed, overpowered by some men. They tied and gagged me and put me in a big burlap grain bag. The big man carried me on his shoulder to a tent. Took about fifteen minutes. Seemed forever. Bounced me around to where I was in pain everywhere. Once we got to the tent the lead man told the other two to take me out of the bag and ungag me. Then I was confronted by what I assumed was the lead man, Sergeant Stoesser. He accused me of setting him up and blaming him for my not having delivered those orders. When I persisted that I'd delivered the orders and it seemed to me that he'd been careless in his handling of 'em, he called me a liar. I threatened him by saying I had a mind to go straight to General Hill and tell him 'bout how I'd been ambushed and kidnapped by his headquarters staff sergeant. I also told him if he was smart he'd make a clean breast of things to General Hill."

"Do you know the names of the other two men who ambushed you?"

"No," replied Tad, "except I think they both work with Sergeant Stoesser."

"Well, that'll be easy enough to find out." Watson seemed pleased to hear about the ambush episode. "Should help our case considerably. Is there anything else I should know?" asked Watson.

"No. That's about it." Tad did not want to convey any lingering doubts or feelings.

"You're familiar with the court martial procedures, I presume?" asked Watson.

"No. Not really. That is, well, we all hear about these things, but I've never seen one," Tad replied hesitantly.

"I'm afraid you still won't have seen one because you're not permitted in the actual court room except when you're testifying. And please remember you can't leave the premises while the court martial is in session. Most of the time you'll just be sitting in the witness area."

After pausing a few seconds, Watson continued, "You know, don't you, Dwyer, the defense will attempt to punch holes in your account of the events. They may goad you or bait you and try to discredit you. The only advice I have is to keep calm and poised. Think before you answer. Make sure you've understood the question. And when I question you, just tell your side of the story the way you just did just now. That'll do fine."

112

Tad was feeling quite relieved. This guy Watson knew what he was doing and how to go about it. He was straightforward and to the point, but in a nice sort of way. Tad felt good about the whole thing.

Except, of course, the whole thing was a goddamn lie and Tad felt ashamed that he'd stooped so low as to attempt to pin his stupidity upon an innocent fellow soldier, even if the fellow soldier was an asshole. But he wasn't going to back down. No matter how ashamed he was of his own behavior, he'd stay the course. He'd play his bluff through to the very end.

The court martial of Sergeant James Stoesser was docketed for Monday, November 3, 10:00 a.m., at a large house that was being used as an annex for headquarters staff.

Tad was sitting in the parlor of a home obviously owned by a family of means. The drapes, the settee, and the chairs all gave witness to elegance and refinement. The pictures on the wall, the accoutrements, and the manner in which everything was so clean and trim and nicely arranged, all bespoke a master and a mistress of class and taste. Perhaps this was the home of a famous politician? Maybe a Maryland aristocrat, or a bureaucrat?

Several other soldiers were ushered into the room with Tad. A major came in and told them not to discuss with one another anything about the pending case. Tad immediately recognized Stoesser's two accomplices from the kidnapping episode. They each looked at Tad and Tad at them. Tad broke out with sort of a sneering smile. Neither of them said anything to him nor did he speak to them. Tad still thought the kidnapping episode was his biggest break because it would cast suspicion on Stoesser as a frantic and fearful defendant. He wondered how Watson would handle it.

Tad's thoughts turned back to that day at the tavern next to the Chesapeake Hotel: I wonder if Leeanne and Mandy were planted by the defense? Maybe they were sent to get me to talk about the lost orders. Tad finally put that thought away, inasmuch as neither Leeanne nor Mandy had been ushered into the witness room.

As Tad sat waiting in the parlor he couldn't help but reflect on where he was and what he was doing. He half wanted to scream out to anyone who could hear: "Hey, y'all. I'm the guilty bastard! Put me in chains and drag me away. I'm the one who lost the orders. Let that bastard asshole Stoesser go. He's innocent. Stop this farce right now. I did it. Do you hear me? I did it."

The general court martial was convened. Seven officers were

summoned, one acting as ranking officer. The court was duly sworn in the presence of the accused and the proceedings began.

The ranking officer of the court read the charges:

On the ninth of September, 1862, sometime in the mid-afternoon hours, at Divisional Headquarters of Major General Daniel Harvey Hill, Sergeant James L. Stoesser C.S.A., noncommissioned clerk to headquarters staff, received and yet did not properly log-in and duly process a dispatch addressed to General Hill. Said dispatch being Special Order 191 from General Robert E. Lee.

"Sergeant James L. Stoesser, how do you plead?"

"Not guilty, sir," he replied crisply.

At this the officer in charge nodded to the counsel for the prosecution: "You may begin, captain."

Captain Roland A. Watson, counsel for the prosecution, called first one and then the other of Stoesser's two henchman.

"The prosecution calls Philip A. Decker."

"Your name, rank, and duty, Mr. Decker."

"Philip A. Decker, Private, Confederate States of America, serving in General D. H. Hill's headquarters staff under Sergeant James Stoesser."

"Private Decker, please tell us where you were, and what you were doing the night of October 17, 1862."

"Well, if the seventeenth is the right date, I can't swear to that your honor, but if that's the date y'all said this happened, then I guess it is. Well, duty was light. We was settled in after the long trek from Harrisburg. Sergeant Stoesser had told us that General Hill suspected him of misplacing some orders, and that Stoesser needed my help in doing some private investigation work to prove he hadn't ever received those orders."

"Go on."

"Well, the three of us, that is Sergeant Stoesser, Corporal Schumann, and myself set out to ambush and get the guy who claimed he delivered the orders. We got him and brought him back to our headquarters tent for questionin'."

"To what guy are you referring? Do you know his name?"

"I didn't know his name at the time. Later I learned it was Dwyer. Lieutenant Dwyer."

"And exactly what did you do with Lieutenant Dwyer?"

"We ambushed him, gagged him, tied him down, and put him in a sack and carried him to the tent. He was a terribly heavy load. Took 'bout fifteen minutes of totin', I'd say. Liked to think we'd never get to that tent."

"Then what?"

"Stoesser did all the talkin'. Stoesser asked him why he was doin' this."

"Doing what, private?"

"Tryin' to blame Stoesser for losing those orders. Stoesser called Dwyer a downright liar. Said Dwyer never delivered those orders to Hill's headquarters." Private Decker appeared nervous as he kept wiping beads of perspiration from his forehead with a red bandana.

"Keep going, private, you're doing fine."

"Well, that's about all there was to it. Dwyer denied it and said Stoesser was careless, and he'd a mind to go straight to General Hill and report this whole thing. Stoesser and Dwyer had more words and finally Stoesser told me to untie Dwyer. Then Sergeant Stoesser told Dwyer to leave and to keep his mouth shut about us bringing him there. Then Dwyer said something about he'd make Stoesser look mighty foolish if he persisted in trying to blame him for his own carelessness."

"For whose carelessness, private?"

"Sergeant Stoesser's carelessness sir."

"Thank you, private."

The counsel for the defense rose for a cross-examination of the witness.

"Private Decker, at this time I have only one question for you. Do you remember ever receiving any delivery of orders from Lieutenant Dwyer, either on the ninth of September or any other date around that time?"

"Objection!" Counsel for the prosecution rose to his feet.

"Sustained."

The counsel for the defense rephrased his question.

"Corporal, to the best of your knowledge, had you ever seen Lieutenant Dwyer prior to this bagging episode?"

"No, sir."

"You're quite certain?"

"All I know is I don't remember ever seeing him before we ambushed him."

"Thank you, Private Decker. That'll be all."

Again Captain Watson rose to his feet.

"The prosecution calls Mr. Allen B. Schumann."

Corporal Schumann was summoned.

"Your name, rank, and duty, Mr. Schumann."

"Allen B. Schumann, Corporal, Confederate States of America, General Hill's headquarters staff."

"Corporal Schumann, please tell us where you were and what you were doing the night of October 17, 1862."

"I take it that's the night me and Decker helped Sergeant Stoesser with the baggin' of that lieutenant?"

"Yes, corporal, October 17 is the date that Lieutenant Dwyer was forcibly removed to a tent."

"Well, all I did was help ambush the lieutenant and tie him up and gag him and stuff him in a bag. He was too heavy for me to carry, but Decker was able to handle him all right. Put him over his shoulder and trudged for about fifteen minutes or so. Poor Decker, that lieutenant was sure a heavy load."

"Tell us what happened next."

"We got him into a tent and took him out'a the bag and removed his gag. Kept him tied though. Then Sergeant Stoesser lit into him 'bout how he'd made Stoesser look real bad in the eyes of General Hill."

"Why was that, corporal?"

"Cause General Hill blamed Stoesser for being careless 'bout incoming orders. Seems the orders got lost or misplaced and General Hill was sure it was Stoesser's fault."

"Had this ever happened before?"

"Oh no, sir. We'd temporarily misplace something, but not really lose it."

"Tell us about temporarily misplacing something. What's that all about?"

"Well, you know how it is in moving headquarters stuff in battle and on the march like we've been. Everybody comin' and goin' and bein' on high alert. It's easy to misplace stuff in that kind of a situation."

"Tell us how that evening got resolved, corporal."

"Near as I can remember Stoesser asked Private Decker to untie the lieutenant. Then each made a threat to the other. Stoesser tells the lieutenant to keep quiet about this here meetin', and baggin' and all, and the lieutenant tells Stoesser that if Stoesser were smart he'd simply go to General Hill and tell him 'bout the missing orders—that General Hill would understand."

"Thank you, corporal."

Again, the counsel for the defense rose to question Corporal

116

Schumann.

"Corporal, at this time I have only one question. To the best of your knowledge, had you ever seen Lieutenant Dwyer prior to the so called bagging episode?"

"No, sir."

"You're quite certain you never received any dispatches or deliveries from Lieutenant Dwyer?"

"All I know is I don't remember seeing him ever before."

"Thank you, Corporal Schumann."

"The prosecution calls Mr. Taylor Arvin Dwyer."

"Please give your name, rank, and duty."

"Taylor Arvin Dwyer, Second Lieutenant, Confederate States of America, General Lee's headquarters staff serving under Major Edward Groves Wilson." Tad tried to mask his nervousness by paying rapt attention to Captain Watson. He hoped no one noticed his sweaty hands.

"Lieutenant, please tell us about the delivery of Special Order 191, on the date of September 9."

All those within Tad's earshot listened intently while Tad repeated his version of the story. Tad seemed poised. He took his time, being careful to make sure he sounded genuine.

Then came the part that Tad dreaded most. The counsel for the defense got out of his chair and came forward. Tad found himself repeating Billy Dean's words. "Keep calm. Keep your wits about you," Billy had admonished him.

"Lieutenant Dwyer, I'm confused about something you said. If I heard you correctly, you testified that in delivering the orders to General Hill's headquarters you'd made a wrong turn that cost you about ten minutes. Would you please tell me about making the wrong turn."

Tad was on thin ice. He hadn't seen the layout of Hill's division and the relation of headquarters staff to the division. He wished now he had taken the time to check the exact layout of Hill's headquarters. Tad would just have to continue his bluff and his gamble based on the fact he'd seen many divisions and headquarters staff, and that each divisional regiment supposedly had ten companies. Each company was lined up behind its captain's tent.

"Easy. I got confused by the several divisional regiments, each with their companies and the rows and rows of tents. As courier, I'd never been assigned to deliver to General Hill. When I got near the area of the infantry tents, I mistakenly turned where I thought the alley would be which would lead to the headquarters area."

"Do you recall the names of any of these alleys?"

Tad knew better than to invent a name. The less he said the better.

"No, sir. I don't remember any names."

"Well then, how'd you find your way to General Hill's headquarters?"

Tad's armpits were soaked with perspiration. His mouth was dry. He managed to scrape some saliva from the roof of his mouth and swish it around, moistening his lips. He took time as he measured every word. "Well, once I realized I was headin' into the regimental and company tent area, I knew I'd made a wrong turn. So I retraced my steps back to the point where I made the wrong turn. I then made the correct turn and soon found headquarters with no further trouble."

"You didn't stop to ask anyone?"

"No, sir."

"Did you insist on a receipt as you gave the orders to Sergeant Stoesser?"

"No, sir."

"Why not? Isn't that standard procedure?"

"It is now, but it wasn't then."

"You mean to tell me that couriers didn't have to receive confirmation of delivery of orders?"

"Until then we were encouraged to get confirmation, but it wasn't stressed very much. After General Lee heard about General Hill's copy being lost, he told us to make sure we got a receipt." Tad remembered the meeting that night when he overheard Lee tell his generals about the lost orders, and how henceforth a written receipt of confirmation would be a policy with strict enforcement.

"Tell us why you didn't have your own mount."

"My primary job was as an aide to Major Edward Wilson. I was sort of a jack-of-all-trades. You know, a gopher. Did all kinds of things. At that time I didn't do a lot of courier duty, so I had to go to livery every time I needed a mount."

"Are you still without a mount lieutenant?"

"Yes, sir. I mean no, sir, I now have my own mount."

"That will be all for now. Thank you, lieutenant."

Tad was uneasy about the politeness of the defense counsel and the way he said 'thank you, lieutenant.' Tad sensed, or perhaps feared, a trap being set that he could not presently make out. Nevertheless, he'd told his story. He'd held up well under the surprisingly brief cross examination and he had, he thought, revealed himself to be honest, forthright, and most important of all, credible. There was no mention of Leeanne or Mandy, so he concluded that the episode at the Chesapeake Hotel was not a set-up.

"The prosecution calls General Daniel Harvey Hill."

Since General Hill was the plaintiff in the case it would seem logical that he'd be called upon to testify. Some thought it was a mistake to subpoena a high-ranking officer in such a case, but Captain Watson wasn't taking any chances of losing this case by not having the plaintiff testify.

"With due apology, your name, rank, and duty, general."

"No need to apologize, captain. I am Daniel Harvey Hill, Major General, Confederate States of America."

"General Hill, may I ask why you've seen fit to bring charges against Sergeant James Stoesser?"

"Because time and time again, I lectured my staff, and particularly Sergeant Stoesser, about the importance of keeping things organized. It seemed to me they were always being careless about things and not enough attention was paid to details, like proper filing procedures, and the transmittal of messages."

"So you've had problems with your staff long before the present problem arose?"

"Yes, sir. I'm not very pleased to have to admit it, but yes. I've had ongoing run-ins, especially with Sergeant Stoesser, and I've warned him repeatedly that it's a serious matter and I wouldn't stand for carelessness."

"Thank you, general. No more questions."

Counsel for the defense arose. Slowly, deliberately, and amid several murmurs and gasps that surely there was no need to cross-examine a major general, the counsel for the defense came forward and addressed General Hill.

"General Hill, the defendant, Sergeant James Stoesser, today stands trial for failure to log in and properly process Special Order 191. I am puzzled, general, by the fact that apparently without these orders you knew exactly what to do and what disposition to make of your forces later the night of September 9, and on the ensuing days of the tenth, eleventh, and twelfth. Would you please help me understand this?"

"I had another set of Special Order 191, which I had received from General Thomas Jackson."

119

"Then why, general, is it so important that the other copy of Special Order 191 be accounted for?"

Hill felt himself to be in a double bind. On the one hand, he dare not admit he was originally quite put out that he hadn't received his own copy of Special Order 191, and that he felt slighted by General Lee. On the other hand, if he did *not* admit to being slighted by Lee, he would be revealing himself as somewhat of a persnickety fuddy-duddy, overly concerned with detail and minutiae.

As Hill thought about it now, he wished he'd let sleeping dogs lie. Now he was risking his own reputation by bringing charges that could've been handled better by an internal house cleaning.

"Simply because the orders were profoundly important, and the fact that I had in my possession another set of the same orders does not alter the fact that there was serious negligence on the part of Sergeant Stoesser."

"Thank you, general. That will be all."

In due order, the defense called Private Decker, Corporal Schumann and Sergeant Stoesser. Each again denied ever having seen Lieutenant Dwyer prior to the night of the ambush episode. They all played down the ambush incident as if it were simply a prankish attempt to test the veracity of Lieutenant Dwyer.

In less than two hours the court martial was concluded.

We find for the defendant, Sergeant James Stoesser. This court stands adjourned.

Tad, of course, was not present, being detained with the other witnesses in the parlor. Sergeant Stoesser came out of the courtroom jubilant, shaking hands and patting his counsel on the back. There simply was not enough evidence to convict him. The issue should never have been brought to trial. General Hill had revealed himself as not only a stickler for proper procedure, but as a somewhat intolerant and vindictive officer, and perhaps negligent himself in not attending to his own housecleaning. Truth be told, he should have sacked Stoesser a long time ago.

Tad was relieved. As a witness for the prosecution one would think he would've been disappointed at the verdict. But he was torn. He'd made that bargain with himself. If Stoesser had been found guilty, he would've had to make a total confession, depending on the severity of the sentence. While Tad was glad his resolve to confess would not now be put to the ultimate test, he was bothered by another likely possibility. Finding the defendant innocent of the charges focused added attention upon him as the only other likely suspect in the unsolved case.

"Lieutenant Dwyer, I'd like to interview you."

Tad looked at the young man who addressed him. The man had brown eyes, dark hair, medium complexion, a well-trimmed beard, and was dressed neatly in a suit, dress shirt, and tie. He sounded quite friendly.

"I'm Arnold Latham of *Harper's Magazine,* and I'm doing a story on the court martial. I'd like to hear more about your perspective on it."

Tad's thoughts were in full gallop. He glimpsed a split-second vision of his future as if granted to him by some benevolent force. The vision gave way to internal words of sharp warning: "Keep your mouth shut, Tad! Shut! All the way shut! Trial's over and done and that's the end of it. You'll not speak further of it. Do you hear, Tad? Promise you'll keep your mouth shut."

"Thank you, Mr. Latham, but no thanks. The trial's over and done and I choose to put it behind me."

"Well, you understand I must write about it regardless. I just thought you'd like an opportunity to tell your side of the story."

"As I said, thanks but no thanks. I just told my side of the story in yonder courtroom and I choose to leave it at that. Good day, Mr. Latham."

Tad concentrated on the handsome face of Mr. Arnold Latham, telling himself to memorize his features and his profile as best he could. This man represented a threat to him. But Tad's baptism into courtroom proceedings had not been in vain. He recognized the threat.

CHAPTER THIRTEEN

I tell you, Billy, General Hill had to be embarrassed by that verdict. I'm guessin' I'll be safe now. I figure if he doesn't bring charges against me, nobody will."

"Yeah, but you better be careful," Billy replied. "I still don't like that *Harper's* guy messin' with this. You did right to say no to the interview. I don't trust him." Tad, reminded of his initial low opinion of the writer, nodded in agreement.

That night, Tad reflected on it. Billy's right, Tad reasoned. Arnold Latham could be trouble. But things've worked out so far. I've just got to keep my mouth shut and not get involved in any kind of discussion about it with Latham, or anybody else, for that matter. Then if a magazine article does come out, I'm not saying a word about it to anybody, except maybe Billy.

By November 25, the news had spread all over, to the trenches, the tents, the taverns, the streets, and the towns. France had followed England's lead and extended formal recognition to the Confederate States of America, but nothing seemed to change as the two great armies remained facing one another to the west and north of Baltimore.

Red was disgusted: "Far as I can tell, recognition by England hasn't made a bit of difference, so what difference is France gonna make? The Union gives no sign of givin' in. The armies are still squared off. Our ships ain't broke any Yank blockades to get supplies to us. I don't see where recognition has changed a damn thing. We're still tired 'n' cold, wet 'n' hungry."

Bert Weatherly disagreed. "Just give it a while, Red. I think in the long run we're gonna see some real changes."

"Maybe," Red allowed. "I shore hope you're right. I just wish this whole mess was over with. I'm sick and tired of it."

Meanwhile, the siege of Baltimore held. Mortars, Parrotts, and Napoleons banged and blazed away about every three hours. The Army of the Potomac was still dug in half a mile south of where Meade halted his advance. The rebel forces were split, with the artillery holding siege around the north and west of the city and the infantry exactly where it was from the onset.

When the skirmishers and patrols of the two infantries weren't shooting at each other, the pickets and vedettes from the opposing forces often enjoyed a round of officially forbidden, but common, verbal exchanges.

"Hey, Reb! Any y'all learned to read yet?"

"I reckon we can read a little. We damn shore read enough to know the English and French are a'comin' in—on *our side*. That's purty good readin'."

"Got any extry tobaccer, Reb?"

"Might have ... if you got a little extry coffee."

"Call off your men, and give us about 15 minutes to get it."

"Aw-right, then. Truce at, uh ... 2 o'clock sharp, Yank."

Although the back and forth between the Yanks and Rebs was generally civil and humorous, the banter sometimes became a contest to see who could hurl the best insults, not all of them good-natured. On each side, the aim was the same: Match the enemy, then go him one better.

"Hey, Yank—yeah, you, o'er yonder: Does yore old man work for a living, or is he a soldier, like you?"

"I druther for my old man to be a soldier than for my old lady to be like yours, chawin' tobaccer and spittin' 'er juice on the kitchen floor."

"I heared you Rebs was usin' darkies to dig trenches and do *mules'* work."

"Yep, but just the females, Yank, just the females."

"Hey, Yank! What's this we heared about ol' Mister Lincoln takin' personal command of y'all's army? Better make sure he keeps his stovepipe down. Thair's a right big price on his head, y'know."

"Wish you was right, Reb. If ol' Abe was to be our general, we wouldn't be carryin' on this nonsense for long. We'd have you licked in no time a'tall."

Remarkably, amid the mutual taunts, an implicit code of honor was observed devoutly by both sides. Should a soldier in either gray or blue have perpetrated an ambush or attack during a trade truce, it would have been condemned as a most reprehensible and cowardly act.

It was November 26 and the chilly gray dawn was typical for that time of year. As the darkness fell a few seconds earlier each day, every night had seemed to become a shiver colder.

At midmorning the snow began falling steadily in huge, feathery, six-fingered flakes that soon shrank and became wetter. That was the beginning of the Blizzard of '62, to be remembered for generations to come. It would force the two opposing armies to focus on survival, not on each other, not on the war, not on anything else.

For the next four days, North America was at peace. No cannon roared, and the Parrotts and Napoleons were quiet. There was no exchange of fire from the cold hands of the skirmishers, the vedettes, and the pickets. No field orders were barked, no wounded men screamed. The dangerous blizzard stilled all. Its freshly fallen snow was the most treacherous possible. Before it shrank, partially melted, and refroze solid, the soft powder could smother the toughest infantryman. Venturing too far beyond his tent to answer a call of nature could cost a soldier his life.

Some of the men fashioned crude snowshoes of flat planks a foot wide and two feet long. Aboard these contraptions, a man could walk a short piece without sinking, but he'd tire quickly, and if he fell, or lay down, he could become engulfed in the snow before he realized the hopelessness of his situation.

One poor Reb, overcome by cabin fever just two days into the blizzard, went outside, strayed away from his familiar surroundings, and was lost before he knew it. Exhausted after trudging in widening circles through the swirling squalls, he sat down to rest, and drifted off to sleep, never to wake. Out to dig a new latrine days later, a detail of men found his body. He was leaning forward, with his head against his knees and the hint of a smile on his face, from all appearances content with the world upon his departure from it.

For those four days in November of 1862, howling wind and driven snow immobilized every crawling, creeping, walking—and even flying—thing. Finally, on the thirtieth, birds took back to the sky as the winds died down and the long-lost sun came out. Clothed in a flowing gown of virginal white extending as far as the eye could see, the earth looked radiant and beautiful and innocent.

That bright morning, both armies began to stir, each commencing its slow dig-out. Soldiers took turns wielding shovels, and the landscape soon was covered with aboveground trenches outlined by steep embankments of snow. After days of enforced inactivity the men welcomed the exercise—throwing snowballs, especially.

By the afternoon of the thirtieth, the men had cleared enough space to conduct drills and get moving again. Given an opportunity to resume swapping insults and retorts, the forward pickets warmed to the challenge.

"Snow too much for you, Reb? You shoulda knowed better than to come this far north."

"Tain't nothin' compared to what we had back in Memphis in '56. Lasted five days. People liked to a'starved to death 'fore it was over."

Then, as if to signal respite from the wintry ordeal just endured, an extraordinary idea blossomed.

"Hey, Reb! Wouldn't it be sumthin' to have a snowball fight, 'stead of throwin' cannonballs at each other?"

"Keep talkin', Yank! We'd just as soon whup yore ass one way as another'n."

Within an hour, a flag of truce was raised and representatives of both sides came together to discuss the particulars of such an event.

"Let's not have any officers."

"But we got to have leaders."

"Well then, we'll allow no one higher than noncommissioned officers. No rank higher than first sergeant. How that be?"

"Fine. And no cavalry and no artillery. Just us foot soldiers."

"Good idea. Cavalry thinks they're such hot stuff. Look down on us. And artillery always got those big guns to protect 'em. It's us infantry that gets the worst of this here war anyway."

"You bet."

It didn't matter who was talking, Yank or Reb. Both infantries shared the same fate. Infantry were infantry and they all thought alike. The foot soldiers absorbed more wounded and dead than any other service.

It took little time for both sides to agree upon basic procedures. Neither army would seek advanced permission from its own command to participate in the fight. Both sides feared the higher brass would overrule such shenanigans. They decided each side would attempt to *con* their commanding brass to go along with the idea. At 6:00 p.m. that evening the highest ranking sergeant on each side would simply inform his commanding officer that his division had been challenged by the enemy to a snow battle. The battle plan and rules would be presented in such a manner that the commanding officer would not be able to forbid or rule against the fight without appearing to be a shameful, gutless, coward.

The rules were stated clearly. Truce would begin at 7:00 a.m. and end at nightfall. The snowball fight will commence at 10:00 a.m. and, unless one side or the other has surrendered, all hostilities will cease no later than 3:00 in the afternoon. Prisoners will be taken to opposing sidelines and held until freed by invasion or 'til battle's end. There will be no trading of prisoners. No ammunition is to be prepared prior to the 10:00 a.m. start of battle.

All of a sudden there were too many rules. Prisoner compounds, number of combatants, number of reserves, leaving the field to outflank the enemy, and procedures for prisoners were covered in detail to the point that everyone was bored. The only three rules that both sides felt strongly about declared there that the simple snowball would be the only allowable form of ordnance, and the throwing of snowballs with one's hands the only allowable form of projection. Absolutely forbidden were foreign objects inserted or hidden within a snowball.

Some thought the rules too restrictive.

"What's this? A game for sissies?"

"Yeah, why can't we play no holds barred?"

"*Cause war is no-holds barred*. And we've had enough of that. For once we're going to have fun and that means having rules," a sergeant replied. "And if you think rules are for sissies, just stick around."

There was only one remaining hitch. What if either the Yank or rebel high command absolutely forbade the snowball battle?

They agreed if it came to that the entire plan would be cancelled. But they also decided it might be a good idea to strengthen the *con* by presenting the higher brass with a written document of challenge from the opposing side. This would have the effect of making the whole thing look quite serious and legitimate and much more difficult for the higher-ups to countermand. The two division commanders were Brigadier General John Sedgwick, U.S.A. and Brigadier General Richard S. Ewell, C.S.A. Neither was reputed to be very tolerant of nonsense and horseplay, but perhaps each could be persuaded to give this terrible war a day off.

The arrangements committee agreed to meet under flag of truce at 7:00 p.m. that evening or as much later as necessary until both sergeants had returned from the presenting of the challenge and rules to their respective commanders.

Neither commander liked the idea. Sedgwick exploded. "I've been had! Been sandbagged. Practically handed an ultimatum. How can I not say yes? If I say no, the Confederates'll think my division's a bunch of cowardly spoil sports. Don't like this idea. Not one bit."

Ewell's reaction was even more negative. "You what?" He sounded like a parent who knew very well what trouble or mischief the kid got into, but asked the question anyway. "Can't believe you'd do such a stupid thing. How could you? Given me no choice in the matter. If I refuse, Sedgwick'll make me the laughing stock of the whole damn Union army. I'm telling you, sergeant, I'll see those stripes come off faster'n you can sew 'em on." His sharp temper lit out at the sergeant so as to be heard by everyone within several hundred feet.

And so it was. The *con* worked to perfection. Both sergeants were worked over the coals, but when all was said and done, neither commander fought back with any gusto. No doubt Ewell would be reprimanded by General Lee, and likely Meade would have something harsh to say to Sedgwick. Nevertheless, in the light of the vast amount of killing and suffering on both sides, it seemed innocent enough to declare a one-day truce.

At 7:00 a.m. on December 1, the sergeants and their respective staffs met to set the boundaries and take care of any last minute problems. The early streaks of dawn were barely visible. By about 7:20 the rising sun had burst upon the white-crested earth and gave one the feeling that life upon earth was the most glorious and the most thrilling experience one could ever imagine. It was good that there weren't many beautiful mornings like this, for if the men gave pause to ponder the killing business, and what it was accomplishing, there might be a mass exodus from the ranks of both armies. One could imagine the commissioned officers of both armies rising some beautiful dawn only to discover their rank and file had departed during the night for places unknown, and henceforth only those who gave the orders would fight the war.

At 10:00 a.m. sharp a bugler sounded forth the call to arms. By agreement, the battle began with both armies concentrated on their respective end lines. All deployment and maneuvering would be from that initial starting point.

The Southern battle plan was to charge as quickly as possible to the nearest thicket, in order to create a semblance of a snow fort that could shield men and ammunition. This would then serve as a forward command post.

The Northern forces did almost the same thing in an advanced grove of trees. Neither side hastened to attack the other, since the preparation of the defensive site took precedence.

Both armies busied themselves in the mass production of ammunition.

By about 10:40 the first encounter of the battle was underway. In contrast to minie balls and artillery fire, the sky was filled with thousands and thousands of white pellets sent on their way by force of human arms. Men went down. No mistake about it. This was tough fighting. A projectile could slam into a man's ear or nose or eye and take him down—even knock him out.

There was attack and counterattack. There was wave after wave, firing faster than ever compared to gun warfare with its laborious and clumsy re-loading. After a man threw eight or ten balls in sequence he'd kneel down in the snow and fashion more pellets and then catch up to the attacking front.

The most eerie thing about it was the absence of certain noises, be it gunfire or cavalry hardware. In the stillness came the sound of men yelling and screaming but without the sound of explosives.

The Yank boys were better attired. They had gloves, woolen coats, and hats that covered their ears. Most of the Rebs had coats, but no hats other than the familiar kepi. Only a few had gloves. Before long the men developed raw, freezing hands, fiery red in color. Hands and feet became numb. Some men had to crawl to safety because their feet were totally without feeling.

At each end, near the flag and the prisoner compound, a band played the familiar tunes of war. "The Bonnie Blue Flag," "Dixie," and "When Johnny Comes Marching Home" could be heard at the Reb headquarters. At the Union headquarters one heard such tunes as "The Battle Hymn of the Republic," "The Battle Cry of Freedom," and "Yankee Doodle." The bands had the effect of cheering people up and providing a focal point for those not directly involved in the fight.

About this time Red was running around like a man possessed. Of course, he wasn't even supposed to be fighting because technically speaking he wasn't in the infantry. But being the talker he was he'd maneuvered himself right into the forefront of the day's activity. Several times he'd rallied the Reb forces. Now he was out of ammunition, out of energy, but he was *not* out of anger. He'd become so caught up in his own personal rage he failed to note his comrades had fallen back, and now he was almost totally surrounded.

Suddenly aware of his situation, he fired his last snowball straight down into the snow rather than at anyone, and flung himself down into a snowdrift. He pounded his fists into the snow, and shouted, "Son-of-a-bitch! Son-of-a-bitch!" over and over again. He quickly became totally exhausted and plunged himself face down in the snow.

Several armed Yanks stared open-mouthed at this crazy rebel, and waited until he calmed down before they approached him.

"Hey Reb, are you okay?" a Yank asked, kneeling down beside Red.

Blinking back the streaming tears, Red looked up into the face of the Yank kneeling beside him, and saw a look of genuine concern.

Red began to sob, the tears flowing down the side of his snow-scarred face. "What the hell are we fighting for? I don't mean today. I mean in this goddamned real war? What's the point of it?"

"What's your name, Reb?" asked the man who had first knelt beside him.

"Dawkin, Red Dawkin. Some folks call me Talker."

"I'm Nathaniel Phillips. Friends call me Nate," the man who knelt beside him said, and extended his hand. As Red took Nate's extended hand, the tears continued to run down his cheeks.

"Pleased t' meet you Nate," Red mumbled awkwardly.

"Lotta men cried since Sumter," Phillips replied solemnly. "Reckon lots of us wish we could let go and be done with this mess."

Red just sat in the snow and stared at Nate Phillips. "I wish I could tell you what I'm feelin', but I can't. Just got real tired out throwin' snowballs and all of a sudden I felt exhausted. Then I was overcome with this feelin' of anger at the whole gol darned war. Don't give a shit any more 'bout who's right and who's wrong. All I know is I'm tired of the blood and the killin' and the whole stinkin' war. I reckon I'm just goin' crazy."

At this, Nate sat down next to Red and put his right arm around him, much as a father puts his arm around his son. Nate said nothing. After about thirty or so seconds Nate stood up and held out his hand to Red. Pulling Red to his feet, Nate looked Red straight on and said, "Red, I believe you're about the wisest man around, certainly not the least bit crazy." At that the two men walked to the Union compound where Red, according to the rules of the day, was interned as a prisoner.

"Hot darn," said a Yank onlooker, "I got me a real story to tell my grandkids. If'n I live long enough to find me a wife."

By now there were almost twice the number of Reb prisoners compared to their Yank counterparts. At 1:40 p.m., a blast of the Yank bugles sounded charge. All at once a grand assault pressed forward in triple rows with about half coming from the left side of the thicket closest to the Reb compound, and the other half coming in circular flank from the northern border, heading west toward the rebel flag. Within fifteen minutes the attack came pouring in upon the few remaining defenders of the Southern Cross.

In one swift movement the flagpole was removed, and two Yanks ran with it toward the Yank end. A rearguard covered the retreat of the men until they secured the flag safely in the Union compound.

The flag was planted in the snow next to the American flag, yet it was lower and off to the side, so that the Stars and Stripes occupied the prominent elevation.

But the Rebs refused to surrender. Actually, they were breaking the rules because their flag had been fairly captured. But nobody seemed to split hairs over such technicality. Having long since used all their reserves, they reformed their lines and made one last effort to free their prisoners from the Yankee compound. The sight was magnificent, with one final fury of charging Rebs, snowballs flying wildly at the Yankee defenders. The Rebs got within forty feet of the prisoner compound before they were rebuffed with a counter barrage of snow missiles that surpassed any other bombardment of the day.

Still, they refused to surrender.

It was now painfully obvious to everyone the South had lost. By 2:20, there was no one left to contend for the captured flag.

It was over! After this last onslaught was repelled the triumphant shouting of the victors echoed across the landscape.

The prisoners in each compound were released, and almost as if by some sense of instinct, all the participants and reserves headed to the center of the muddy-icy battlefield.

In spite of fatigue, numbness, and frostbite, the soldiers from both sides cheered wildly as they met in the center of the battlefield. The scene was one of pandemonium. An uninformed observer would've had trouble making sense of the wild cheering and celebrating.

The cheering ended as the men, as if prompted by an unseen stage director, formed ranks. One long row of Yanks, extending almost from sideline to sideline, faced their opponents who were similarly lined up. Facing each other and having the chance to eyeball each other as never before, a perceptive bugler called them to attention. Then, without any spoken orders, they joined in a spontaneous salute, a salute that transcended friend and foe, South and North, gray and blue.

The sight was never-to-be-forgotten. Hundreds on the field of battle and on the sidelines were either in tears or close to it. Perhaps this was a sign of what was to come? Here were the valiant men of the two armies standing opposite one another. One side was victor. One side was vanquished. Yet at this moment in time they were as one. No one seemed to care about winners and losers right now. They looked each other dead in the face, holding right hand at forehead.

Never in the history of warfare had the eyes of equals met like this.

Suddenly, there was an exchange of cheers and yells even louder than before, so loud that anyone who heard it that day would never forget. Men were shaking hands and some were hugging each other. In an instant, there was no one left on the sidelines as all the support personnel and onlookers took to the center of the battlefield.

Red and Nate Phillips had located each other and stood side-by-side as the combined bands joined together in playing "Tenting On The Old Camp Ground" and "Home Sweet Home." Courageous men from both armies could be seen mixing with each other, arm-in-arm, even as they tried to choke back their tears.

Many refused to let the day end. Some unseen force seemed to hold them together as they lingered, savoring the spirit of the moment. Finally, with the breeze becoming ever more chilling and the sun sinking ever more in its westward trajectory, they went their separate ways, now to resume the business of killing each other.

CHAPTER FOURTEEN

In the North the crescendo of anti-war sentiment and the ever-growing political opposition to the policies of Lincoln, combined with formal recognition of the Confederacy by both England and France, were converging to bring overwhelming pressure on Lincoln to end the war.

Lee knew this to be a fairly accurate assessment because he had daily access to Washington and New York newspapers. The Northern press was increasingly anti-war with daily demands for either Lincoln's outright recognition of the Confederacy as a nation or his resignation from the presidency if unwilling to end the war.

However, Lee had become increasingly pessimistic. He bent the ears of his two most accessible colleagues, Major Wilson and Colonel Chilton. "If we do not prevail in the next several weeks we may be forced either to retreat or surrender. Surrender is out of the question, and I find retreat almost unthinkable. But we cannot continue the siege much longer. With dwindling troop strength and scarcity of supplies, food, and ordnance, I don't see how we can hold through the winter. It's almost impossible to transport food from the Shenandoah Valley. And we've heard nothing from either England or France."

Lee and his generals were in seclusion on the night of the great snowball fight of December 1. Lee was not closed-minded, but he was fairly strong-willed once he'd determined the course he thought ought to be taken. While he did seek others' opinions, he did so more as a gesture of courtesy and with the anticipation they would say what he wanted to hear. In truth, Robert E. Lee, much like Abraham Lincoln, did not handle contradictory opinions or criticism very well.

On that night, Lee seemed more receptive to a truly open council of war than he'd been at any other time on this campaign. He asked the same basic question of each of his generals: "What would you do if you were in command, knowing your plans could not be overturned, not even by President Jefferson Davis?"

First Longstreet followed by A. P. Hill, Walker, McLaws, Ewell, and D. H. Hill. Each spoke their mind, but the net result was a standoff between a defensive posture and an offensive posture.

"Gentlemen," Lee proceeded with reserve, "President Davis has cautioned both ways. All of you have pretty well summed it up. There are advantages either way and there are risks either way. It's been good for me to listen to you because it's helped me clarify my thinking."

Lee now caught everybody by surprise. "We stand dismissed until 8:00 a.m. sharp tomorrow morning. I will have plans ready. In the meantime, get a lot of rest and make sure your troops are honed for battle. Absolute secrecy is essential. Confide with no one."

The day following the snowball battle, December 2, was another beautiful day, very cold with only cirrus mare's tails clouds. For many men of both armies, especially Sedgewick's and Ewell's men who participated in the snowball fight, it was a disappointing day. The men seemed to be in a state of funk, as one corporal put it. They had tasted freedom in the shelter of truce for a twelve-hour period and many had experienced some kind of reconciliation with a heretofore bitter enemy. Warfare separated people and fed on embittered prejudices. Fraternization, even in a competitive frame, tended to cut through the hateful images and permitted the adversaries to see each other in a different, more human light.

Yet the mood of peace and tranquility soon evaporated as both armies prepared for the upcoming clash.

Lee worked throughout most of the night, drawing up all the necessary plans and the orders, which had to be clear in every detail. After only two hours of sleep he was ready to lay out every aspect of his final plan to his generals. He thought to himself that this just might be the most important single meeting of his life.

Just after the 8:00 a.m. meeting began a shout and loud voices from just outside the tent distracted Lee. He immediately made for the entrance.

"What's going on out here, lieutenant?" Lee's voice rang with anger.

"We spotted a man eavesdropping outside the tent, general, and we've apprehended him. Believe he was alone but we'll take him for questioning," Lieutenant Taylor Arvin Dwyer replied.

"For now, just get him away from here. Put him under restraint with a heavy guard detail. I want the tightest security around here we've ever had. I'm holding you personally responsible to see that no one, not even our own people, are within twenty feet of this tent. We'll question the prisoner later. Understand, Dwyer?"

"Yes, sir." Tad had never seen Lee so visibly worked-up.

Indeed, very few people had ever seen Robert Lee quite so agitated or heard him bark out orders with such unrestrained anger in his voice. Lee's generals were almost as shocked by his outburst as they were by the fact that a likely spy had been caught right outside headquarters tent. Everyone in the tent grasped the gravity of the situation. Lee's battle plans had nearly been outlined in detail for the enemy.

After things settled down, Lee regained his composure and carefully outlined his plans. "We'll begin at 3:00 p.m. this afternoon by deliberately assuming a defensive posture. Then we'll attack and quickly retreat, so as to invite the enemy to pound at us. If this does not work immediately, we'll attack again and again, until the enemy counterattacks. It is important that this be a drawn-out affair. Also, our cavalries must be visible to the enemy. All four cavalries must take pains to be *seen and observed* and this must be done not just once, but several times, and especially very late in the day, at twilight.

"Then tonight the four cavalries will head west some ten miles. I want it to look like a very wide flanking operation. I want Meade to think we're attempting to flank him.

"Meanwhile, as the cavalries move out, we abandon the siege of Baltimore and move all our artillery to the front of our entrenched lines facing Meade's forces."

All in all, it was a good meeting and Lee had allowed the men a lot of freedom to contribute, or even to complain if they chose. Lee knew very well the animosity of subordinate generals in other Southern armies, especially the feelings against Braxton Bragg in Kentucky. He did not feel anyone was double-dealing him or creating dissension behind his back. But he knew full well that not all of his staff fully believed in this latest plan.

*****

Even the best-laid plans must be cast aside when an opposing commander strikes first. Robert E. Lee was stunned when Meade struck with a furious assault late in the afternoon of December 2.

The attack caught the Confederate forces by complete surprise. Meade hit the Confederate center with a twenty-minute artillery barrage before sending in thousands upon thousands of infantry. Within an hour, Meade sent infantry against the Confederate center, the right, and the left.

A few days earlier Meade had addressed his generals: "As I see it, there are three primary reasons for lost Union battles such as both Bull Runs and the Peninsula: failure to attack on several fronts at the same time, withholding reserves, and misusing cavalry. I intend to attack center, right, and left simultaneously. I believe isolated attacks, first on one front and then another, only serve to give the defenders a chance to move forces from right to left or left to center. Further, I'll not hesitate to use reserve forces at any crucial point of battle. To my way of thinking, withholding forces may save lives but at the cost of losing battles. Third, I'll use cavalry as a separate fighting force, not field support for infantry."

Early in the fight, travelling from headquarters to McLaw's division, Tad came upon a grove of trees where there were three desperate Rebs calling for water. Tempted to stop and give aid he remembered what Major Wilson said to the couriers: "We work against ourselves if we stop to give aid and comfort to our fallen comrades. There are special details for this purpose. You serve best by pursuing your objective without pausing to give a hand to the dying and fallen, no matter how pitiful their plea or cry."

And so Tad tossed his canteen to the fallen men without dismounting. He gave no other help. He felt guilty as hell but he knew he had an important duty that simply had to take priority. Besides, he was becoming more and more hardened to the scenes about him.

Tad kept moving as fast as he could. He was to be back within an hour. He breathed in smoke and tasted the dense sulfur-filled air. Everywhere about him men were falling back. Some were faceless and some blind. The screams were cries of pathos and agony. Many men had seen the elephant many times, but never as close as this. The trenches were filled with men of both armies. Finally he was face to face with General McLaws who answered Tad, practically shouting.

"Tell Lee I think we can hold. Our defenses are still intact, and the breakthrough of Sedgwick's division has been repulsed. But we need Hill's backup 'cause Meade seems intent on breaking us no matter what it costs him."

Tad pushed his mount to a gallop as he headed back to headquarters. He retraced his steps only to discover the line of battle had once again returned to the original line of the rebel entrenchment. While the Confederate lines were not being advanced, they were certainly standing up to at least double their own numbers.

"McLaws suffered a breakthrough by one of Sedgwick's companies, but it was repulsed. He said he wants back up."

"Did it look to you they were in danger of being blown through?" Lee asked.

"No, sir. But it looked very severe, with terrible losses."

"Do you concur with them that Hill should be brought forward?"

Tad couldn't believe that General Lee was asking him for his own assessment of the situation, yet he made no hesitation in his reply.

"Yes, sir. I believe it's essential. Meade seems intent on hammering his way through our lines, even if it costs him thousands."

Lee turned to Chilton and voiced his deep concern. "This's what I fear most. Meade can afford to lose thousands. We can't. I'd give anything right now for two or three more divisions."

Chilton could only listen.

"You're dismissed, Dwyer. Get some rest, but don't go far. May need you soon."

After dismissing Tad, Lee sent two couriers, each by a different route, to General D. H. Hill with orders to move his entire division to the immediate rear of McLaws.

As evening settled upon the armies, there appeared to be a stalemate in terms of territory gained and lost. Yet the fallen bespoke a message of waste, and perhaps, absurdity. It was the bloodiest single day of the war. The Union had lost close to five thousand men. The Confederacy lost about half that number. Lee knew he couldn't stand even one more day with this kind of loss.

With this in mind, Lee summoned his four cavalry commanders. Canceling all of his previous orders, he armed Stuart, Forrest, Morgan, and Hampton with revised orders that could pave the way for either final glorious Confederate victory or the last hurrah of ignominious defeat. Lee's decision was either reckless and foolish or daring and courageous, depending entirely on whether or not things went according to plan. Results would soon enough indicate which.

Meade's army to the west of Baltimore was thoroughly engrossed in holding Lee's main army in stalemate. This gave Lee the opportunity to do something entirely different with his four cavalries. He did not talk about it beforehand and so it came as a great surprise to his four cavalry commanders.

Lee's orders to Start, Forrest, Morgan, and Hampton, were to move with haste to the northern outskirts of Washington, forming a huge semicircle along the line of the Union artillery defenses.

Eighteen forts and at least twenty-two major batteries encircled the northwestern, northern, and northeastern sections of Washington. Fort Stevens, the northernmost fort, was but five miles from the Capitol building. From Fort Totten, in the northeast sector, a single rifled Parrott could thrust 100-pound shells six miles. If these Parrotts and Napoleons were to be swung around and turned toward Washington it would be easy to destroy the executive mansion or the Capitol building.

Between the forts a strong line of batteries extended from Fort Lincoln on the northeast to Fort Sumner to the northwest. Dozens of field forts and batteries located on lunettes, earthen structures shaped to embrace the fieldpieces, were at intervals of 800 to 1000 yards. All in all, there were over 900 pieces of cannon and mortar ringing the city. The chief engineer of the Washington defenses, Union Brigadier General John G. Barnard, had done his job well.

Placing Jeb Stuart in supreme command of all cavalry, Lee reaffirmed his orders to send the four cavalries westward about ten miles. But then, instead of heading toward Meade's flank, as originally planned, Lee redirected Stuart to make a dash with all four cavalries southwest to Columbia. Lee fixed his eyes upon Stuart as he explained what he wanted the four cavalries to do.

"At or around Columbia you are to proceed with great speed to the northern defenses of Washington and capture as many forts and battery installations as possible. As each battery is captured, *turn all the movable cannon directly toward Washington City,* including the Capitol building, and as many other government buildings as possible. Tell your men to begin firing as soon as they capture and turn a battery."

Stuart interrupted, "And if we can't turn a cannon? Some of these cannon are huge—beyond our capacity to move in the slightest."

137

"Spike it," Lee responded without hesitation. "There are hundreds of Parrotts and Napoleons and mortars that can be turned. I'm sending forty captains of artillery with you, ten with each cavalry. Your cavaliers are sufficiently resourceful to master quickly the fundamentals of artillery bombardment."

This was much more difficult than it sounded inasmuch as it necessitated finding forty additional horses and pairing them with artillerists. Nevertheless, Lee wanted to take no chances. These artillerists now become cavalry could mean the difference between victory and defeat.

The task was accomplished by hook and by crook. Horses were confiscated from every field command and stolen from nearby farms. By daylight on December 3, four corps of cavalry, total some sixteen thousand strong, were moving stealthily through the Maryland countryside toward Columbia. Once at Columbia, a twenty-five mile trek to the south would put them on the northern outskirts of Washington.

With first light on December 4 the combined forces of Stuart, Forrest, Morgan, and Hampton were in position in a semi-circle around the north side of Washington. The four cavalries were free to begin their attacks whenever they were in position. Resistance was light. Each battery was defended with about eighty men, about 80 percent of a full company of infantry.

Storming a battery was treacherous, at least until the cannon was fired. If troops attacked from the flanks immediately after a cannon had been fired, it was virtually impossible for the cannon to be reloaded. If there were three or four cannon located in a particular battery, it became much more difficult to attack. Nevertheless the force of numbers favored the Rebs.

Battery Omega proved to be a particularly difficult battery for the men of Company D, Division II, of Morgan's Corps. Battery Omega consisted of four, thirteen-inch sea coast mortars, weighing eight and one-half tons. The shells weighed 220 pounds, with a range of 4,300 yards. It was situated high atop a knoll. Earthworks underneath the ramparts housed some of the detail, as well as serving as an arsenal. Its backside descended steeply downhill, and hence it was very difficult to approach from the rear, especially on horseback. The front and sides were on a gentle rolling downhill plane. The battery was well defended, with chevaux-de-frise extending in a broad semi-circle at the base of the front, and on both flanks.

Long after other batteries had been captured and turned

upon the city, Battery Omega remained in Union hands. Fighting was intense, with first the Confederate cavalry attacking, and then the Union defenders counterattacking. Sheer numbers prevailed and the Yankees were finally overwhelmed. Never did Union forces show more bravery, courage, and sheer persistence than they did at Battery Omega. There was no surrender. Thirteen prisoners were taken at the very end of the battle when the Rebs swarmed the battery. The remainder of the Union company, Company F., First Maryland Volunteers, was killed. Now in possession of the Rebs, the immovable cannon was spiked.

Wade Hampton reflected Lee's admonitions: "Target accuracy is not important! Only general direction and maximum distance. The whole idea is to aim in the direction of government buildings and to reign terror. If your fusillade fails to strike specific buildings it doesn't really matter. The purpose is to create havoc, chaos, and panic. Keep firing until you exhaust your ammunition."

The cavalry swept from one lunette to another—one battery to another—one fort to another. By mid-morning upwards of 200 Parrotts, Napoleons, and assorted mortars were firing toward Washington City. Cavalry losses were statistically light, but in a manner of speaking, they couldn't have been heavier.

James Ewell Brown Stuart was off to the side of the main action, watching a company of Union infantry taking a stand against a company of Confederate cavalry at Fort Totten. Stuart didn't see the lone Federal gunman running hard in retreat. As he ran off into the nearby woods the Yank caught a glimpse of a gray horse with a rider in a plumed hat. The Yank stopped, paused and took aim. One shot in the abdomen took him down. Although Jeb Stuart did not die instantly his wound proved to be fatal. He would live only until the next day. In this splendid maneuver only eighty-three Rebs were killed, yet one of them, the pride of the Southern *cause*, served as the eyes of General Lee.

Upon Stuart's death, Bedford Forrest assumed overall command of the four corps of cavalry, much as on an earlier day, Jeb Stuart had assumed temporary command of the Stonewall Division. John Singleton Mosby assumed command of Stuart's cavalry.

The war that began at Fort Sumter now came home to the Union Capital. Widespread devastation left Washington in a state of utter chaos. Escape and evacuation became virtually impossible.

By dusk on December 4 the center city seemed to collapse under enemy fire. As the Confederate cannons bombarded the city, the sky filled with exploding shells. Canister was falling everywhere. Fires raged throughout the city as numerous government offices and warehouses burned to the ground. The Capitol building, although taking several direct hits, remained standing. An arsenal, just north and east of downtown Washington, took a direct hit and a series of explosions ensued which brought every living being into the streets to see what happened. The ensuing explosion reverberated for miles. Destruction and fire ravaged the landscape to the point of total carnage. On the streets, pandemonium took over—people searched desperately for a way to escape the bombardment, but they knew that leaving the city would only lead to being captured or killed by the Confederates.

While Lincoln was at the telegraph office, the President's House, a huge and impressive white structure on Pennsylvania Avenue, took a direct hit. The ensuing fire was quickly contained. Several hospitals were hit as well as dozens upon dozens of private dwellings.

Congress was in emergency session. After several close calls, and numerous exploding shells, the Representatives and Senators got down to the business of attempting to force Lincoln's hand and bring an end to the war. The bombardment was having exactly the effect for which Lee was fervently hoping.

The Peace Democrats were in control and even the Republicans offered little opposition. The drama had played itself out and the people of the North had had enough. The ideology of abolition may be considered ethical and moral, but when it came to white civilians and children losing their lives, and others their homes and the fruits of many years of labor, there was nothing left in support of the abolitionist position, at least in Washington.

The cabinet was in a secret meeting at the home of Secretary of State Seward. Seward and Chase dominated the discussion as the cabinet attempted to work out a plan whereby they would face the president with an ultimatum to either end the war or resign from office. Stanton and Welles were opposed to the whole idea and refused to attend the meeting.

CHAPTER FIFTEEN

The young man sat up in his bed. His eyes were glazed and his jaw set in firmness of purpose. He had his usual audience of one.

"The Lord has anointed me to be the instrument of his vengeance on a sinful and corrupt people. Through me He has pronounced his righteousness upon the face of the earth. Who can escape his judgement? Who can endure his wrath? It is no matter that one is black and one is white. White and black are as nothing in the pages of the Almighty. The nations are as a drop in the bucket, saith the Lord of Hosts. All ye that sell the righteous for silver and the needy for a pair of shoes, they that trample the head of the poor into the dust of the earth and turn away the afflicted shall burn because they have rejected the law of the Lord. All ye that pretend to righteousness while starving your servants shall no longer stand. Let justice roll down like waters and righteousness like an ever-flowing stream. Amen and Amen."

Right this minute Corporal Hiram Clark Mills was delirious, although most of the time in recent weeks he gave every appearance of complete normality. Ever since regaining consciousness after being hit at Second Bull Run he would lapse into spells in which he spoke in tongues. He would seem to make sense and then slowly drift off into a babble that nobody could understand. He carried on much in the manner of an Old Testament prophet who made pronouncements about the impending doom of the people if they didn't repent and forswear their ungodly ways.

Mills was a handsome looking man with a ruddy complexion and a winning smile that revealed a deep dimple on each side of his face. He stood about five foot eight, usually clean shaven but now

141

showing about ten days of bearded stubble. He had grayish-green eyes and thick dark brown hair.

Mills was now recuperating at Field Hospital Number Three, six blocks north and east of the President's House, not far from the arsenal that had taken so many direct hits. Mills suffered from hallucinations that contributed to his belief that he was the appointed one of God to bring an end to the terrible carnage of war. A native of Ohio, Mills had enlisted in the 59th regiment of Ohio Volunteers and had distinguished himself in the Seven Days battles in McClellan's Peninsular campaign. He'd seen heavy action at First and Second Bull Run.

On August 28, at Second Bull Run he was wounded above his left hip. Infection had set in. He was sure to die. Due to the press of hundreds upon hundreds of severely wounded, the doctors spent little time with Mills. Everyone assumed he would die. Mills survived six days and nights of unconsciousness. When at last he regained consciousness it appeared he'd lost his mind. Whether the ensuing struggle for life contributed to the young man's delirium will probably never be known. Mills despised Abraham Lincoln with a passion that turned to poison in his deranged mind. His abject hatred for the president took root during the day and a half he lay wounded and waiting for help on a battlefield surrounded by the dead and dying.

After a time, and against all odds and prognostications, both his body and his mind made excellent progress toward recovery. The infection abated and the flesh wound healed, although Mills was left with a slight limp. His hallucinations gradually diminished, occurring only sporadically since early November. During this time, Mills was confined to a special ward with all the other mental cases.

Little did anyone know what was going on in Mill's mind during his period of recuperation. As the hallucinations decreased his rational mind appeared to take over its normal functions. To the casual observer it appeared that Mills was regaining soundness of mind. On the inside, however, a sinister plot was being hatched and nourished.

Mill's recovery was so ostensibly complete he was granted leave time each day. Since exercise was deemed necessary for his full recovery, Mills was free to go anywhere he desired between the hours of 10:00 a.m. and 4:00 p.m., with no restrictions whatsoever. This freedom came with the full and unqualified support of the doctors and other medical personnel who remained terribly overburdened with the wounded from both the Battle of Carlisle and the fighting around Baltimore.

Because of almost everyone's preoccupation with matters of a more serious nature, no one noticed just when it was that Mills started walking the streets of Washington. To an observer it would appear that Mill's daily walks were purposeless and mindless wanderings. Beginning in mid-October, Mills walked in wider and wider circles so that he became well acquainted with the layout of the city. He became especially well acquainted with the area around the State and War Departments.

One day, quite by chance, he saw a tall, gaunt man emerge from the War Department. Mills instantly knew it was the president. A small entourage surrounded him. There didn't appear to be any formal military bodyguard, only a few companions. Mills followed at some distance. Lincoln turned into another small building. Mills noted the time of day. Not wanting to arouse suspicion, Mills crossed over to the other side of the street. He noted that Lincoln had entered the offices of the War Department Telegraph Service.

After many days and countless hours of observation, Mills was quite familiar with Lincoln's daily routine. Ordinarily, Lincoln would spend one to two hours at the telegraph office, but after the defeat at Carlisle and the siege of Baltimore Lincoln was spending growing amounts of time at the telegraph office awaiting news from the front.

Mills' plan was simple enough. When he felt the time was right he'd make certain he arrived at the telegraph office just a few minutes before Lincoln. If Lincoln didn't show up on time, or didn't even show up at all on that particular day, it would not matter to Mills. Mills convinced himself that one sure way to bring his intended mission to ruin would be to force it. Mills could wait. Time, at least for a while, did not matter. Mills figured the greatest risk to be the people in the telegraph office. They may become suspicious. Nevertheless, he reasoned, better to chance having to explain his presence there than to foil the plot by being impatient and over-eager.

Mills intended to be exiting the office through the small air lock entryway as Lincoln and his companions entered. They would pass close to each other, almost face to face. Mills would be in uniform, with his corporal stripes on his overcoat in plain view.

The most difficult part of the plan was securing a sidearm. Corporal Mills had a rifled musket prior to his injury, but that was long lost. Besides, that wouldn't do him any good because he needed a small sidearm he could easily conceal.

One day in his trek around Washington, Mills was on the southeast side of town in an area of run-down shacks and stores. Clearly this was a part of town that one would call impoverished. There were grubby-looking people who appeared to be aimless. The only people who showed any expenditure of energy were the children playing in the snowy pathways and streets. Not many women were to be seen. The men stood near doorsteps, conversing in small groups. Mills felt very out of place but he gave the appearance of one who was completely in charge of his physical, mental, and emotional well-being. Erect in posture, and trim in demeanor, Mills cut a fine figure. He looked so fine and proper one would never guess his treacherous deed was pending only the acquisition of a proper weapon.

Amidst the shacks and stores known as Wharf Row, on Canal Street near L Street, Mills found a salvage store. He entered cautiously and wandered through the assorted racks of gear and military clothing and supplies. He felt slightly nauseated from the powerful smell of mold and mildew. There were all kinds of military paraphernalia but no small side arms. Although he was reluctant to inquire, he knew this was probably his best chance of securing a reliable weapon.

"Anything in particular you looking for?"

"I'm looking for a small sidearm to replace my lost Colt."

"We don't sell side arms, sir."

"Friend of mine said he bought one here . . . 'bout a month ago," Mills said, having no trouble fabricating his story.

At this, the disheveled-looking clerk took him to a back room and told him to wait there until he could locate the owner.

Within a minute or so, a middle aged man approached Mills. The man gave the appearance of being a slick entrepreneur, one who was very careful not to say too much or to leave himself open. He was clean-shaven and well dressed. His hair was combed back and gave the appearance of being greasy.

"I hope you understand, sir, that I don't ordinarily deal in firearms," the man said politely, yet firmly.

"Yes, sir," Mills replied in crisply. "But this friend of mine said he got one here. I was hoping you could help me replace the one I lost in battle. I was wounded at Second Bull Run and am just now recovering. Lost everything I owned."

To this point Mills had told the absolute truth. Mills thought he'd spoken with enough credibility and straight-forwardness to convince the owner of his veracity.

"I understand," the man said, nodding his head. "Perhaps if you could come back this evening, I could introduce you to a friend who might be able to help you."

"No. Must be back at the hospital. Still being treated. I'm only free from 10:00 to 4:00. Could I possibly meet with this friend of yours now?" Mills suspected there really was no friend.

The owner suddenly found himself in the position of losing a possible sale. Greed overruled caution.

"You understand I'm not permitted to sell sidearms and such, without some identification. How do I know what you tell me is true?" the owner asked nervously.

Mills produced his papers even though he knew the entrepreneur didn't have the slightest concern about his identity or what he was going to do with a sidearm. Mills guessed the entire inventory of arms and ammunition was either hot or of dubious origin. He figured the owner's real concern was that a competitor or informer might be setting him up.

"Look," replied Mills, sensing now that he'd stumbled into a shady operation, "I don't care where you got this stuff or how you operate. All I want is to replace my Colt. Can you help me?"

At this, the man motioned to Mills to follow him. "Shouldn't do this. Understand, you were never here and you don't know me. Never saw this place. Agreed? And don't be tellin' any of your friends like your friend told you."

"Agreed." Mills understood perfectly, and nodded his head in agreement. All the better, he thought to himself, for that way you won't be knowing or caring what I'm going to be doing.

Carrying a lantern, the man led Mills through another back room to a flight of stairs leading to a basement storeroom. Once down the stairs the man told Mills to wait for him while he went further back in the dark cellar. The owner lit a candle for Mills and then he took his lantern and disappeared for several minutes. Upon returning he presented Mills with a choice.

"I only have these three. This Colt .44 caliber, U.S. Army model, or this .36 Navy version, or this Adams .44, five-shot chamber from England."

Mills methodically held each, lifting and lowering and sighting. He fondled each, much as one would feel a bolt of cloth, a sheath of leather, or any newly acquired treasure.

"You have ammunition?" Mills would not choose a revolver for which this man could not provide ammunition.

"How much ammo are you talking?" asked the proprietor.

"I like to carry about a dozen shots, and of course some powder."

"No problem. Just tell me which gun."

Mills thought quickly. The .44 caliber was a bit heavier, and more powerful, but a .36 was more than enough to do the job.

Mills released a sigh of indecision.

"C'mon. Not got all day."

Forgetting entirely to ask about price, Mills voiced his decision: "I'll take the Navy thirty-six with the ammo and powder. Oh yes, I almost forgot, throw in some chamber grease too."

"Fine." The owner was anxious to be rid of this guy and wasted no time in calculating the bill. "That'll be $22.00 dollars for the Colt and, let's see, $2.80 for the ammo and powder, and another buck for the grease."

Mills knew this was a very high price. A corporal's pay was $18.00 per month. But this was of no account to Mills. He had plenty of money. He wasn't in a position to be choosy and he didn't want to waste time hassling about price. He absolutely needed what this man had to sell.

Mills handed the man twenty-six dollars.

"Get change upstairs."

"Forget it." Mills could care less about twenty cents.

Mills then deftly disassembled the Colt, putting the ammo and the barrel in his pants pockets—the handle with the small bag of powder in the inner left pocket of his overcoat, and the chamber and tin of grease in the inner right pocket. Mills followed the owner up the stairs into the back room.

Upon reaching the top of the stairs the owner turned and again admonished Mills: "Remember when you walk out of here you don't remember where you bought this stuff and you never saw me in your life. We understand each other, corporal?"

"Yes, sir."

Mills moved quickly through the streets of Washington, heading north and slightly west. He wanted to get back to the hospital in time to load his weapon and then hide it.

Today was December 2. There were huge drifts of snow on the ground from the great blizzard and it was very cold. He was very glad for his overcoat, both for its warmth and for its bulk, which would hide his Colt.

Upon arriving at the hospital, Mills knew just where to go. The latrine was the safest haven around. He needed the privacy that can only be afforded by a one-holer.

He removed his overcoat and quickly set to work in the shelter of the privy. He slid the chamber onto the handle and then inserted the barrel, making certain that it was firmly connected. Mills was an expert at estimating the amount of powder to be poured into each chamber. One by one, he poured in the powder and then inserted the pellet. Then he used the tamper mechanism to seat the charges, gently tamping each of the six charges of powder and pellets.

He opened the little tin of grease and put a dab of grease into the exposed opening of each of the six chambers. Early in the war Mills learned the hard way that if you didn't top off each chamber with a dab of grease you run the risk of double firing. He once fired two shots and a spark from the second shot spread to a third chamber, setting off an explosion that almost cost him his hand.

When Mills finished loading each of the six chambers, he disassembled the Colt. Knowing there would be no opportunity to test fire his Colt, he carefully re-examined each step of the process. Exercising great care, he then wrapped the loaded chamber in a handkerchief and placed it and the barrel and the handle in three separate inner pockets of his overcoat. Then, taking a knife, he slit the linings inside both of the large pockets of his overcoat so he could free up his hands inside the coat. He would now have full use of his hands and could assemble the Colt as he walked down the street. Satisfied with his work, he put his coat back on and headed to his hospital ward where he placed his coat on one of the three hooks on the wall behind his cot, right where he always did.

On December 3, Mills was not permitted to leave the hospital. Word was that Meade was attacking to the north and it was best if patients stayed in quarters.

By the morning of the fourth the cannon were raining havoc on Washington City. No one knew what had gone wrong with Meade's attack. Everybody was shocked that the Confederates were so close to downtown Washington. News was slow to arrive at the hospital and in its absence the grapevine spread rumors. One rumor had Meade surrendering. Another had secesh crashing through Meade's lines. A third had Lee himself leading a charge of cavalry.

Patients were again confined to the hospital, but by early

147

afternoon Mills decided his chances of leaving the grounds were very good. He determined to get moving on his mission of deliverance. When no one was in the ward, he put on his overcoat and walked nonchalantly out onto the hospital grounds as if he'd not a care in the world. He strolled around the grounds several times. On his third trip around he simply drifted through the open gate and out into the adjoining street. No one noticed.

As he walked he put both hands in the outside pockets of his overcoat and then brought each hand in through the slits to the inside. Taking in hand the three parts of the Colt, he assembled it with ease. He slid the chamber onto the handle and followed this with the barrel. Except for cocking the gun, he was ready.

Within twenty minutes he was across the street from the telegraph office. Mills couldn't believe his good fortune when within minutes he saw Lincoln and several associates approaching from a distance. Mills wanted his timing to be perfect, so he waited until they were within about fifty or sixty yards of the telegraph office. At this point he quickly crossed the street and entered the office as he had done on several dry runs. As he crossed the street, hands inside his coat, he carefully cocked his Colt, and then withdrew his hands so they were plainly visible.

Inside nobody seemed to notice him. The place was noisy and people were very occupied with their work. Mills felt certain that if anyone recognized him they would remember him as having been there before and they would think he was nobody to be concerned about.

He entered and then paused. He brought both hands close to his mouth and blew into them, warming them with his breath. He kept reminding himself to show his hands. He waited until he saw the forms of Lincoln and his associates walk past the front windows. Mills was calm and poised. This was the moment of deliverance from the curse of war and killing. His timing was perfect.

An aide held open the main door. One by one the party entered through the small air lock entry to the inside door. Lincoln would be the second one through. Mills started to make his exit so as to catch the president just inside the entry. As the lead man in the president's party turned to back him out of the way, Mills pulled the Colt swiftly out of his overcoat pocket and fired it point blank into the left chest of the president. As the president recoiled, Mills triggered a second shot. The two nearest aides seized Mills and wrestled him to the floor where he was quickly overcome and disarmed.

For the briefest span of time the struggles of earth stood still amidst the shores and skies of eternity. The future of the fledgling democracy hung in the balance as its protector and guardian hovered between life and death. For centuries the earth had been ruled by all kinds of tyrants including dictators, holy emperors, kings with divine right, demagogues, and feudal lords. On the shores of North America a bold experiment in representative democracy had taken hold under a constitution. Since 1789, a federation of states had managed to cede a significant portion of their prized state authority and autonomy to the higher authority of a central government, with a balance of legislative, executive, and judicial powers. And, now, in a matter of five fleeting seconds, this democracy would forever lose eleven of its member states, leaving the remaining twenty-three to survive on their own. No one could know or possibly foresee what the future held for either North or South, free or slave, rich or poor, male or female.

The small entry hall became a crowded den of confusion. The dying president, his assassin, and aides were so entwined with one another there was scarcely room to maneuver. The president was carried inside the office and laid on the floor. He was unconscious and his pulse was weak. Death looked to be but a matter of minutes.

One of the aides was so beside himself he took his sidearm and aimed it at Mills, who by now was tightly bound.

"Die, you miserable bastard traitor." But before the aide could pull the trigger one of the others knocked the gun out of his hand.

"He must be allowed to live so he can be tried."

"Why not let's do it right now? We saw him do it. He's guilty."

"Course he's guilty but we must protect his day in court. Must learn more about his reason and motive."

The president lived another five and one-half hours.

CHAPTER SIXTEEN

I do solemnly swear that I will faithfully execute the office of President of the United States and will to the best of my ability, preserve, protect and defend the Constitution of the United States.

Vice President Hannibal Hamlin, a former governor of Maine with a record of service in both the House and Senate, was sworn in as the seventeenth President of the United States at 10:30 p.m. on December 4, 1862. Hamlin was of medium height, and he had a strong face with a wide mouth and a strong nose. His hairline was receding and he had a bald spot on the back of his head. Within twelve hours of being sworn in, the new president was besieged by demands for peace from almost every conceivable agency and arm of government.

On the morning of December 5, the cannonade of Washington continued. Along the lines between Lee and Meade there was only sporadic skirmishing. Tad was at headquarters when the word came that Lincoln had been assassinated. There were wild cheers and everybody was asking if the war was now over.

General Lee came forward and scolded his staff, albeit in a soft and conciliatory tone: "I see no need to celebrate the death of one, who more than any other human being who ever lived, sought to bring to fruition the dream of democracy. I remind us all that this war is not over. There've been no peace overtures from the Union, nor any sign that there soon will be. Until such time, I suggest that we all go back to the business before us."

At about 11:30 Lee received a telegraph from Jefferson Davis: "If there is an armistice or surrender in the field you will be in touch with me immediately before taking any action. If there is an overture of general armistice or surrender that comes to me via the U.S. State Department I will be in communication with you."

Within the hour Lee received a second telegraph from Davis: "The United States has capitulated. Truce in effect at 1:00 p.m. today, December 5. Meet our delegation at the Court House in Fredericksburg, Virginia 1:00 p.m. tomorrow, December 6, for executing terms of surrender."

Staff Sergeant Red Dawkin called out to Tad just as Tad was exiting his tent. The two men nearly collided. "Sorry, sir," Red said.

"What's up?" Tad asked.

"General Lee wants you. Said I shouldn't come back without you."

Headquarters was in a commotion. Chilton greeted Tad. "Be ready to leave within the hour to accompany General Lee to Fredericksburg."

As Lee tended to all sorts of administrative details, he handed a copy of his orders to Chilton. "Please re-write these immediately. My hand is better, but my writing is still questionable. Please hasten to see these orders are sent to every command within the jurisdiction of the Army of Northern Virginia. I urge special haste to inform the commanders of cavalry and those commanding the batteries of cannon around Washington." Then Lee added, "With any luck no more men will die or be maimed in this terrible war."

General Lee then set out toward Fredericksburg with a party of fifteen. As they departed Lee ordered the lead cavalryman to unfurl a white flag.

Chilton immediately arranged for aides to write multiple copies of Lee's orders.

December 5, 1862, 1:00 p.m.
Headquarters, Army of Northern Virginia, The Confederate States of America
Robert E. Lee, Commander.

Effective immediately, December 5, 1862, all fronts within this command shall cease all offensive action. No one shall fire unless fired upon, and then only after due attempt is made to inform the aggressor of the truce now in effect between the governments of the Confederate States of America and the United States of America.

All units on patrol, or in advanced position, shall fly the flag of truce at all times. No person within this command shall provoke, or otherwise allow himself to become a party to any action which shall in any way endanger the terms of this truce, or the honor of those belligerents in the CSA and the USA who have agreed to this truce.

Every general and colonel shall be responsible for publishing these orders and alerting those within his command of the urgency in abiding by this truce.

Robert E. Lee, Commanding General, Army of Northern Virginia.

Preliminary sessions commenced at the Court House in Fredericksburg at 10:00 a.m., on December 7. Gathered together were Presidents Jefferson Davis, C.S.A. and Hannibal Hamlin, U.S.A. with Vice President C.S.A. Alexander Stephens, Secretaries of State Judah P. Benjamin, C.S.A. and William Henry Seward, U.S.A., Secretaries of War, James Alexander Seddon, C.S.A. and Edwin McMasters Stanton, U.S.A. In adjoining rooms were other cabinet level civilians and high ranking military, including C.S.A. generals Joseph Johnston and John Cabell Breckinridge and U.S.A. General Henry Halleck. General Lee would be the last to arrive.

"Where do you stand on the issue of slavery?" A reporter for the *Washington Daily* asked the new president.

"I believe slavery is immoral. It is contrary to the laws of nature and nature's God. The United States of America is now absolved of all guilt in the matter of the institution of slavery. Henceforth it is entirely a matter for the eleven Confederate states."

"Since you believe slavery is wrong, why are you ending the war?"

"I would have much preferred to continue the war, but the people demand an end to it. The House and Senate are in no mood to continue the war. To let the Confederacy go its own way is not too large a price to pay for the return to sanity and peacetime tranquility and commerce."

Hannibal Hamlin was powerless, and he didn't possess the dream or the vision that was Lincoln's. Although Hamlin strongly opposed slavery he was not the politician that Lincoln was. The truth was that he was in Fredericksburg because he had neither the courage nor the strength of political power to resist the wishes and dictates of the House, the Senate, or Mr. Lincoln's cabinet.

The movement toward armistice began almost as soon as Lincoln was pronounced dead, or so it seemed. The Senate Democratic caucus demanded an immediate end to hostilities and the opening of peace talks with the Confederate government. The House Democratic caucus voted rights of secession to the eleven rebellious states. The Republicans, appearing reluctant, nevertheless acceded to the Democrats. At its caucus late Thursday night, the cabinet, except for Secretary of War Edwin M. Stanton and Secretary of the Navy Gideon Welles voted to grant freedom to the eleven rebellious states.

With the death of Lincoln, there remained few who held fast the dream of an undivided union of states. It was as if Lincoln himself had been the warp and the woof, the sole protector and defender of a strong centralized union. Once he was gone there was no way the Union could survive undivided.

As the time for formal talks was close at hand hopes and expectations were high that the matter could be concluded with dispatch and by evening the land would be at peace. Nevertheless, few people could anticipate the radical demands of Jefferson Davis.

The Confederate caucus took on an unexpected tone when President Jefferson Davis announced that he was going to press for fourteen states instead of eleven. He was prepared to demand that Kentucky, Missouri, and Maryland be included in addition to the original eleven. He would also oppose the giving up of sixty-two counties in western Virginia.

Davis was speaking to his vice president, Alexander Stephens, his secretary of state, Judah P. Benjamin, and the rest of the Confederate entourage. Stephens wasted no time in questioning Davis about the three border states. "On what basis can we expect the North to give us Missouri, Kentucky, and Maryland?"

In his response to Stephens, Davis was adamant. "This's no surrender—it's blackmail! We'll have no part of such an arrangement. Valiant men from Kentucky, Missouri, and Maryland died for the Confederacy. The Stars and Bars bears stars for Kentucky and Missouri. And we'll not give up western Virginia."

What Davis failed to realize was that if he prevailed in his feelings about Kentucky, Missouri, and Maryland, there would likely be no immediate end to the war.

The Confederate States had succeeded in convincing the United States to cease all attempts to prevent them from seceding from the former Union of States. The Union had, in effect, lost the will to continue the fight and so now appeared willing to recognize the complete independence of the eleven Confederate states. Edward Stanton had drafted a surrender document that was approved by

President Hamlin and the remaining members of the cabinet. Both the speaker of the House and the majority leader of the Senate concurred. The United States consented to the secession of eleven states with the exception of sixty-two counties in the western regions of Virginia.

"I'll never agree to such humiliating terms. Who do they think they are? It's the Union that's askin' for peace, not us! It's them that want this war to end, not us! As far as I'm concerned we can leave this place right now and get back to fighting by tomorrow." Davis remained in a state of agitation, constantly wringing his hands and wiping perspiration from his brow.

None of the military personnel dared to counter Davis, but Alexander Hamilton Stephens would not be intimidated. Stephens was a man of slight build. At about 90 pounds, he was extremely frail.

"Begging the president's pardon, sir, but I believe the terms offered by the Union delegation are fair and ought to be given a thorough hearing. They're obviously not going to agree to an unconditional surrender. Not now and not ever. At least not unless England and France invade New York and Boston and wreck havoc on the entire Yankee nation. You know that isn't likely to happen. Furthermore, I can readily understand why the Union won't give up Kentucky or Missouri. These two states never did secede like the rest of us. True, they provided men to our armies, but they've never taken their seats as partners in the Confederacy. Maryland's case is even less defensible than Kentucky and Missouri. And we surely don't want to risk losing everything we've fought for by trying to hold on to the western part of Virginia. And the rest of the terms make all kinds of sense. The safe treatment and return of combatants and the freedom of waterways. My God man, what's come over you?"

Nobody had ever seen this side of Stephens. He was livid. At this point he became even more personal: He looked Davis straight in the eyes and continued his tirade.

"I think, Mr. President, that you've done splendidly. You've persevered. You've fought the good fight. You've achieved everything we set out to achieve. You've defeated the mighty Yankee nation. You've won a great victory. It's the Yankees who've come seeking peace."

Stephens choice of the word, *you*, was an obvious appeal to Davis' vanity and pride. The room was hushed as Stephens continued.

"So we lose Kentucky, Missouri, Maryland, and a Yankee piece of Virginia. So what? They were never with us anyway. Not really. Not in any legal sense. Where were they when we called for money and support? Where were they when we really tried to recruit for our ranks? No, sir. I vehemently disagree that we should go back to fighting. We've won a great victory and are we now to disdain it for the sake of pride and honor, or God-knows what other personal reason?"

Those in his hearing were aghast at this little man's audacity in standing up to Davis.

At hearing this, Davis was so filled with anger he seemed to choke on his words. He was distraught to the point of being temporarily incoherent. Finally, dismissing Stephens out of hand, he managed to put him down: "Stephens, you never were much of a friend."

Silence pervaded the room. No one dared speak. No one rose to break the ominous silence. What had been anticipated as a joyous occasion of celebration had suddenly turned into a wake. Both Davis and Stephens stood alone. No one voiced a single word of support for either of them. Davis remained immutable in his demands.

Sessions were scheduled to begin at 1:00 p.m. when General Lee was expected to arrive. Davis acted disappointed that Lee had not yet arrived. He had hoped Lee would be in attendance at the morning caucus. Certainly, Davis thought, Lee would stand with him on the issue of the three border states.

Lee and his staff had circled around Washington, because Lee preferred not to expose himself and his small entourage to the Union military located just about everywhere on the Maryland side of the Potomac. The going was slow, with slush and flooding affecting the footing of the horses.

Upon arrival, Lee was ushered quickly into the suite of private rooms set aside for the Confederate officials. Davis wasted no time in handing Lee a copy of the articles of peace. Davis was quick to tip his hand to Lee. "Here's the Yank proposal—for what its worth." Lee replied that he would need a few minutes to read the proposal before he made any comments.

Davis, Benjamin, and Stephens, along with Joseph Johnston and John Breckenridge, waited in silence as Lee read the various sections of the proposal.

Finally, he looked up and said, "President Davis, who wrote these terms?"

"Surely, general, that's obvious. They've Union written all over 'em."

Lee, without giving the president a chance to ask him what he thought about the articles, dominated the retort. "And what is your position in regard to these terms?"

Davis looked surprised. "General Lee, I presume you'll agree with me when I say I find them totally unsatisfactory and absolutely unacceptable." Davis' face turned as red as the drapes hanging majestically in the windows. Lines of stress ran down the veins of his neck and his Adam's apple protruded.

"What in particular do you find unacceptable?" Lee said softly as he maintained a firm and stoical stance. He fixed his eyes on Jeff Davis much as a predator spies its prey and never takes its eye off the object of its attack.

Davis gave a quick and succinct answer. "General Lee. We can't give up Kentucky, Missouri, Maryland, and sixty-two counties of Virginia. I've no real quarrel with the remainder of the terms. But I must say I feel the Yankee government is trying to put one over on us. We meet here ostensibly to receive their surrender and we end up bowing to their proposals for peace. I shared my feelings about this in our caucus this morning. Wished you'd been here."

Davis could hardly conceal his anger at what was now happening. Lee looked around the room. He moved his head slowly and deliberately, as if sizing up his audience. He knew General Johnston best. He'd never met Vice President Stephens, who, as rumor had it, was a shadow vice president and had little authority. He'd never met Judah Benjamin and was only briefly acquainted with General Breckenridge.

Nobody had the opportunity to apprise Lee of the remarks made at the morning caucus by Alexander Stephens in response to Davis's position. It was now obvious to Lee that Davis was against acceptance of the Union terms, but he had no idea what position the others held. Lee guessed to himself that Stephens would echo Davis and that Breckinridge, a former vice president of the United States, probably believed Kentucky should go with the Confederacy. After all, Breckinridge was almost as renowned a Kentuckian as the great Henry Clay.

But no matter. Lee wouldn't let this deter him. Regardless of where Davis and the others stood, Lee knew very well where he stood.

"I'll be brief. These terms, whether to your liking or not, are probably the best terms we could ever dare hope for. We've no hope of claiming Missouri and Kentucky, much less Maryland. I think we could make a good case to trim away seven of the 62 counties in western Virginia. Other than that, the terms seem reasonable and logical. Free navigation of the Mississippi with rights to the Ohio River from the Cumberland and Tennessee through Kentucky sounds right and fair. Return of the weapons of war, resources, and men is routine as is the right to establish diplomatic relations. And midnight tonight is none too soon.

"More important than my opinion of the terms is the question of whether or not we're in a position to continue the war toward the end of a more favorable decision regarding Missouri, Kentucky, and Maryland. My response is an emphatic no! We are badly crippled. We were victorious at Carlisle, but with great losses. We've done well at Baltimore, considering that Meade had us on the ropes not once but twice. We lost Jackson. Two days ago we lost Jeb Stuart. We lost over forty colonels and over twenty brigadiers. Yankee supplies and Yankee troops are endless."

Davis started to interrupt, but Lee wouldn't yield.

"Our *cause* has been blessed by a beneficent Providence. With Lincoln's death the Union has made a decision to give us what we asked for and what we fought for. Eleven of our states joined together in a sacred compact to stand or fall with each other in our effort to disassociate ourselves from the Union. Missouri, Kentucky, and Maryland were never part of this compact. We've now been offered precisely that for which we sacrificed and fought so dearly. I've done my best for you. I don't wish to sound arrogant or as one who insists on his own way, but I think it nigh unto impossible to do better than we've done."

And then, as if to focus his full demeanor and attention upon his commander-in-chief, General Lee spoke directly to Davis.

"Sir. It's not my wish to oppose you. You may have my resignation or replace me if you wish. But you asked my opinion. My opinion is that if we refuse this proposal we open again the door to months or years of further agony and useless sacrifice on the field of battle and in our towns and villages. We'll soon spend the remaining vitality of our young men. And when that happens the life and breath of our future is spent also. Make no mistake about it, I wish Missouri, Kentucky, and Maryland had declared for the Confederacy. But the fact remains they never did. That's my position, sir. I have nothing further to say."

The room felt like a mortuary. Nobody dared breathe, let alone volunteer a further word. Everybody in the room except Lee had heard Davis' tirade in the morning. Now it was obvious to all except Lee that Davis was in some kind of a bind. His morning position was in direct opposition to Lee. All except Lee knew that Stephens and Lee were in total agreement about the proposed peace terms being acceptable. If Davis were to assume by the silence of the others that they agreed with him, he might be making a huge mistake.

Rather than responding to Lee's opinion of the terms, Davis asked that he might have a private consultation with his secretary of state, Judah P. Benjamin, and his recently appointed secretary of war, James A. Seddon. Davis was clearly counting on both Seddon and Benjamin to support his position.

Seddon, assuming the position of secretary only three weeks prior, was the fifth secretary of war since the inception of the Confederacy. Everyone knew that whoever occupied the seat of secretary of war would be a patsy. Few people could stand up to Davis. If they did they placed themselves in jeopardy. Gustavus W. Smith was the previous occupant of the secretary of war position, lasting less than a month after replacing George W. Randolph, who had served from March of 1862 until early November.

Judah Benjamin had a great legal mind. He was a staunch supporter of the rebellion, and gave everyone the impression that he'd fight to the death if need be.

The fate of the Confederacy now appeared to reside with the collective decision of four men, Davis, Stephens, Benjamin, and Seddon. Since Davis and Stephens were in disagreement, Benjamin and Seddon possessed the power to create a deadlock or swing the vote in either direction.

"Well," began Davis, "I must say I was taken back by Lee. Of course Lee doesn't have the whole picture. If he did, he'd understand why I take the position I do."

"Why is that?" asked the vice president.

"Because Lee is only one general in one theater of war. Other generals may see it differently, especially Hood and Bragg."

Stephens was quick on the retort. "President Davis, you know perfectly well you've relied more on General Lee than upon any other general of our army. You counted on him originally as your military advisor. When Joe Johnston was wounded you gave Lee command of the Army of Northern Virginia. You know as well as I do that Hood is boisterous about Hood and that you're high on Bragg although he's done practically nothing. It's my opinion that not only is Lee correct in his analysis, but your position is indefensible. Frankly, I don't see where there's much of a choice."

At this, Davis ignored further redress of Stephens, whom he obviously now held in the lowest of esteem. "What's your position, Benjamin?"

Secretary of State Benjamin was slow to speak.

"I've listened this morning, and now this afternoon. My position is based entirely on my understanding of the legal position that binds our eleven states in this war. My emotions are entirely with you, Mr. President. I wish we could command the allegiance of Missouri, Kentucky, Maryland, and western Virginia. But I fear this is impossible. We have *no legal* basis on which to make this claim. Furthermore, we have *no moral* claim. The people of those states, were they forcibly included in the Confederacy, would prove to be a millstone around the neck of the rest of us. I fear it wouldn't be long before each of those states would be involved in their own secession from the Confederacy. As for the counties of western Virginia, I think the Yankees would agree to 55 counties. Seems to me all they really care about is keeping the B&O within the Union."

At this Davis was downcast. Turning to Secretary of War Seddon as his last hope, Davis put the question: "Where do you stand?"

"Sir, I think you're to be admired and congratulated on your enthusiasm and loyalty to the cause, but in truth, I think that we'd best be done with it. I think . . ."

Before Seddon could utter another word, Davis interrupted.

"I've had enough of your shit, Seddon. So that's it. You're all standing with Lee and against me. I never thought it'd come to this. I'm deeply disappointed. Think you're making a terrible mistake that'll come back to haunt us. I've the greatest respect for General Lee but we should never allow the military to dictate civil policy."

Stephens was quick to rebut.

"That's absolutely wrong, sir. I gave you my decision and the reasons for it, prior to Lee even being here. I remind you that Benjamin and Seddon and I are civilian, not military. And I think you do grievous error to take this decision personally, as if it were a personal betrayal of yourself."

Once again Davis was livid. Again he struggled for words, as if he'd not sufficient breath to speak.

John F. Crosby

"I'll take this decision as goddamned personally as I choose, Stephens, and I'll thank you for not telling me how I should, or should not, interpret your rejection of my leadership."

That was it. If Davis attempted to override the will of the three, the matter would have to be referred to the Confederate legislature. Of course, any decision on terms made today would have to be referred to the legislature anyway, as a matter of protocol. But there would be a world of difference between a pro-forma ratification and a genuine debate over the issues of Kentucky, Missouri, Maryland, and the counties of western Virginia.

The 3:00 p.m. hour for convening at the conference table was fast approaching. Stephens, Benjamin, and Seddon emerged from the small office. Davis remained. As the three emerged they were beset with questions from the reporters representing the Confederate states. As a matter of both protocol and courtesy, Stephens indicated any response would properly come only from the president.

Who can say what thoughts went through the mind of Jefferson Davis as he sat alone at the table, a solitary figure with head slumped down upon his arms? Here he was utterly alone in the privacy of his own counsel. He wondered what historians and future biographers would make of Lee's betrayal. And what would the people of the Confederacy think of their vice president and secretaries of state and war?

From this day forth Davis would paint the picture of victory. He would forever after give a public endorsement to the rightness and correctness of the terms of surrender, but he would never live down this moment of private humiliation. Never again would man or woman ever get close to Jefferson Davis. Never again would he share his innermost thoughts and feelings with any but his most trusted immediate family. He would henceforth nourish the feeling of having been maliciously betrayed, especially by General Lee. He would wear this feeling with pride until his life's end. In later years he'd even compare himself to the Christ figure who'd been so callously betrayed by Judas Iscariot.

What did it matter? He stood alone. He felt weak and defeated as he summoned up the strength and courage to face the Union delegation.

Upon completion of a written statement, Davis emerged from the small conference room. He kept his own counsel, giving no word or sign of his decision. He motioned to the entire entourage of Confederate statesman and military aids that it was almost 3:00

160

p.m. Time to return to the main chamber. He chose to be the last to enter the room. He walked slowly to his place at the head of the long table, directly opposite his counterpart at the other end, Union President Hannibal Hamlin.

Davis composed himself to the point of embarrassment on the part of those about him. Finally, clearing his throat as if to presage a grand and eloquent address, he spoke:

"We, the elected president and vice president of the Confederate States of America, together with several of our appointed cabinet officials, and several representatives of the military, do agree, with one exception, to the proffered articles relating to the cessation of hostilities existing between our two governments. The sole exception to be resolved is the number of specified counties in the region of western Virginia, which we submit must not in number exceed this list of fifty-five counties."

At this, Davis handed a list to an aide, who walked the length of the long walnut table and delivered it to President Hannibal Hamlin.

Davis continued: "With the number of counties being no more than fifty-five, as specified, we accept these terms of armistice and peace. We do this with the stipulation that our actions, in reference to the proposed terms of peace, require formal ratification by the Senate of the Confederate States of America.

"We do therefore propose a continuation of terms of truce presently existing. If the Confederate States of America ratifies this agreement no later than midnight, December 31, 1862, a state of peace shall henceforth exist between our two nations.

"However, and please be very clear about this, the issue of the fifty-five counties of western Virginia and the necessity for ratification by the Senate of the Confederacy are *not negotiable*.

"I propose we reconvene promptly at 3:30 p.m. to affix our several signatures to these documents. If these terms are *not* acceptable to the authorities of the United States we shall consider the truce presently existing between us to have expired as of midnight, December 8, 1862."

At this, President Davis stood up and turned to exit the room. His brisk and silent movement served to accentuate the fact the he would make no further concessions and that there would be either a *yes* response or a *no* response from the Union officials without any further proposals or counter-proposals. The silence was ominous. One could hear a pin drop at twenty yards. The time was 3:10 p.m.

The Confederate delegation left the room without any greetings or salutations or any other form of acknowledgement to Union personnel. Once out of sight and sound of the Yankees, the Confederate delegation swarmed around Jefferson Davis, heaping thanks and praise upon him, congratulating him for his courageous and statesmanlike stand.

Everyone knew Davis had bitten the bullet by yielding to the arguments of reason set forth by Alexander Stephens and Robert E. Lee. For his part, Stephens made a purposeful gesture by going over to congratulate Judah Benjamin and James Seddon, for it was they, more than any others, who cast the deciding votes.

At 3:35 p.m., December 7, 1862, it was over. Union President Hannibal Hamlin affixed his signature to the accord of agreement along with that of Secretary of State Edwin M. Stanton.

The room was subdued. The atmosphere was somber. Men of the North and South, fellow countrymen no more, were somehow paradoxically reunited in spite of victory for one and defeat for the other. There would be wounds to heal and scars to remind. Nevertheless, there would be no more fighting, no more killing, and no more agonizing sounds from the living dead at eventide upon the field of battle.

The word surrender was never used. There would be no formal ceremony of surrender, such as the offering of swords and the stacking of arms. Henceforth, any conversations and any matters arising from unfinished business would be channeled directly through the respective secretaries of state. It would likely be a month or two before the usual protocol would be implemented including the creation of embassies and ambassadors.

For now, the respective elected officials of both countries clasped hands, with military personnel engaging in mutual salute.

By 5:00 p.m., both delegations had departed to the sound of peeling church bells throughout the hamlet of Fredericksburg. There was peace upon the land. The sons of the Confederacy had reason to rejoice—they had won their freedom. The second war for independence in less than one hundred years had been fought upon American soil, and for the second time, a lesser power had separated itself from the greater power.

Would the Confederate States of America now grow and flourish as did the original thirteen colonies upon their freedom from the crown? On this day of Southern victory nobody would answer such a question, because no one dared ask.

PART 2

CHAPTER SEVENTEEN

Upon his return from Fredericksburg, Tad wasted no time in reporting to staff headquarters. As soon as Red saw Tad enter the tent, he reached into his breast pocket for an envelope.

"Got a letter for ya, Tad," he said. "Must be pretty important, it's marked urgent."

Tad glanced at the address, reciting his favorite line to Red about bad news. "Must be bad news 'cause good news's never marked urgent," Tad said, beaming his broad smile as he spoke.

Second Lieutenant Taylor Arvin Dwyer.
Headquarters Staff, Army of Northern Virginia, C.S.A.

Now what? Tad thought as he nervously pulled out the sheet of paper. Certainly not another summons for a court martial?

Nov. 19, 1862
    Come to Johnson's Island, Ohio, as soon as possible. Please get me out of here.

Captain Louis Randolph Dwyer, Johnson's Island Federal Prison, c/o Postmaster, Sandusky, Ohio

Tad shared the letter with Red. "Damn! Good news, my brother's alive! Bad news, he's a prisoner of war."

163

"Probably can't get leave. Nobody can go anywhere until the Confederate Congress ratifies the terms," Tad grumbled to Red.

Tad hadn't heard a word about his family since receiving a letter from Jane telling him of his brother Arthur's death on April 6 at Shiloh. She mentioned in that letter that she was writing Louis about Art, but that she was uncertain as to where Louis was. Last Tad heard Louis was with Kirby Smith in Kentucky.

Tad had no idea how Louis became a prisoner. Nor did he have any idea as to his state of health. Was Louis severely injured, or incapacitated? Is he able to be moved? Tad's mind filled with one scenario after another. Tad wasted no time in tracking down General Chilton.

"What's up, Dwyer?"

Tad showed Chilton the letter.

"I'll see if I can get the general to give you a minute. But don't take long. He's terribly busy just now."

Within two or three minutes Tad was face to face with General Lee. Tad wasted no words. "General Lee. Just received this message from my brother. It must've come when we were in Fredericksburg. I'd be obliged if you'd read it, sir."

Lee took the letter and after a few seconds replied, "Son, I certainly understand. You may go to your brother just as soon as ratification is confirmed. But I must warn you, I've heard you may be called to testify in a spy trial. The event may occur within the next several months, or it may not happen for several years, but the Confederacy will persevere in the prosecution of these types of cases."

"Yes, sir. I understand. I hope it doesn't come to that, but if it does, I'll be glad to do my part."

"Tell you what, Dwyer. Let's have Chilton do all the paper work now so that when ratification comes all that will remain to be done will be to enter the date and sign the paper. Then you'll be all set to go to Ohio."

"Thank you, general."

Tad had forgotten all about the man who was caught eavesdropping outside General Lee's tent when Lee was going over his battle plans with his generals. Tad was so preoccupied with Louis' condition that the possibility of a spy trial was far from his mind.

December 8, 1862
Captain Louis Randolph Dwyer

United States Prison Compound, Johnson's Island
c/o Postmaster, Sandusky, Ohio

Received yours of the 19ᵗʰ of November, yesterday, Dec. 7th. Cannot come immediately but will endeavor to begin journey as soon as formal ratification is accomplished. General Lee has agreed to my absence and will supply me with necessary papers. Ratification of peace terms must be prior to Dec. 31, 1862 or hostilities resume. In the meantime, do everything in your power to improve your circumstances. I don't know any details but you must take courage knowing relief is in sight.

Affectionately, Your Brother, Taylor Arvin Dwyer.
Headquarters Staff, Army of Northern Virginia, Confederate States of America, Robert E. Lee, Commander.

*****

Formal services for President Abraham Lincoln were scheduled to be held in the East Room of the Executive Mansion on December 10. Until then, Lincoln's body would lie in state in the rotunda of the U.S. Capitol. Following the state funeral Lincoln's bier would begin its long trip on the rails to Springfield, Illinois. Accompanying Mr. Lincoln was the recently disinterred casket of the Lincolns' twelve-year-old son, Willie, who had died just nine months earlier, on February 20. Little Willie's death of typhoid was a bitter pill for the president and Mrs. Lincoln. Some say Mary Todd Lincoln was never herself again.

The travel plans called for the B&O to carry the funeral cars to Baltimore. Then the Northern Central to Harrisburg and then back eastward to Philadelphia via the Pennsylvania. From Philadelphia to New York City on one of the New Jersey roads before taking the route of the New York Central to Albany, Rochester, and Buffalo. Then by various roads to Pittsburgh, Cleveland, Columbus, and Chicago, before the final trek to Springfield, Illinois.

Hundreds of thousands lined the streets and the rail beds all across the route. Never had people mourned the loss of a leader as the Union mourned Lincoln—this in spite of the fact that most people were genuinely ambivalent. They were grateful that the slaughter was now over, yet they grieved the loss of him who led the fight to preserve the Union.

Lincoln would be loved more in death than in life. The people of the North, except for the abolitionists, were glad for the end of Mr. Lincoln's war, as they called it. It wasn't that they approved of slavery. In fact, the great majority did not. But they were no longer willing to pay the price that the terrible fighting was continuing to exact.

While Lincoln's train traveled to its final destination, the two nations became fixed on Richmond, where ratification of the terms of the Fredericksburg treaty was placed before the Confederate Senate.

The debate, as expected, centered entirely on the issue of Missouri and Kentucky. There was no opposition to Maryland remaining with the Union. And there was only token opposition to the question of losing the fifty-five counties of western Virginia. An executive of the Orange and Alexandria Railroad unveiled a huge map showing how the B&O Railroad would henceforth be traversing the new Union State of West Virginia rather than the Confederate State of Virginia. No one else seemed to care about losing either the fifty-five counties or the B&O.

John C. Breckinridge was invited to testify specifically as to why he, a well-known native son of Kentucky, took the position at the Fredericksburg peace talks that Kentucky should remain with the Union. Well over six feet tall with deep blue eyes and a handsome physique, Breckinridge commanded rapt attention:

"I would love for Kentucky to be with the Confederacy. I much prefer it for many reasons, not the least of which, it is my birthplace and my home. At first Kentucky attempted to remain neutral. But once General Grant occupied Paducah on September 6 of '61, Kentucky was squarely in the Union fold. Then, on September 11, the Kentucky Legislature passed a resolution ordering all Confederate troops out of the state. It's true that the Kentucky Legislature never officially acted on the issue of secession, but not to act, as in this case, is to declare for the Union. After the battle of Perryville, which, as you will recall, was a decisive Confederate victory, General Bragg evacuated all his troops to Tennessee, thus leaving Kentucky almost completely in the hands of the Union.

"Oh, yes, I know there's been a splinter group of secessionists who claimed to represent Kentucky in our Confederate Congress and that one of our battle flag's thirteen stars represents Kentucky. But all of this is to no avail as long as the vast majority of Kentuckians remain loyal to the Union. In short, I believe it would be wrong for us to include Kentucky in the Confederacy against her will."

After Breckinridge sat down, there was a distinct hush. Davis still had a few supporters who insisted on continuing the struggle to include Missouri and Kentucky, regardless of the logic or the cost. Finally, as if the day would be incomplete without him, Robert E. Lee was invited as a special guest and to testify. Lee was soft-spoken and quite candid about the terms of secession:

"Gentlemen, I stand before you as one who loves his native Virginia. As a Virginian I pledged my oath to the *cause* of our Confederate states. I am proud to say that if Missouri, Kentucky, and Maryland had voted for secession and entered willingly and with full measure of support into our confederation I would never have agreed to the terms of peace we accepted at Fredericksburg.

"But this is not the case. History will note that these three states did not cast their vote with us. I think it would be impolitic and just plain wrong for us to attempt to bring them into the Confederacy, asking them to bear allegiance to our Constitution.

"In my humble opinion I believe, as I told President Davis in our deliberations back in Fredericksburg, we have succeeded in achieving every objective to which we committed ourselves back in the spring of 1861. I am very proud to stand here today and give my unqualified endorsement to the terms of peace. Beyond this, I have nothing further to say. Thank you."

Cool heads and voices of reason prevailed. On Friday, December 19, 1862, twenty-one long months since Fort Sumter, the Senate voted overwhelmingly in favor of ratification of what would be henceforth known as the Treaty of Fredericksburg.

The second American war for independence was finally over.

*****

On the twentieth, Tad did not feel he could wait for his long overdue pay. The red tape would take many weeks, maybe months. He'd just have to make do with some cash he'd garnered at the poker tables since the end of hostilities. As soon as he received final permission and the signed and dated papers from General Lee, Tad began making his way northward to Pennsylvania. Since the Baltimore & Ohio was badly torn up west of Baltimore, he decided his best bet would be to take the cars running on the Northern Central to Harrisburg. Once at Harrisburg, he'd board whatever rails he could find that would take him to Pittsburgh, or even to Syracuse or Rochester. From any of these three cities he could surely find fairly rapid transportation to Cleveland and thence to Sandusky.

In Harrisburg, on Sunday, December 21, Tad encountered the unexpected. He recalled how they'd shelled Harrisburg and many of the buildings had been reduced to rubble. Everywhere there were signs of fires that had raged into extinction. Roads were torn up and chaos was in evidence in every direction. It occurred to Tad he wasn't only in former enemy territory, he was in the most devastated of all northern cities except Baltimore.

After Tad detrained, he set about finding the terminal that could connect him either to the west or north. His uniform was obvious to everyone, as was his gold second lieutenant bar on each shoulder. He hadn't gone very far before he found himself caught up in a crowd of angry-looking men who apparently had nothing better to do than to extend jeers and insults to any passerby who seemed to make a likely target. Tad looked the perfect candidate.

"Hey Reb! What you doin' up here? Don't you know this here's Yank country and you ain't welcome, you good for nothing son-of-a-bitch pimp."

"Slave owner! How come you're not down in Dixie where you belong? You should be eatin' watermelon and spittin' out seeds with your nigger friends."

At this last remark, Tad started to react. Instead of ignoring them, he turned his head just enough to let them know he'd heard their taunts. He started to speak and then just at the brink of jumping into a fray he caught himself and sealed his lips.

The crowd took on the profile of a hungry mob. Men in tattered clothing held long iron pipes. Some held crowbars at the ready. Even the women looked eager to exact a piece of flesh or a flow of blood. For most it was an occasion for sport at Tad's expense. It was a chance to avenge the siege of Harrisburg.

Tad kept walking until it was no longer possible. The taunting increased as the small crowd grew larger and more belligerent. Within another half-block he found himself surrounded by the swelling crowd. He stopped. There was nowhere to turn. He ignored the insults, but he couldn't ignore those who began to kick and punch him. After someone landed a punch on his left ear, Tad swung back and had the satisfaction of seeing the man slump to the ground.

This gave the angry crowd the pretext it needed. Tad felt

fists pounding at him from every side. Someone shoved him to the ground, his face pressed into the dirt of the street where he was savagely punched and kicked. Every retaliatory move on his part brought twenty to thirty more kicks and blows from this band of bullies whose frustration knew no bounds. As he spit out the dirt and blood in his mouth his tongue settled into the hole where once he had a tooth. The merciless pounding was all over within two minutes. He was a convenient scapegoat upon whom anyone and everyone could vent their anger and their hatred toward the South.

Wiser heads notified the police, who arrived and dispersed the crowd without making any arrests. Not wanting to antagonize an angry mob, the policemen merely called out, "Move along! Move along now, you've had your fun. Move along." Laughing and talking amongst themselves, the crowd dissipated, satisfied they'd made one Reb sorry he'd set foot in Harrisburg.

Tad lay in the street, motionless and speechless. He was still bleeding from his mouth but the cut on his forehead had begun to clot. He felt like every bone in his body was broken. His legs felt weak and rubbery. He tried to stand, but his legs buckled under him.

He, who was on a journey to rescue his imprisoned brother, was now himself a prisoner of sorts. He was free to go, but he could not move. He was free to move, but his limbs would not obey him. Each time he managed to rise to his knees he slumped over and fell backwards. Finally he blacked out.

When the police took a good look at him they were aghast at the severity of the bludgeoning. In their view wanton beatings such as this had no place in this fine Northern city, even if rebel forces had ravaged it. At least that was purposeful, even if the purpose was unacceptable to the Yankee viewpoint.

The police secured an ambulance to take Tad to the local U.S. Sanitary Commission. The commission operated a field hospital that had been extremely busy during the bombardment of Harrisburg but was now almost empty.

Tad was unconscious for nearly three hours. When he awoke it was early evening. He didn't know where he was but he had no trouble recalling what happened. As he lay motionless, putting together the events that had laid him low, he heard the muffled sounds of women talking to one another. The voices suggested to him winsome femininity and comely faces. He heard no male voices.

Within a few minutes Tad found himself in the presence of two ladies. His first recollection was listening to these ladies talking about the bombardment of Harrisburg back in September. He overheard the younger woman talking about losing her father in the fusillade. A cannon shell landed within ten feet of where he was standing. He'd worked as a journalist for the local newspaper and was covering the story.

The other woman was older, more matronly. The younger one called her Nancy. Nancy reminded Tad of his mother, Mary Hill Arvin Dwyer. How he loved his mother. As he lay there he recalled the day of Arthur's birth. Everybody was excited. Tad, Lucy, Jane, and Louis were going to have a new sister or brother. But with Arthur's birth came their mother's death.

Now Tad would never see his mother again. The old memories played through Tad's mind as if they had happened yesterday. He recalled the funeral with the reverend and his tear-jerk sermon about being with the Lord Jesus and forgiveness for sinners. Forgiveness for what? Then the cemetery. The casket into the ground. Ashes to ashes and dust to dust. Oh how terribly lonely he had felt—empty and forsaken. The pain of loss was excruciating. Nine-year-old Tad, the firstborn child, became a man before his time.

Tad, remembering his role in the barrage of Harrisburg, decided to keep his own counsel about his whereabouts on that particular day. For now, although he was wracked with pain, he was being nursed as no man was ever nursed. He was receiving tender and loving care that couldn't help but blunt the terrible pain throughout his body. The women cleansed and dressed his wounds. They sponge bathed him. They fed him tea and chicken broth. He no sooner finished eating than he tired and dozed off. When he awoke it was a beautiful sun-lit December morning.

Later Tad found himself apologizing to the ladies for the war: "Not that the South was wrong in seceding, but I and countless others owned no slaves and had nothing to do with slavery. Being from Tennessee, I felt I had to fight for secession and the *cause* of states' rights."

Tad wanted them to know he had no ulterior motive in coming to Harrisburg. "Was transferring terminals. Came in on the Northern Central. Wanted to find a train that'd get me west to Ohio. Must get to my wounded brother. He's a prisoner of war at Johnson's Island."

"Where is Johnson's Island? I've heard of it but can't say I know where it is," the younger of the two nurses responded.

"It's near Sandusky, Ohio, out near where Sandusky Bay

blends into Lake Erie." Tad was glad for the conversation.

Of a sudden Tad realized that no one knew who he was, not even his name.

"I'm Tad Dwyer."

"Pleased to meet you, Mr. Dwyer. My name is Sandra Abernathy. We did know your name, though. Had to find out who you were. Standard policy when someone's unconscious like you were. Hope you don't mind."

"Naw. I had two pieces though. A haversack and a knapsack. Hope everything's all right. Nothin' missin'."

"Yes. We have two pieces plus your clothing. We washed your clothing but couldn't get all the blood stains out. Your shirt was ripped nearly to pieces. I have no idea if anything is missing from your knapsack and haversack. In a day or so, when you're up to it, you can go through your things and make sure everything's in order."

Tad had so much time on his hands he tired himself thinking about the future. What would he do when he found Louis? What would he do when he was back home in LaVergne? Why couldn't he fall in love with a fine, lovely woman like Sandra and be contented? Raise a family like his brother Louis? Look at that nurse Sandra Abernathy! Can't keep my eyes off her. She's beautiful! Look at that hair. Sort of honey blonde. Her eyes sparkle and her nose is tiny and a bit perky. Chin just right. Appears to be well-endowed. Seems full of love and caring. Damn, sure would like to marry somebody like her.

Tad reminisced about the women in his life. No serious relationships. He thought about a couple rolls in the hay with a girl friend when he was barely eighteen or so, and losing his self-respect in a few brothels early in the war. Tad's musings took him back to the time he tried to talk himself into being in love. I must've been about twenty. Nice gal. Betty Jo Morely. Very attractive. Nice figure. Well-rounded. Sure got me excited, but I never had any real feelin's for her. Feelin's like really caring about her and wantin' to be with her permanent like, not just for sex.

Tad sank deeper into a mellow and tender mood.

Sure wish I could be in love. Really in love, the kind of love you hear people talkin' about. The kind of love where you go nuts over the girl and feel squeamish inside and feel you just have to be with her 'cause you feel so incomplete without her. Kind of love where even *after* sex you want to stay close to her and hold her and be with her, instead of rushin' to get the hell away from her. Damn, I love sex as much as the next guy but I want love too. Real love. The kind that lasts.

On the third day, Tad began to feel better. His strength was returning and he could move his limbs without grimacing or wincing. On the morning of the sixth day Tad was released. The nurses had managed to repair his uniform. The shirt was beyond repair and the ladies had somehow secured a new one. Sandra suggested to Tad that he might be better off wearing civilian clothes, at least until he was out of this war-ravaged part of Pennsylvania.

"I appreciate your concern and am very thankful for your care and all the help you've been to me, but I wouldn't feel right not wearing my uniform. Tell you what, though, I'd be mighty relieved if you'd see me safely on the train."

Nancy Langley countered: "We'll be glad to do that for you, Lieutenant Dwyer, but only if you'll agree to remove those gold lieutenant bars from your shoulders. At least until you're out of Harrisburg." Tad nodded that maybe that would be a good idea.

Tad and the two nurses rode in a borrowed carriage. Tad, with his back toward the front, suddenly sucked in his breath. His eyes fell upon a man whose face was indelibly imprinted in his mind. Over there outside the front door of a general store was the man whom he'd seen in Harrisburg back in September, while he was waiting for the mayor of the city to render a decision on General Lee's request for surrender. Tad would always remember that face. Somehow it remained etched in his memory. He was of medium height, had strong blue eyes, sagging eyebrows, a weak cut of jaw, and a sizable and sharply trimmed moustache. He gave the appearance of being a man of means, well dressed, with strong and erect posture, carrying a walking stick. Tad recalled that in some manner his physical appearance had been intimidating. Furthermore, he remembered, someone had referred to him as Will. Will who? He couldn't recall.

Pointing to him, Tad asked if either of them knew who he was. Both ladies turned their heads to get a good look. Sandra said she'd never seen him before. But Nancy Langley commented, "I don't know his name, but I've heard he's a Southerner who came here during the war. Why do you ask? Surely he wasn't one of those thugs who beat you up?"

"No, but I feel I've seen him somewhere before." Tad paused for a second. He decided under the circumstances it was better to let the subject drop.

They all lingered at the terminal. Tad was reluctant to board the cars. Neither of the women seemed anxious to leave before the train departed. Tad hugged Nancy and told her how appreciative he was for all she'd done. Then he turned to Sandra. He really wanted to kiss her but he restrained himself. He gave her a warm hug and kissed her on the cheek. Still holding her he said, "I'm truly sorry about your father. I feel partly responsible." Sandra appeared to choke up. Tad continued, "Words can't express my gratitude for you takin' such good care o' me." Tad started to let go when Sandra kissed him square on the lips. Tad held onto that kiss for as long as he dared.

Tad continued to wave as the train pulled out of the station and the two figures became smaller and smaller specs on the horizon. Damn, Tad thought, should've gotten their address so I could write a proper thank you. But it might be better to write a letter to the editor of the newspaper. That way the whole city'll know of their kindness as well as the brutality of those guys that beat me.

After another three days on the rails, waiting in terminals, and sleeping on hard wooden benches, Tad arrived in Sandusky. It was Tuesday, December 30, two days before the New Year. Would Louis be alive? If alive, would he still be at Johnson's Island? Would he be mobile? He had no idea what to expect. He had very little money. Had nothing to sell. Could hardly even sell his labor because his body was still racked with pain.

Tad made his way to the waterfront and talked his way on board a U.S. Navy scow headed for Johnson's Island.

"Have they started to release prisoners yet?" he asked the helmsman.

"Yes. Started last week. Fifteen or twenty each day. Those that've left appeared to be the healthiest. So I hear."

"Ever hear of a Captain Louis Dwyer?"

"No. Can't say I have. He kin of yours?"

"My brother."

"You secesh really not welcome here. After what you did to our country. Glad it's over, though I'm sure sorry to see the Union split forever," the helmsman remarked.

Tad muttered to himself, that perhaps one day the country would reunite. Within a few more seconds the stream of thought was lost from memory. For now, Tad only wanted to find Louis and be on his way home.

As Tad debarked he couldn't help notice how drab Johnson's

Island looked. Gloom seemed to hang over the island. The overcast sky was gray with wisps of darker clouds. Seagulls were screeching their familiar cry for prey. The air felt foreboding, as if it would begin to snow any minute. The wind felt constant, although today it was not over seven or eight knots. Tad walked by the drab wooden barracks, and wondered what it must have been like for his brother to live in this gray, god-forsaken place.

Everything seemed to be an experience of sitting and waiting, and then being sent on, from one clerk to another, and then to the captain, and finally to the commander in charge. In two hours of waiting he produced his credentials three times in as many stations. Finally, the officer in charge told him: "Down the center of the barracks, fourth bed on the left."

Louis appeared to be dozing. Tad could hardly contain himself. Louis awoke with a start. He appeared to be all right. Tad leaned over and hugged his brother's head. Probably hurt Tad more than it did Louis. Tad started to cry tears that'd been stored up over many months.

When Tad regained his composure he asked Louis about his health.

"How bad is it, Louis? I got here quick as I could once the terms were ratified. You got my letter didn't you?"

"Yeah. Thanks. Made me feel a hell of a lot better knowin' you were comin'. Made a lot of progress since then. Think I'm gonna' make it. If y'all can get me home, I know I'll make it. I still feel pain in my right foot, but Tad, I don't even have a right foot! I thought for a while I was a goner, but that was more the combined effect of dysentery and being half-crazy from pain. I think I'm strong enough to move, if you're strong enough to help me."

At this, Tad gave a sarcastic kind of smothered laugh. "Hunh . . . don't count on me being strong. Feel weak as hell." He told Louis about the Harrisburg beating, and how he'd been rendered unconscious and delayed six days.

"My biggest concern is money. I haven't received pay in over two months, but I couldn't wait around Lee's headquarters knowing you were here. So, I'm down to almost nothing. You have any?"

"Yeah, if it hasn't been stolen. I got paid shortly before Perryville and I had over sixty dollars on me when I was captured. I managed to hold onto it until they amputated my foot. It's supposed to be in safe keeping at the commanding general's office here on the island. Don't know if it'll buy anything up here though. Maybe have to get across the Ohio River before it's of any use."

"Well, let's start making arrangements. I'll go to the captain in charge right now and see what we have to do."

Surprisingly, the paper work was completed within two hours, but as it was now late afternoon, they decided to spend the night in prison and depart first thing in the morning. The base military personnel were most accommodating. Tad welcomed the government-issue army cot.

When all the arrangements were complete and they had finished their evening rations, Tad said to Louis, "How about filling me in on the details of your injury and capture?"

"Not 'til you tell me what's been happenin' with you, especially in Harrisburg. Truth be told, I think you look worse than I. Your eyes are puffy and those black and blue marks aside your ear don't look so good."

Tad told his Harrisburg story: "I'll tell you, those two nurses were the finest thing I've seen in this war, except maybe that day at the end of the snow ball fight." Tad told Louis all about the snowball fight and how many of the men had come to see each other in a different way that day.

"That's 'nuff about me. Tell me about you."

"Well, I was taken prisoner at Perryville, Kentucky, on the eighth of October. I was captured while leading my company in a charge against Carlos Buell's right flank.

"Several of our divisions were successful in turning the left flank of Buell's command. I was in command of Company B of Daniel Smith Donelson's regiment and we were attempting to turn Buell's right. We were caught in a deadly artillery barrage. That's when I took a hit. I caught a shell fragment in my right foot. Right soon after that we were overrun and surrounded. We could've fought to the death, but what's the point? Surrender wasn't all that bad.

"My foot didn't appear to be serious at first, but by the time I arrived in Sandusky gangrene set in.

"They put me in a hospital in Sandusky, but it got worse and so sometime in late October—I don't remember the date—they amputated just above my ankle. After a couple of days they brought me here.

"I came down with dysentery almost as soon as I arrived. I was desperate. Felt certain I was gonna die. Night before I sent that message to you one of our guys became delirious and hallucinated about all kinds of things. Finally, at about 4:00 a.m. he quieted down. In the morning they discovered the reason he quieted down was rigor mortis. As soon as it was daylight I wrote you that letter. I was desperate. Can't remember the date. Anyhow, I wasn't at all certain where you were, but I guessed it would be wherever Lee was located."

Louis hesitated for a minute. He choked back some tears.

"Sometimes I feel this horrendous pain in my right foot. But, Tad, I have no right foot. Drives me crazy.

"Got to tell you big brother, I don't give a good goddamn 'bout this war any longer. My only goal's been to survive. The bitter freezing winds whip across Lake Erie and penetrate these walls like water fills a hole. The nursing care is tolerable and the majority of the guards are decent and kindly, but there are a few cruel and beastly ones.

"Several of our guys froze to death. They tell me Johnson's Island was built to house 'bout 1,000 officers. Until just the other day there must've been 2,000 of us, mostly enlisted men. The place is infested with rats, and it's not unusual for guys to catch 'em and cook 'em."

Tad listened intently. He began to feel he'd been very lucky compared to Louis.

"Louis, I hate to admit this, but until now I'd not heard of Perryville. Where is it?"

"It's in central Kentucky, about fifty miles mostly east and a little south of Louisville. It was quite a battle! Both armies stumbled into each other because they were searching for water. Finally met at Doctor's Creek off the Chaplin River near Perryville. I hear we had about 800 fewer casualties than the Yanks. Sent Buell's troops back almost a mile. Some say it was a standoff. I don't agree. But it was all for nothin' cause the next day Bragg and his entire army, except for us prisoners, headed back to Tennessee, which didn't make much sense to me, seein's how we had driven Buell back and had the upper hand."

By 9:00 a.m. the next morning, December 31, the Dwyer brothers were in a launch on Sandusky Bay. Louis carried his haversack. He managed his crutches without too much trouble. In a kindly gesture, the quartermaster provided Louis with two blankets. And, thankfully, the Confederate money was all there.

CHAPTER EIGHTEEN

Happy New Year, Louis."

"Happy New Year, Tad."

The day was spent hurrying, waiting, sleeping, boarding, sleeping, riding, waiting. By train on January 1 from Sandusky to Toledo and then from Toledo to Cincinnati. Day two would be a steam packet from Cincinnati to Louisville. Finally, on day three, the third of January, the cars from Louisville to Nashville.

Other than a few derogatory remarks outside the terminal in Toledo, nobody really bothered them. Going from the train to the wharf in Cincinnati Tad caught the newspaper headline.

MILLS FOUND NOT GUILTY BY WAY OF INSANITY

Much as the Battle of First Bull Run, the trial of Hiram Clark Mills became a spectacle of major proportion. In the days since the assassination Mills has been characterized either as a ruthless murderer who deserved to be hanged for his dastardly deed or as an angel of mercy sent to do the will of divine Providence. One side demanded his execution and the other side called for his vindication. Several key witnesses gave testimony regarding Mills' state of mind just prior to his injury at Second Bull Run. They characterized him as a homespun Billy Yank who would never harm a flea. The defense based its entire argument on the effects of his terrible injury. The doctors who treated him claimed that the severe effects of his infection could possibly lead an otherwise normal person to become completely irrational. The jury was charged at 2:30 p.m. In less than an hour the jury reached its verdict.

"I feel bad for Lincoln," Tad commented, "but I'm sure glad the war's over. Far as I can tell nothing but misery all around."

"Wish we could've won without him bein' killed like that," Louis responded.

In Cincinnati, things seemed easier and much less tense. The packet side-wheeler was very old and dilapidated. It was badly in need of repair and a paint job. Tad looked at the two boilers and wondered about their integrity. The layboard boiler looked patched and the starboard was quite rusty.

Aside from worry about the state of the boilers the trip was enjoyable. The Ohio was not yet iced up although there were large formations of ice along the shoreline. The weather remained cold and damp with occasional light snow flurries. Neither Tad nor Louis seemed to care because the eating was so great. The two of them became gluttonous, devouring turkey, roast beef, ham, mashed potatoes, gravy, grits, green beans, and plenty of coffee.

After this great meal Louis unburdened himself to Tad.

"Don't know what's in store for me. Don't know how 'Lizabeth will be."

"Why's that?" Tad asked, his face showing a look of surprise.

"Well, it's a long story. Reckon you can surmise some of it. Lookin' back on the events leadin' up to the spring of '61, I think it's fairly obvious that I joined the army to escape. Know that sounds funny, but as I scrutinize myself I keep thinkin' I joined up to get away from 'Lizabeth's dominatin' ways and from my job."

"How's that?"

"Simple. Before leavin' for the war, I fought with 'Lizabeth almost constantly. Most of our fights were the result of my reaction to her. I'd overreact at most everything. I'm much easier going than she is and I'd often comply with her in order to keep peace. But the strain got real heavy and I found myself in constant opposition. I reacted badly to things she'd say and the things she wanted to do."

"Like what?"

"Like pushing to join the Young Adult League. You know, that group that sponsors cotillions and garden parties and all kinds of high-brow social things. 'Lizabeth wants to be part of the Nashville social set. Always wants to be seen by the right people. Important to her, I guess. Don't ask me why. Not for me though. I tell you, Tad, it was almost unbearable. She'd push and push until finally I'd give in.

"At times she reminded me of Pa. Remember how he'd get on us. I'd be very contrary and bullheaded. Couldn't stand his bein' on me like that. Well, same way with 'Lizabeth. Whenever she'd get bossy and preachy I'd become downright resistant and stubborn. Lose my temper. Then I'd placate her, try to play the peacemaker. Kept givin' in to her. You know, sort of appease her best I could. Yet the more I appeased her and tried to keep the peace the more determined she was to get her way. And the more resentful I became."

"How'd the kids handle all this?" Tad asked with genuine concern.

"They took it better than I did. Didn't know anything different. Felt sorry for 'em."

"How old are they now? I've lost track."

"Betty's seven and Blaine's five. Seems they just fell in line, marchin' to their mother's tune. They seemed to be happy children. Least when I left. Didn't seem to mind their mother's pushin' 'em. 'Lizabeth manages the house like her father manages his employees, like some sort of domestic officer."

"What was her father like?"

"Her father? He was somethin' else! Blaine Morgan Townsend. An imposing figure if there ever was one. An authority guy. He gave his children the best of everything. Least 'til his sons proved such disappointing failures. Her mother died when 'Lizabeth was 15. After that 'Lizabeth was the only one who could please her father. In return he indulged her every whim. The old man idolized her and she returned the favor. But more than that, he instilled in her a very strong drive for material success and social prominence. 'Course you better believe her two older brothers resented her. Probably still do."

Tad said nothing. Just nodded to Louis to continue.

"Asked her father for 'Lizabeth's hand in marriage and the old man kept me for over two hours. 'How do you propose to support Elizabeth? How'll you be able to support a family? What've you done with your life? Why do you think you're right for Elizabeth? Do you love her? What does love mean to you? Are you sure you're not just infatuated with her?'"

Tad gazed at Louis and forced a weak smile, but made no attempt to say anything.

"At any rate, I left that grueling session with a feeling of hopelessness. Sure wished I'd broken it off right then. Remember thinking at the time I'd never be able to measure up to the old man's expectations. Always be trying to prove myself to him. So what'd I do? Instead of getting out like I should've, I marry her and go to work for him. How stupid could I be? Allowed myself to be pushed right into a management job in his importing business. You know he owns distributorships all through the south. Became a rat race. After eight years I didn't just hate my job, I despised it. I hated every minute I worked for that bastard. He was always goadin' me to push the salesmen to break new records each month."

At this juncture Tad volunteered some thoughts. "I really had no idea about all this. First, I had no idea father got on your nerves the way you describe. Hell, I just let his directives just roll off me. Guess I just took it for granted you were happy and well settled. Heavy stuff. And I certainly had no idea you hated your work all that much. Why didn't you quit?"

"Yeah, why didn't I quit? Who knows? Money was good. Should've. Maybe you've forgotten, Tad, but I was one of the first from Nashville to enlist after Fort Sumter. In the name of the southern *cause* I saw my chance to escape. At least for a while. Thought maybe I'd be killed. Maybe I'd be maimed for life and have a good excuse not to measure up. I remember the argument I had with 'Lizabeth when I told her I was going to enlist. She thought I was crazy and irresponsible."

"Let the younger men go to war. You have a wife and two children. You can't just leave us."

"That's just what she said. So I answered back. 'Don't you understand? The Confederacy needs officers and I have the qualifications and the training. I must go. It's my duty.' Then she screamed at me . . . "

"'Your duty, Louis Dwyer, is right here in Nashville.'"

"Then I took more shit from her old man. Boy, did he give me a mouthful."

"See Tad, no doubt about it. The war gave me a perfect excuse to leave. Now that I'm home what'll I do? Except for my foot everything looks the same. Not trained in a profession and I dread the thought of going back to work for Townsend. At least I'll have a few months to ponder my future. Need some time to heal. Know what I mean, big brother?"

"I'm not much help, Louis. Never realized you were so unhappy. Guess I was all engrossed in my own stuff." Tad wanted to tell Louis about the lost order, but he quickly discarded the idea. Better keep that stupid bit of nonsense to myself, he concluded.

"Hey. You've been great. Just hearin' me out. Feels good to tell you all of this. Wished I'd told you all this back 'afore the war.

Truth is, I wish either you or Pa would've knocked some sense in my head 'fore I ever married."

Within another hour the packet docked at the Louisville wharf. As they managed their way through the streets they began to feel at ease. There were no snide remarks from passersby. No put-downs to the emblems of the Confederacy. Some cheers, a few jeers. A few people just glanced at them and then shook their heads sadly as the two pathetic-looking figures made their way to the Louisville & Nashville depot. Most people seemed not to notice. There were no more Nashville trains till Saturday morning so they had no choice but to catnap as best they could though the night. It was a difficult place to sleep.

On the morrow they boarded the cars and slept some more. They felt they were practically home. Many thought Kentucky to be the most divided state in the Union. There was even a Confederate Kentucky Brigade that didn't dare return home until the war was over. Everybody called them the *Orphan Brigade*. Rumor had it the Orphan Brigade was one of the most valorous of the war.

Louis told Tad about an incident involving the Orphan Brigade he'd heard about at Johnson's Island. "During an action there were masses of Confederate wounded who'd been cut down after advancing out of their entrenchment. The wounded were left where they fell because rescue efforts would produce more bloodshed and further loss.

"But several men of the Orphan Brigade, choosing not to wait for a truce at days end, ran forward anyway. Disarming themselves, they carried white flags of truce, jumped their earthworks and ran to the wounded who were screaming for help. Each Orphan hoisted a wounded man to his shoulders and ran back to the Confederate breastworks.

"The Feds saw what was happenin' and they held their fire, just staring at these foolhardy rebs. After the Orphans made several more forays the Yanks actually began to cheer and applaud those brave guys. Must've rescued between twelve and fifteen men that day. One or two Union guys even fired a volley in the air as a salute."

For a while there was silence. Then Tad spoke.

"It's great to be in Kentucky, even if Kentucky's now part of a different nation. So far it hardly seems different." Tad had always thought of Kentucky as a Southern state. "Seems funny they bein' part of another country from us."

They arrived in Nashville by early afternoon. Tad's eyes lit up and he smiled happily at the welcome. People in the Nashville terminal were celebrating and cheering. There was a military band, evidently on duty all day as trains were still arriving from all points. The music was like medicine to Tad and Louis. The band kept playin' "Dixie" and "The Bonnie Blue Flag."

There was no one to meet the Dwyer brothers. In Louisville Tad had tried to find a telegraph office, but to no avail. Tad quickly arranged for local transportation to take them to Louis's home in the fashionable western end of Nashville. Louis noticed the barren deciduous trees, and several evergreens that seemed bigger than when he last saw them almost two years ago. Much of the countryside was devastated by the war and the never-ending need for wood. Most of the fences were gone. The exterior of his Greek Revival homestead looked about as he'd remembered it. It was now mid-afternoon.

Louis began to perspire and he felt his heart beating.

Tad paid the driver and they managed to climb the three steps to the columned verandah. Louis thought it best to knock rather than burst in on his unsuspecting wife and children. There was no answer. Another round of knocks. Still no answer. Finally Louis turned the knob and the door opened.

"'Lizabeth? 'Lizabeth? I'm home! It's me. It's Louis. Anybody home? 'Lizabeth."

They set their haversacks, blankets, and other belongings down. Louis, now quite adept at hobbling around on a single crutch, went into the kitchen. Peering out the back door he saw his wife, Elizabeth Anne Dwyer, picking flowers in the side garden. She looked every bit as beautiful as Louis remembered. Her hair was done up with a few strands hanging down over her forehead. She was wearing a green calico dress with a sunbonnet on her head and a basket over her arm. She was tiny of build. Her face was thin. The strain marks on her lower forehead, just above her nose, seemed to be a bit more pronounced. Her eyes were very expressive. Louis always liked her smile because it brought out her dimples.

"Hi, 'Llizabeth," he shouted out the back door so that there was no possibility she could not hear him.

"Louis? Is that you? Is that really you?" She dropped the basket of flowers and ran toward him. He hobbled down the back steps to meet her. They met with open arms. He hugged her and kissed her and squeezed her until she was almost breathless.

"Oh, I'm so glad to see you. Everyday I kept wondering if today would be the day. The children will be thrilled."

Then she noticed his leg. "What's happened to your leg? It's not . . ."

She couldn't bring herself to use the word.

"Yes," Louis responded, "I mean no. My leg's all right, but I lost my foot."

There followed an awkward period of silence as Elizabeth tried to absorb this upsetting bit of news. She'd not truly envisioned her husband as being anything other than a whole person.

"Are you all right? Is it healed? Will you be able to walk and, and be . . . you know, will you be normal?" Elizabeth asked, unable to mask her concern that her husband would be different.

"Just got out'a prison. No, it's not all healed yet. I'm weak, but I'm beginnin' to feel better. I'm not completely recovered, but when I am, I'll be good as new. I'll have a wooden foot that'll fit inside a shoe just like everybody else. I doubt I'll be able to run or hike much, but I'll be able to lead a fairly normal life. Might even be able to dance a little."

Tad remained on the rear porch, watching the reunion between his brother and Elizabeth. He couldn't help but hear the exchange between them and he found it disturbing.

"Tad, how good to see you!" Elizabeth exclaimed as she hastened to the porch. "Hope you're all right. Goodness, it's a shock to see you both. I mean, it's a nice shock, but well, my heart is just pounding." Tad gave her a light hug and kissed her on the cheek.

"You're looking well, Elizabeth. I hope you're feeling well. And the kids? Where're my nephew and niece?"

"Oh they're with grandpa and grandma Townsend today. Always on Saturdays," Elizabeth replied, as if surprised that Tad hadn't remembered.

Oh, yes, it's Saturday. Tad thought to himself. How thoughtless of me to forget that it was Saturday. Thirty lashes, Dwyer. God! How does Louis stand her? Bet he forgot 'bout Saturdays too!

"Well, Elizabeth, I'm anxious to be getting home. Could you spare a horse? And, Louis, how about coming to LaVergne tomorrow? I'm sure Dad and Jane will be anxious to see you."

"Yeah, sounds good," his brother replied eagerly.

As Louis said this, Elizabeth raised a hand to her mouth and exclaimed, "Oh my goodness, you haven't heard! You didn't get my letter?"

"Heard what?"

"You haven't heard about your father?"

"What about him?"

Elizabeth was taken back but she remained very well composed and very matter-of-fact.

"Your father was killed . . . back in November."

This brought Tad and Louis to a halt. They knew their father was getting up in years, but to be killed? Tad and Louis were stunned. They could hardly believe their ears. The two brothers looked at each other, each lost in his in thoughts as he tried to absorb the news. To Tad, Louis' face mirrored how he felt.

"My God, Elizabeth, what happened?" Tad asked, almost in denial.

"Well, several divisions of Bragg's army were moving to Murfreesboro. Father Dwyer volunteered his services as an aide in the supply of the commissary. You know your father. Could never slow that man down." Elizabeth paused and then continued, "Some Union skirmishers encountered our boys on the road south of LaVergne. Father had a load of supplies and he was heading to Murfreesboro. Nobody knows for sure what happened. The best they could figure was Father's wagon got caught in a crossfire, and he took several shots in the chest. The horses kept running. When they finally stopped, there was your father slumped across the seat. They said he never had a chance, and couldn't have suffered long."

Then, completely insensitive to the immediate emotional state of Louis and Tad, she turned the focus onto herself, "I wish you two could've been here. The war around here got plenty nasty. Let me assure you that living in Nashville hasn't been easy," Elizabeth hastened to explain. "Union forces occupied this place since shortly after Grant took those two forts up near the Kentucky border. Nashville's been a Union transportation center, and we've all been caught in a living hell. And sometimes those Yankees were mean, especially in the way they talked to womenfolk." Elizabeth became all worked up and started to cry.

While Louis tried to comfort his wife, Tad's thoughts went back to his father. Never measured up to his expectations, thought Tad, but he was a good man and I always felt he loved us kids more than life itself. Never reacted to him the way Louis did. Never reacted to his preachin' at us the way Louis did. Hell, I just paid him no heed. Did what I wanted anyway.

"I assume he's buried in the family plot in the churchyard at LaVergne," Tad inquired of Elizabeth.

"Yes, I remember the day clearly. Services weren't much.

Hardly anyone there. It was terrible. Lucinda seemed to take it well, but Jane took it very hard. Last time I heard she was still all in pieces."

"Well then, I must get home. Can hardly wait to see her." Tad paused as he looked Louis in the eyes. "I still think you should come tomorrow. How about coming about mid-morning and we'll make a day of it? On second thought, being Sunday, why don't you bring Elizabeth and the children?"

Louis nodded. "I'll be there."

"Oh, must you tomorrow? I was hoping you could go with me to see Mom and Dad. They'll be so relieved to see you," Elizabeth asked, placing her hand on Louis' arm and her needs above those of her husband.

Elizabeth turned to Tad. "Tad, I think you should stay the night here. That way you'll get to see Betty and Blaine and get a good night's rest before going to LaVergne. Louis and I'll be over early in the week."

Not wanting a confrontation with Elizabeth in front of his brother, Louis joined with Elizabeth. "Sure, Tad, great idea. Stay the night. Been a long day."

The children arrived about 5:30. The Townsend family carriage driver, a black servant by the name of Jason, delivered the children to the front steps just as Louis was dressing after his first real bath in almost a year and a half. Of course Betty and Blaine were thrilled to see their father, but they couldn't understand why their Daddy hugged them so tightly and started crying. Elizabeth took them aside and explained about their daddy being hurt in the war and losing his foot.

"I'll be good as new in a few months. I'll be able to walk normal and go up and down stairs. Probably not be able to run like you kids but after awhile nobody will ever notice much difference."

At such a moment, and only as a child can do, Blaine asked: "Did you bring us anything, Daddy?"

For once Elizabeth proved to be the tactful mother, "Your Daddy brought himself home from the terrible war. That's present enough."

In spite of the joyous evening and the great dinner, Tad could feel the strain between Elizabeth and Louis. Something didn't seem right. Things didn't feel right. Later that night Tad could hear the muffled sounds from Louis and Elizabeth's bedroom. Certainly they weren't the muffled sounds of loving sex! To Tad it sounded more like questions and answers followed by rebuke and criticism.

On the morrow, after a time of sharing and conversation, Tad took his leave. Elizabeth instructed Jacob, the Dwyer's groundskeeper, to prepare the Tennessee Walker for Tad. As before when Tad started to mount the horse he was completely overwhelmed with emotion. He turned to Louis and opened wide his arms. They held each other for several seconds. Tad tried to hold back the tears, but he couldn't. They both cried.

"Take care o' him, Elizabeth," Tad yelled out as he mounted the horse. "He's the only man left in this family 'sides me."

As Tad rode off he added to his last sentence, "And I need him to be strong."

As Tad made his way through the various short cuts between Nashville's west side to the southeast, he could see the many signs of war and occupation by the Yankees. Union military equipment was strewn everywhere. There were storage depots along side acres of Parrotts and Napoleons lined in rows.

Never again, he muttered to himself, never again.

Tad was experiencing a multitude of emotions. His father was dead. His brother Art was dead. And Louis was married to a shrewish woman who seemed intent on managing anything within her reach.

As the Tennessee Walker picked its way along one of the decimated short cuts, Tad began to wonder what kind of sex life Louis had. For his part, Tad couldn't even imagine Elizabeth being sexual. Poor Louis! But then, Tad thought, sex was probably the least of it. Was Louis happy? How must it feel to be dominated by Elizabeth? What would it be like now, at least for a few months, until Louis was all healed? But she was Louis' wife and he would respect her for no other reason than that. Unless, or until, Louis gave him reason to do otherwise.

Tad rambled toward the fork leading to the LaVergne road. Almost everything looked familiar. The trees were bare except for the evergreens. He noticed four or five charred barns. He wondered if they'd been destroyed in battle or deliberately torched.

He reached the Dwyer homestead in less than two hours. At about fifty yards Tad started yelling out, "Jane Dwyer, Jane Dwyer, your brother's home from the war! Jane Dwyer, Jane Dwyer, your brother's home from the war." Hearing the greeting, she ran outside to see if it was really Tad.

As soon as Tad dismounted, she reached out to put her arms

186

around him, bursting into tears.

He held her a minute. Sort of rocked her, standing-up style.

"Oh Tad, did you hear? Pa's gone. Killed driving a wagon near Murfreesboro."

"Yes, Elizabeth told us. No, we didn't know. I brought Louis home from prison. He was a prisoner on Johnson's Island, just off Sandusky on Lake Erie. Wounded bad. Lost his right foot."

"I don't know how much more I can take. Are you all right? Side of your face looks bruised?"

"Yes, I'm hurt some, but I'll be fine."

Jane Hill Dwyer was four years younger than Tad. She'd never married. She'd never even been asked. Pretty enough. She had dark brown hair, brown eyes, and a very pretty face with a lovely complexion. In addition to being attractive, she was very smart. People used to say when they gave out brains they held back a portion of Tad's to give to Jane. Maybe that's why she never received a proposal of marriage. Men were scared off because she was so smart.

They passed several hours in conversation. There was much catching up to do. First Tad would hold forth, then Jane. Jane talked mostly about their father and his efforts on behalf of the Southern *cause*. Tad told Jane all about Louis and his terrible experience at Johnson's Island. Tad hoped Jane could give him some details about Art and how he got killed. But she knew nothing more than the basic fact of his death in the Hornet's Nest at Shiloh. She had written Tad about that and hadn't learned a thing since. Of course, Tad still had that letter.

Actually, if it hadn't been for their father, the war would have been an economic catastrophe for Jane. Jane basically lived as homemaker for her father. Tad hardly ever sent money home. He didn't have a lot to send. But then, he knew very well he'd plenty enough to gamble with and to squander.

They rode over to the cemetery and stood by the grave of Randolph and their mother, Mary Hill Arvin. Tad was only nine when she died and he thought his world had come to an end. He was the light of her eyes. His thoughts reflected back on the occasion of his mother's death. She died and baby Arthur lived. He remembered it well.

And now Arthur was gone too. Only Louis and Tad of the males were left. Randolph had ostracized their older sister, Lucinda, when she married a Yankee officer in the summer of 1861. Yet the old man always seemed to find ways to keep up with her doings and whereabouts. During the war Lucy went to live with her husband's parents in Illinois. Randolph felt so strongly about the war and the right of states to determine their own destiny, he simply couldn't accept a Yankee as a son-in-law, even if he did prove to be a gallant soldier and capable officer.

"I've ordered matching stones, about yeah high." She held her hand against her thigh as if to show the height of the stones. "I hope that's all right with you?" She looked at Tad with the kind of look seeking approval.

"Of course," he replied. "I'm glad you did. I've always admired your good taste. I'm sure they'd both be pleased.

*****

The next few months proved to be harder for Tad than anything he faced during the war. He became infected with a disease of the mind. Most people referred to it as some form of melancholia. Since Jane was not in touch with any other returning soldiers besides Louis, she had nothing or anybody else with whom to compare Tad's behavior. And Louis did not seem to be suffering from the problem that haunted Tad.

Tad started going into Nashville most every day, making the tavern rounds on a routine basis. He borrowed some money against his overdue pay. He told Jane he just wasn't ready to go to work. He didn't even help Jane with the farm chores. He needed time, he said, to just sort things through. He had so much to absorb and digest. For him the war was not over, not by any means. The memories haunted him. Losing Special Order 191. Telling lies to D. H. Hill. The soldier lying next to him who chided him about being able to handle a rifle, and then actually experiencing the sight of the guy's head severed from his body. Being ambushed by Stoesser and his two cronies. The trial where Stoesser was acquitted. The hanging death of the spy, Ruff. The snowball fight. The beating in Harrisburg and the memory of Sandra Abernathy.

Tad seemed unable to let go of the past. Slowly and steadily he became more and more standoffish and distant. He seemed to become morose. The expression in his eyes became dull and listless. Tad was sinking deeper and deeper into a pit of self-pity and lethargy.

Since Tad talked daily with other veterans he knew he was not the only one having difficulty readjusting to civilian life. It seemed to him that almost everyone he met in the tavern shared the same story. "Nothing's right. Nobody understands me. I'm irritable. Restless as hell. Y'all know what I mean?"

Then his drinking buddies would confirm Tad's feelings by responding in kind, even if they didn't feel as keenly about things as Tad did. Of course, they always told Tad exactly what Tad wanted to hear, thus validating and confirming his misery.

It didn't occur to Tad that as long as he compared his own feelings and experiences with the tavern crowd, he'd likely find men with sympathetic ears. The drinking routine was validating to Tad because he felt reaffirmed in his misery. Truth was there were many others who could hardly wait to get back to the farm or their place of work, but he wouldn't run into these people in the tavern.

To a more objective outside observer the question would not be "What has the war done to Tad Dwyer?" Rather, it would be "What is the demon drink doing to Tad Dwyer?" His only solace seemed to be the bottle. The bottle would give him cheer and hope and energy. Trouble was, as he continued drinking on any given morning or afternoon, the cheer and hope and energy would turn to increasing anger, then melancholy.

Late one afternoon Tad passed out and had to be carried to a carriage and driven home. The driver had to help him out of the carriage and to the front door. Jane was terribly embarrassed as she used her meager savings to pay the fare and a modest tip. She put blankets over him as he lay on the floor in the middle of the living room. He slept well into the next morning and upon waking he remembered nothing of the day before.

During these weeks he was very difficult to be around. Jane tried to deny Tad's behavior, but there came a point when she couldn't. He became aggressive and very hostile toward her. He seemed to be angry most of the time.

When Jane confronted Tad about his bottle problem, as she called it, he became all the more furious.

"It's the goddamn war. You don't know what it's like. Hell on earth! That's what it was and I can't get it out of my mind. Just get out of here and leave me alone."

People would try to talk to him. Jane, Louis, the Methodist preacher in LaVergne. Even several of his cronies at the tavern tried reasoning with him. One day he got into a fight when one of his favorite drinking buddies attempted to challenge him for using the horrible war as an excuse for his drinking. "Come on, Dwyer. Who you tryin' to kid? It's not the war. That's just your excuse. You're a juicer, Dwyer, that's what you are. You're stuck on the bottle and yer tryin' to justify it by cryin' 'bout the damn war."

"O yeah!" countered Tad, fumbling for the most intelligent response he could muster from his drunken stupor, "Y'all can go straight to hell, hear?"

That did it. They were on one another like two boys in a scrap. Tad was so loaded with liquor he could hardly stand up, let alone land a punch. They ended up wrestling one another to the floor and in the ensuing struggle one of them knocked a glass jar off a table. The bottle shattered as it hit the floor. The next thing Tad knew a huge piece of glass from the top of the jar cut through the backside of his right hand and was sticking out his palm. Blood started gushing all over the place.

"Quick, put a piece of cloth round his wrist and twist it real tight," one of the customers called out.

"Like how?" Tad's opponent was too confused to be of help.

"Like you was a wringin' out a wet towel! Here, like this." At that, the man got down on the floor and applied the tourniquet.

"Gotta get this man to the doctor. Bleedin's about stopped, but this glass gotta be pulled out."

There, on the floor of the tavern on a cold, damp, day in mid-February Tad Dwyer hit rock bottom.

Once they got Tad to Doc Hayes' office, the old Doc got through to him in a way no one else could. Either that or the time was ripe for him to quit his denial. Probably both.

"You're depressed." Doc Hayes wouldn't take that away from him. "There's lots of men with post-war blues. It's like there's a big let down after some all-consuming event.

"I'll give you this, Dwyer, you've shared an almost incommunicable experience with a few close friends. And now that it's over you feel lost. Your wartime buddies are gone and there's hardly anyone who can really understand or appreciate what you went through."

"But," the doc continued, "you've made the problem a hell of a lot worse by drinking. The drink just feeds your blue moods, and slowly it becomes a downward spiral, feeding on itself and getting worse and worse. The war's gonna get you yet, Tad Dwyer. You're headed for the grave sooner than you think unless you can get off the juicin' habit, and fast, damn fast. Hear?"

Tad gritted his teeth as the doc pulled the huge shard out of his hand. The doc was as careful as could be, but he also figured the pain might be good for him. Tad wished he could pass out but his mind and body wouldn't cooperate. Instead, he took his left hand and put it to his head and pulled hard at a fistful of hair, trying to divert the pain as the doc removed the glass shard. Then the stitches. Finally tying the last stitch, the doc said, "Oughta do it." Tad looked down at his left hand and was surprised to see a huge wad of hair still in his grip.

That night and in the next few days he had a lot of explaining to do. And everywhere he went the big bandage around his hand invited the question, "What happened to you?"

By late February he was mending well, both his hand and his head. Perhaps, as some said, Tad needed some kind of release from the war. The release, at least a beginning to the release, came in a letter, postmarked February 27, 1863.

Department of War,
Confederate States of America

February 24, 1863

Second Lieutenant Taylor Arvin Dwyer,
General Delivery, Nashville, Tennessee
   You are hereby notified that as of the first day of February, 1863, you were honorably released from active duty in the Army of the Confederate States of America.
   Enclosed, please find a government draft for your back pay in the sum of one hundred sixty-one dollars and 82 cents ($161.82). Be assured that your nation will be forever grateful for your service.
By order of the Quartermaster General,
D. O. Jenkins, Paymaster

Almost two months had passed since Tad and Louis arrived home from Johnson's Island. Now, after devastating melancholy and demon drink, Tad stood four square to his future.

CHAPTER NINETEEN

The Dwyer Hardware Company was now in its second year. Incorporated late in the winter of 1863, the business represented one-third investments from Jane, Louis, and Tad. The three Dwyers bought the property and started the business with money from the sale of the Randolph Dwyer farmland.

Thirty-three acres were sold. Old Randolph had originally willed the farmhouse and the four adjacent acres to Jane and the remaining acres to be divided equally between Tad, Lucy, Louis, and Art. After Arthur's death Randolph revised his will. Since Arthur had no heirs, Randolph left the four immediate acres surrounding the farmhouse to Jane and one-third portions of the remaining land to Tad, Lucy, and Louis. Jane sold three of her acres fronting the Nashville-LaVergne road at a very good price, keeping one acre bordering the south side of her house. She then borrowed two thousand in order to contribute her one-third of the price of the hardware store.

Lucy was greatly relieved to receive a portion of her father's estate, not so much for the value of the property, but more because it meant that her father had not really cut her off. She hadn't been disinherited after all, and that meant the world to her. It was very difficult to be caught up in a conflict between the man of her adult choosing, and the man who'd been her loving father.

The hardware business was good in spite of the fact that all through the South there was severe depression. The South had cotton but little else. There were some truck farms, some corn, some light industry, a budding steel industry in Birmingham, and some foundries in Richmond. Dairy farms were scarce, however, and cattle seemed to do well only on the open plains of Texas.

192

Nevertheless, it was the small farmer who kept the Dwyers in business. The small farmer always needed hardware, as did most people who owned their own homes. And if they didn't own their own home, the landlord certainly needed what Dwyer Hardware had to sell. Of course there were some landlords who never bought anything because they neglected their property, even though they charged their tenants an arm and a leg for a hovel infested with mice and rats.

*****

"Massah Tad, Massah Louis, help! Some men be chasin' me on de side lot. Say they gonna' skin me 'live cause I took de job from some white boy."

Tad rushed out the front entrance of The Dwyer Hardware Company and ran over to the side lot but no one was there. It was difficult to see the entire lot because of all the inventory and implements stored there.

"Tell us about these men, Jonathan. How many? How big were they? Tall? Short? Bearded?"

"I see's two men. One 'bout de size of Massah Tad and other 'bout de size of Massah Louis . . ."

"Jonathan, how many times do we have to tell you that Miss Jane and Mr. Louis and myself are not your masters. You're our hired hand. You're not a slave anymore." Tad was kindly, yet firm about not wanting to be called master.

"Yes, sir. I keep forgettin' I'se not a slave no mo'."

"So tell us what happened."

"Well, like I say, these two men come on me an tell me they wus gonna steal me away and whip me good for takin' a job away from de white boys. I got skeered and ran fas' as my feet could run."

"Did you tell them you were a *let-go* slave?"

"No, sir. I be too skeered to talk like dat."

"What else did they say, Jonathan?" Jane's voice was soft and soothing.

"Well, Miss Jane, dey say dey gonna teach Dwyer Hardware people a lesson and burn a cross front of de store."

Louis turned to Jane and Tad. "I was afraid of this. Lot of people down on us for hirin' Jonathan instead of a white."

"To be expected. I've a hunch they were just puttin' a scare into the boy. Best we assign Jonathan chores that can be done right

193

in close to the store."

"Yes, Tad, but you know as well as I do the locals can hurt us plenty if they think we favor the colored. They'll take their business somewhere else." Jane started to choke up. She hated conflict of any kind.

The Dwyers hired Jonathan two months ago. Jane recalled the day that he first came into the store. He was not quite five feet, had a broad smile, ears that stuck out, and dark black hair. His clothes were filthy and he gave off a terrible odor.

"Ma'am, my name's Jonathan and I'm lookin' for work. Do most anything. Had lots 'sperience working with tools on de land where I wus a slave."

"How old are you, Jonathan?"

"Reckon I'm 'bout 12, ma'am. But I work hard. Do the work of two my size. Carry stuff three times my weight. And I'se not a runaway."

"Do you have papers, Jonathan? Are you free?"

"No, ma'am. Ain't free. I'm *let-go*."

"Where'd you come from? Who was your master?"

"Come to Nashville from plantation in place called Macon . . . Macon, Georgia. Master tole us we wus free to leave 'cause he gone broke and couldn't 'ford to keep us no mo'."

"Do you know your master's name?"

"Sho' do. It be man by de name o' Herkimer. Caleb Herkimer."

"What about your mammy and pappy?"

"Never had a pappy and my mammy died 'bout a year ago from de fever."

The Dwyers decided to hire Jonathan because they needed a hand to do all kinds of chores. Part of his weekly pay was in kind. Louis and Tad fixed up one of the rooms in the back of the store. Jonathan called it his bunk room and he took great pride in keeping it clean and tidy. He had his very own bed and chair and a few shelves.

*****

Life in Dixie wasn't good. It wasn't what people had expected when they first attacked Fort Sumter. Jefferson Davis was now in the fourth year of his six-year term as president, having been inaugurated in February of 1862. Everybody was expecting him to pull the country together and provide the leadership necessary for the Confederacy to become a world power, but it wasn't happening.

In this summer of 1865 there was widespread unemployment accompanied by disillusionment and a sense of hopelessness. The Yankee blockade during the war years had made it impossible to ship cotton. So stores of cotton just piled up. Soon after the war ended massive supplies of cotton were shipped to England. But this proved to be too much of a good thing. Now England was overstocked and the English mills faced a glut. Once again exports to England were almost non-existent.

The most viable market was the Union. About 90 percent of all Southern cotton went northward to the textile mills of New England. However, the price was not nearly what English manufacturers had been paying. Northern mills paid less than half the price of English mills.

As the bottom dropped out of the cotton market, it became very difficult for many of the large plantation owners to maintain the scale of their operations. Consequently, many slaves were given their freedom with papers or simply let go. A *let-go* slave was simply a former slave who had no papers giving proof of freedom. The term caught on. Technically, they were still the property of their owner. Yet, since the owner no longer fed and clothed them, they were considered free, at least in the sense of being free to pursue work. However, a let-go slave had a legitimate claim to freedom inasmuch as the former master had relinquished his or her claim to ownership by not feeding, boarding, and clothing his slave. Even without papers of manumission, Jonathan was legally free.

Many of the let-go slaves made their way to a different part of the country. They felt safer not being near their former masters just in case their former master changed their mind and wanted to reclaim them. By the summer of '65 there were let-go colored people everywhere in the South, from small towns to big cities. And they were all looking for work. Lots of them would band together and move about as a group, finding comfort and safety in numbers. White folk found these wandering coloreds to be quite threatening.

Increasingly, these migrant bands of homeless Negros were becoming a problem. Very few could read or write. Their masters had seen to that. The fact of illiteracy now complicated the problem. The only thing the colored was qualified to do was manual labor. This put them in direct competition with poor whites. Consequently, very few coloreds could find work.

The ports of Charleston, Wilmington, Jacksonville, Mobile, and New Orleans were saturated with legions of coloreds as was Vicksburg, Memphis, and Richmond. The only viable work for a male negro in these port cities was as a stevedore. Many of the men became roustabouts and many of the women became migrant workers. Some women became ladies of the night. Thousands made their way westward to Kansas, Arkansas, and Texas, but there too the prospects for employment were dismal.

Jefferson Davis tried to create a public relief program, but it ended in failure. There was little cooperation between the states when it came to the creation of national laws and programs. The failure was due, in part, to the fact that the Confederate currency had not yet been accepted in world trade. There was simply not enough silver or gold to back up the paper currency. The Confederate war debt was staggering. Over sixteen million was owed to England alone.

The let-go slaves were a burden to the Confederacy. More and more Southern slave owners willingly gave papers to their slaves and encouraged them to "go north where y'all'll find lots of work for which you're well fit."

As a result, crime rates rose. Burglary for food was common. Robbery at gunpoint was fast becoming a common occurrence. Whites were killing blacks at the slightest provocation. White juries were turning out *not guilty* verdicts by the hundreds for the perpetrators of such crimes.

By 1863, twenty-two of the twenty-four states in the United States had ratified the Thirteenth Amendment to the Constitution, but of course no such amendment would ever be accepted in the Confederacy.

In one swoop of legislation, the Congress and States of the Union had plugged the hole that had been responsible for the War Between the States: "Neither slavery nor involuntary servitude . . . shall exist within the United States . . ."

The next evening after Jonathan had been threatened by the two men, Tad, Louis, and Jane closed the doors at six and retired into a back room to discuss problems and attend to the monthly accounts when Jonathan ran into the back store rooms.

"Mister Tad, Mister Louis, come quick. Ders loud noises from de street."

Jonathan followed the three of them as they rushed to the front of the store. Peeking out through a break in one of the windows, they saw a bunch of people all covered with white sheets blocking the Nashville-La Vergne road.

"Dwyer Hardware. Dwyer Hardware. Come out of there, you nigger lovers. We've got a message for you. Come out. Come out. Come out." They repeated these words until Louis and Tad came out of the building.

"Hear us, Dwyer Hardware. This is the only warning you'll get. Either you get rid of that black boy o'yours or this place is ashes. Either o' you got anything to say fer yourself?"

Tad looked at the crowd. Not a face to be seen. Only white sheets covering body and head with two holes for the eyes to see through. Numbered about thirty or so with five or six carrying torches. A huge cross wrapped in grease-soaked rags was planted in the dirt at the side of the street.

After a few seconds Tad spoke out:

"My name's Tad Dwyer and my brother is Louis. We fought for this country of ours so that we'd be free of domination by our Yankee neighbors and could be free to pursue our living as we thought best. Louis here lives every day with a lot of pain and a wooden foot to remind him of the hell he went through at Perryville. We lost our brother Art at Shiloh. Our dad got cut down near Murfreesborough. Now you, our own Southern kin, our own Southern brothers, come here and invade our privacy and peace by threaten' us for hirin' a let-go slave. Now y'all listen to me. I faced death many times during the war and I'm not one speck afraid of any of you. Was a courier with General Lee. So I'm warnin' you, if you harm our hired hand, or our sister, or us, or one square foot of our store, I'll make it my life's work to expose and convict each and every one of you. Y'all ought to be ashamed of yourselves. Dare any of you to take that sheet off your cowardly head and come up here and call me a nigger lover to my face."

Jane was just inside the front door. She cringed as she put her ear to the door, listening to Tad. Her first thought was Tad's safety. Her second thought was that this would spell ruin for the hardware store.

When no one came forward Tad walked over to the cross and knocked it down. At this, one of the white-sheeted pack threw his torch onto the greased soaked cross. Within seconds the cross was engulfed in flames and the white-sheeted people high tailed it out of sight. All except one. One of the torch flames caught his sheet and he was on fire. Panic swept over him as he started to run with the others but tripped and fell. He let out several shrieks but no one was left to help him. Seeing this, Louis and Tad got right on him and smothered the fire. Rolled him in the dirt and gravel. Jane saw the whole thing and rushed to get water. Within seconds the Dwyer Hardware Company had a prisoner.

Once inside, the unmasked prisoner faced interrogation. He was about five and a half feet tall, with a fat youthful face, sagging jowls, and a protruding belly. He looked to be in his early twenties.

"What's your name?"

"None of your business."

"You wanna play that game? We'll just take you right down town to the magistrates office and press charges.

"Name's Jimmy Randall."

Jane brought a towel and a pan filled with cool water. "Let's see that leg."

"Thank ya' kindly, ma'am. Hurts."

"You've got some burn there. Looks ugly. But it's not too deep. Reckon you'll be all right in a few weeks." Jane looked over at Tad as she finished dressing the burn.

Tad continued, "I want names, James. Lots of names."

"Can't squeal on my brothers. Secrecy's 'portant."

"Fine, James. We'll keep you here tonight and tomorrow we'll go to the magistrates office. I'm not in the mood to protect a bunch of cloaked cowards running around threatening innocent people."

Jane drew Tad aside and showed him a copy of a municipal order delivered to the store just a few days ago. It was signed Thomas B. Randall, Constable, City of Nashville.

"You kin to Thomas B. Randall?"

"He's a cousin."

"Wonder what he thinks of all this?"

"Reckon he'll just laugh it off."

"We'll see."

Tad and Louis took turns sitting up all night, guarding their prisoner. Early the next morning Louis and Tad, with their prisoner in tow, were at the magistrates office in city hall. Louis filled out a warrant, pressing charges against James Randall. A date was put on the court docket and the prisoner was released on bail. Tad wondered if anything would come of it. Within another few minutes Tad and Louis couldn't help overhearing a man's strong voice from an adjacent office.

"You stupid jerk! Who you think you are? Word's all around you got caught. Told you not to mess with those people. Bad business! Lucky for you Dwyers put your fire out. You mighta' burned to death. Your buddies all ran, and the very people you threaten turn around and save you. Mighty embarrassin' for me. Could cost me my job. Tellin' you, James, if the mayor gets on me for this you're ass's gonna be in big trouble. Hear?"

Tad and Louis looked at each other and smiled. "Tell you what, Louis, why don't you go on? Long as I'm right here I'd like to drop in on the mayor."

"Yeah. Think I'll go home and clean up. Been a long night. Check in with 'Lizabeth. Be at the store about noon."

Tad was fortunate to catch the mayor. "Name's Dwyer, Tad Dwyer. Wanted to talk to you about the white sheet people. You may've heard about last night's demonstration or whatever at my hardware store."

The Mayor Joshua Armbaugh stood up and extended his hand. "Heard good things about you, Dwyer. How you stood up to those bullies and challenged 'em."

Tad wondered how the mayor heard about the details so quickly.

"What I was wonderin' is what can we do as a city about those folks? Has there been action on the part of the city council? What's bein' done to put an end to this harassment?"

"Mr. Dwyer, you must understand the times we're livin' in. Lots of people upset about lack of jobs for poor whites."

"May be. But most young whites got kin to take care of them. They want jobs, but their life isn't threatened. But the young blacks. That's another matter. Roamin' our cities all through the South. That's why Dwyer Hardware chose to hire a let-go boy. Gave him a home. Pay! Pride! Self respect! Took him off the streets. Helping him get on in the world without stealin' or commitin' other crimes."

Mayor Armbaugh carried on about the state of the South: "We're in hard times, Dwyer, no doubt about it. No cooperation between banks in the South. No help from Richmond in dealin' with let go slaves. Most free slaves goin' north cause they got papers. We got bigger problems. Buell and Rosecrans and Grant practically ruined us. Need to rebuild. Need guaranteed bank loans. Terrible number of farm bankruptcies."

Tad listened politely. "I know the times are hard. I still want to know what we're doing here in Nashville to end this harassment stuff."

"I have a lot of confidence in Constable Randall. He must've been embarrassed about last night. First cousin to James Randall ya'know. Tell you, Mr. Dwyer, what's bein' done is we're tryin' to expose every single person we can. Bring 'em out in the light of day. Hopin' public scrutiny'll bring 'em in line. You catchin' James Randall last night might be the biggest break we've had. Gonna' do everything we can to get James to talk. Need names. The Klan's hurtin' us. Hurtin' our reputation and our businesses."

They talked a while longer and then Tad took his leave. Later that day he shared the conversation with Jane and Louis: "Y'know, Armbaugh could easily be one of them. I doubt it. Don't want to believe it. But just the same he could be. Bears watchin'. In the meantime, I'm gonna' give him the benefit of the doubt and follow the proceedings against James Randall."

*****

Amidst this climate Tad found himself itching to become involved in politics. Several of his friends had jokingly told him that he ought to run for public office because of his penchant for debating and arguing any kind of issue. His mother used to shake her head and lament: "If ever there was anything to argue about Tad Dwyer would win first prize in presenting one side or the other, and it didn't make a speck of difference which. That boy's gonna' make a lawyer sure as I'm Mary Dwyer." Fist fights and brawls were commonplace with young Tad Dwyer. If words couldn't convince an opponent, his fists usually settled the issue. When he was in his early teens his father told everyone, "No, I don't believe Tad is cut out for farmin'. He's probably gonna' be a boxer or read for the bar."

Politics meant working with people, and Tad liked being with people. He had always been involved in local issues and took keen interest in the larger issues that affected the Confederacy. That afternoon Tad shared with Jane and Louis his idea about running for the city council. He expounded on some of his thoughts. "I've heard tell that Virginia, North and South Carolina, Georgia, and Florida may become protectorates of the British Crown. Even if one of our eleven states votes to secede it'll severely weaken us. Worse, if the seaboard states act in concert the whole Confederacy might well crumble.

"We need leadership that'll guide us through this period of

post-war reconstruction. Mayor Armbaugh was right about how Tennessee's been devastated. Farm bankruptcies are at an all time high and increasin' daily. The negro problem's serious, but probably not nearly as threatening to Tennessee as to Alabama, Mississippi, and South Carolina."

Louis responded: "As I see it, the crisis is mainly the lack of capital to finance the building of factories capable of producing the machinery necessary for agriculture. I think banking's the key. Things made worse by the lack of knowledgeable leaders and educated manpower. Seems as though there's nothing left but old men and young boys. Rest've been wiped out."

"If you ask me the biggest problem is states' rights! The very thing we fought for is coming back to threaten us. Not enough central power and authority to get things done." Jane cut right to the heart of the issue.

"You're right. Makes me all the more determined to run."

The decision was made. Shortly after purchasing the hardware business, Tad had purchased a house on Lambert Street, about three blocks from the store. It was a small brick Federal style house. Being a taxpayer and being male were the only requirements for running for city council. He would have to start at the bottom. He was a political unknown. Except for the Dwyer hardware store he had no name recognition. Nevertheless, he was determined to take the plunge.

"You need to go over to city hall and file a petition to become a candidate. That's all there is to it. File for the third precinct. That's the precinct where you live Tad, in case you didn't know," his friends advised him.

Before he knew it, he was certified as a candidate for the Nashville City Council. The election would be in November, but the primary would be in September.

There would be tough competition, at least in the primary. The Republican Party was practically non-existent in middle Tennessee. The competition would be in the Democratic primary where there were three other hopefuls. Tad figured he should be able to win easily over two of the three. "I know nothing about this third guy except he was a Memphis native who came to Nashville after the war and founded a small accounting and bookkeeping business. Name means nothing to me. Raymond O. Jansen." Jane and Louis were both a bit dubious.

In early August, broadsides began to appear everywhere

201

in Nashville's third precinct heralding the name and candidacy of Raymond O. Jansen. Broadsides were posted on almost every street corner. They were to be seen all up and down College Street, Cherry Street, and Front Street bordering the Cumberland River.

Tad soon learned—had he not known before—that he was in a fight. He quickly countered Jansen's broadsides with his own multitudinous signs and posters. His photograph in his dress gray uniform with the second lieutenant gold bar clearly in evidence was an eye catcher. He looked quite handsome with his dark curly hair and his broad military bearing.

But this kind of tactic wasn't enough. He'd have to knuckle down and come up with a platform and program with some real solutions to real problems. One night after enjoying dinner with Elizabeth and Louis at Jane's house, Tad outlined his platform: "I've decided to concentrate on what I know best, which is Nashville's status and role in the post-war economy. The most pressing problems dealing with commerce and trade are ongoing and not easily solved. I see these problems as partly the concern of the state legislatures as well as the Confederate Congress and Senate.

"So I've settled on three local problems. Finding a remedy for the increasing amount of horse manure in the streets; the lack of safe drinking water due to the dumping of sewage into the Cumberland; and harassment by the people in white sheets. I figure people vote according to what touches closest to their homes, their hearts, and their pocket book. Got to appeal to what they can feel and see, and . . . smell." He broke out into a huge grin.

The manure was becoming a terrible problem due to the fact that there was a vast increase in the numbers of horse drawn buggies and carriages on the downtown streets. It was difficult to walk anywhere. One had to walk on tip-toes through the horse manure. If a person were careless, the manure would act like a banana peel and give the necessary impetus for a long slide on one's posterior. It was not uncommon, especially on rainy days, to hear an occasional scream that signaled some poor soul's adventure on the manure slide.

Tad made a quick trip to Knoxville and Chattanooga in order to determine just how they handled their manure problem. The Knoxville city council simply raised everyone's property tax to cover street cleaning. It proved to be highly unpopular, but no alternative method of financing had yet been agreed upon. In Chattanooga, property owners and proprietors alike were responsible for cleaning the streets in front of their own dwellings and businesses. The city had the power to levy fines for those who proved to be uncooperative. Most everyone Tad talked to spoke in negative tones about this system. In fact, it was the most popular subject of jokes making the daily rounds.

Tad whipped up his campaign rhetoric based on open trade without any city tariff, except for taxation of the owners of all privately owned commercial businesses and transportation facilities, including wharves and docks, and other points of entry, such as train terminals. Only city-owned facilities like the municipal train depot would be exempt. The total sum collected would be sufficient to take care of all of Nashville's streets, including those in the residential sections of the city. The typical city taxpayer would be spared. Since only the proprietors of business and transportation linkages and connections would be taxed, Tad took heat only from those sources. The average citizen who labored for someone else for his livelihood liked this idea because it would cost him nothing. Or so it appeared. Also, adequate funding for street cleaning would be a fine source of employment for those presently out of work.

In reality, the proprietors and owners would quickly pass on such expenses to the consumer. Nevertheless, consumers really didn't pursue the matter that deeply. The preponderance of voters was consumers, and they liked the sound of not being taxed. The strategy was a time-honored method of winning votes.

Contamination of the Cumberland was a problem, but Tad decided not to highlight it as a campaign issue. There would be time to deal with this later. He did come down hard on the white sheet people. He attacked them as no one had dared, shaming them for their cowardly and unenlightened approach to the let-go slave problem. Most of all, Tad had the credentials for attacking the white sheet people. After all, he had laid his life on the line for the Confederacy. He said the *white sheets* were the most divisive faction in the city and they succeeded only in alienating the white community. "Can think of nothing that will do more harm and wreak more havoc in keeping new business and trade away from Nashville. In the long run the *white sheets* will discourage tourists and visitors as well as prospective investors in our city and its beautiful Cumberland waterfront potential."

Louis and Jane agreed if Tad were elected, he would retain his one-third ownership in Dwyer Hardware. There would be no reason why he would need to resign from the partnership.

Furthermore, he'd continue to draw full salary as long as he could devote at least eighty percent of his working day to the business. However, assuming he won the election and his duties as a city commissioner required more than twenty percent of his time, salary adjustments would have to be made. Tad's job as a member of the city council paid a paltry sum of $50.00 per year.

Although they didn't speak about it to Tad, Louis and Jane both recognized Tad's involvement in city politics could have a very positive effect on the volume of business at Dwyer Hardware. On the other hand, they also recognized that if for some reason the public should turn against Tad at any time during his term of office, it could have an adverse effect. "Based on the public reaction to the white sheet incident over our hiring Jonathan, I'd say the public is in favor of our position. If anything, patronage and sales have increased," Jane said with enthusiasm about how the Dwyer approach was part of the solution rather than part of the problem.

Tad was an affable person, willing to take risks and to play the political games so necessary for victory. He entered the campaign with a lively attitude. He was upbeat, friendly, sociable, and quite clear about the issues.

That is, until he was surprised to read that his war record was not impeccable. Seems that Raymond Jansen had done a fair amount of sleuthing into Tad's past, trying to get some dirt on him.

Posters and broadsides began to appear asking the question:

DO YOU WANT THIS MAN
REPRESENTING YOU?

His war buddies call him a gambler, and a man who likes to drink. It's a well-known fact that Taylor Arvin Dwyer likes his whiskey, and shoots craps whenever he gets a chance.

Question: What will such a man do for you? What can such a man possibly do for Nashville?

KEEP NASHVILLE DECENT
VOTE RAYMOND OLIVER JANSEN FOR CITY
COMMISSIONER - THIRD PRECINCT

CHAPTER TWENTY

Upon learning of this personal attack, Tad and Jane were soon making plans to go to Memphis. "I need you with me, Jane. You're good at bookwork and such, and you can help me trace this guy down. If he's going to throw dirt at me, I've no choice. I don't like doing politics this way, but damn it, he started it, not me. I never had any intention of attacking him personally, but if Jansen wants to fight this way, then I'll return the favor."

"Besides," Tad thought to himself, "her presence helps me stay straight. Helps me keep my nose clean. I dare not get into any night life scene."

Louis was very upset at Jansen's charges. "I really don't give a damn, but you should hear 'Lizabeth. She's so gullible she takes it all as gospel truth."

"Tell Elizabeth not to worry. Tell her Jane and I are going to Memphis for a few days to see what we can dig up about Jansen. Publicity like this won't hurt us or Dwyer Hardware as long as we can turn the tables on him."

Tad learned long ago that denial of a charge such as being a heavy drinker was the wrong tactic. He reassured Louis, "On personal attacks and charges I'll always disarm my opponent by agreeing with him and then I'll normalize it and put it in a different context. I'll always minimize my behavior as best I can. That way, I take away the sting of his attack and he's got nothing more to say."

One evening, as part of his speech, he responded to Jansen's charges.

"Yes, I've been known to be besotted, 'specially that night after the battle of Carlisle, when we drove those damn Yankees back toward Shippensburg. And I freely admit I liked to play cards and wager some bets. It sure beat goin' bonkers with boredom on those cold winter nights."

Tad came to depend on Jane. He liked her input on things, whether it was business or the election, or the way things were shaping up in the Confederacy. On one occasion after a speech, Jane suggested to Tad that he not mention any of Jansen's charges in his prepared remarks. "Don't mention anything about such charges in your speech. I think it's much better to wait until either you're asked about it or somebody accuses you. In other words, respond only to those who may bring it up." Tad mulled over Jane's advice and decided she was right. Soon this became his usual way of handling such attacks and accusations.

On a more practical note, Tad also realized that if he were to be elected to any political office, it would be absolutely necessary to give no opportunity to future opponents. Often when he was alone Tad scolded himself out loud: "Appearance is everything. I know I can't afford to give the slightest appearance of misconduct. Damn, I've got to be careful how I even look at a woman. And absolutely no card games or alcohol!" Tad meant to be very hard on himself in these matters.

Later that week, Tad and Jane boarded a train for Memphis to see what they could learn about Raymond O. Jansen.

They began their search at the county courthouse. Guessing Jansen to be in his late thirties, they searched birth records for the ten-year period 1820-1829. Not finding any record of Jansen's birth in this time period, they searched the decades 1810-1819 and 1830-1839. Then they searched the files for the recording of businesses within the Memphis area over a twenty-year span. Here again they found nothing.

Then they went to the property tax roles. Nothing!

At lunch, after a fruitless morning on their second day, Jane suggested, "Why don't we check the military records. Let's see if he ever served."

"Great idea."

By mid-afternoon they had what they were looking for. This was all Tad would need. Publicize this and he was home free.

By the end of the week the broadsides were everywhere around Nashville:

ATTENTION
LOYAL CITIZENS OF NASHVILLE

Would you vote for this man? Would you want him to represent you as Commissioner in the Third Precinct?

According to the office of military records in Memphis, Tennessee, Raymond Oliver Jansen purchased a military <u>substitute</u> for himself on May 18, 1861. The military substitute then promptly deserted the ranks, June 14, 1861.

TAD DWYER ASKS FOR YOUR VOTE.
LIEUTENANT DWYER PUT HIS LIFE ON THE LINE FOR YOU, FOR TENNESSEE, AND FOR THE CONFEDERACY.

VOTE DWYER ON TUESDAY, SEPTEMBER 11.
MAKE YOUR VOTE COUNT

Jansen complained that what he did was perfectly legal. But Tad had learned to fight fire with fire. If Jansen could so callously impugn his character by deliberate reference to his being a gambler and a drinker of hard spirits, so also could Tad call into question the character of Raymond Jansen.

True, Jansen had done nothing illegal. But who would want to waste their vote for such a gutless person? Few people respected those affluent *mommy's boys* who bought their way out of military service by hiring a substitute.

Election day was but a week away. The four contenders would meet on a public platform. The occasion was a rally for the purpose of getting the public interested enough to vote. Public apathy was the downfall of many politicians, and this rally was definitely to Tad's advantage.

All four candidates would speak on Saturday afternoon, September 8, just three days before the Democratic primary. The speeches would precede an open basket dinner. The rally would be held on the open green on Third Avenue.

Tad wanted to speak last. If not last, he at least wanted to speak after Jansen rather than before him. He wanted to make certain Jansen wouldn't drop any last minute bombshells.

207

Jansen, however, had cooled down. He had no new charges or innuendoes. Tad figured the guy was at least smart enough to leave well enough alone. After Tad's last broadside telling of the military buyout, the public seemed to be much more forgiving of Tad's wartime shenanigans and not nearly as gullible about the things Jansen was saying.

With four candidates it was doubtful if anybody would win a majority. Most people figured there'd have to be a run-off between the top two candidates.

But by 10:30 in the evening of the primary election, Taylor Arvin Dwyer had won more than a plurality. He'd garnered a clear majority of the votes. "So what if he drank or gambled a bit too much during the war? He's only human."

Then, on election day, Tuesday, November 7, 1865, Tad won handily over his token Republican opponent.

*****

Tad found out quickly that performing the day-by-day duties of precinct commissioner on the city council was a thankless and oftentimes boring job. Of all his duties he liked domestic intervention the least. Mayor Armbaugh insisted that all council members were expected to investigate reported domestic quarrels of constituents in their respective precincts. One female constituent demanded that Tad protect her from her husband who was beating her and her children. Tad investigated and then filed papers to have the man put in jail for thirty days. No sooner was this accomplished than the husbandless wife presented Tad with her now unpaid household bills for groceries, clothing, and rent.

A male constituent, married to his wife for nineteen years, complained to Tad that for almost two years his wife had denied him conjugal rights and wasn't there something Tad could do about it? In talking with the man's wife, Tad learned that they had eleven children—the youngest was almost two years old.

No matter what he did or how he voted, there were sure to be some who weren't pleased with his effort. He had to admit to himself that it was a lot more fun campaigning and getting elected than actually serving. There was something energizing about political confrontation and the excitement of the political arena, but the day-to-day routine was terribly dull.

In the summer of 1867, Tad set his sights on a seat in the state legislature. He'd made quite a record for himself in his position on the city council. There were even people in Knoxville and Chattanooga familiar with his work in dealing with the Nashville's sanitation problems. He was widely known by the mock title the *Manure King of Nashville.* Not a very desirable way to achieve fame, but the pay-off in name recognition was excellent. *Tad Dwyer, the man who cleaned up our city. Tad Dwyer, the man who keeps our taxes down. Tad Dwyer, the common man's mouthpiece. No horsing around with Dwyer.*

Local transportation officials, as well as entrepreneurs, were not very happy with his taxation program adopted by the city council. Nevertheless, the program was working well. People respected him. Being part owner of a small business meant that Tad paid the very tax he had helped instigate. People were impressed that a businessman would author such a bill and campaign for it. "Well, Dwyer owns a hardware store so he'll have to pay the tax like anybody else. Sounds good to me."

As Tad predicted, the business community simply passed the costs on to the consumer in small doses. The typical consumer hardly realized that the bill for clean streets was being paid out of his own pocket. Everybody in Nashville reaped the reward of a more beautiful and attractive city. And the sanitation department employed a lot of people who otherwise wouldn't have jobs. About thirty percent of these jobs were filled by let-go slaves.

In the fall of '67, after serving almost two years as a commissioner on the city council, he was elected to the state legislature. His district included Nashville and the surrounding three county areas. He resigned from the city council as of December 31, 1867, in order to take his oath of office in the ensuing Tennessee Legislature on January 1.

The only thing missing, he told himself, was someone with whom he could share life. Someone like that beautiful lady in Harrisburg, Sandra Abernathy. Someone whom he could love and who would love him. A smart woman like Jane. Not a shrew like Elizabeth. Gawd, how does Louis stand her? Poor Louis. Seems so unhappy. At least Louis doesn't have to work for his father-in-law anymore. And Dwyer Hardware is doing great.

But in the midst of the political whirlwind, these thoughts soon faded into the background.

Tad wanted to keep the electorate in a frame of mind where, hopefully, they would want more. Tad always said a smart politician is very careful to run just fast enough to get caught.

At any rate, Tad Arvin Dwyer proved to be a very popular politician with little serious opposition. He was re-elected to another two year term in the state legislature in '69 and then again in '71. His reputation was spreading throughout the legislature as a man who was adept at compromise and mediation. Tad was a man of action who got results. He could bring warring factions together. He could forge compromises in the face of stubborn resistance and selfish pride, like the time he got Ambrose Davidson to support one of David Swansea's bills.

David Swansea and Ambrose Davidson were both honest and intelligent men, yet their dislike for each other had reduced them to the point where, at times, both had become ineffective legislators. They were unable to represent their constituents effectively because they somehow got into the game of opposing whatever the other supported. Each had a large following and always swayed a large number of legislators. Tad was aware that both men were avid horsemen, and he used that knowledge to bring about the passage of a piece of critical legislation.

Tad invited Ambrose Davidson to join him for a drink after a house session was adjourned. After lighting up his cigar, Tad commented on how much better some cigars were than others.

"That reminds me, Ambrose, I understand that Dave Swansea is putting his horse Stars and Bars out to stud. I imagine he'll sire some real championship stock."

Ambrose took the bait. "He is? Hadn't heard. I've got a mare that should be ready real soon. Love to have a foal from Stars and Bars. But you know Swansea! He'd put Stars and Bars down before he'd ever agree to let him service any mare of mine."

"Ambrose, nothing's out of reach for those willing to stretch a mite. How serious are you about wanting a foal from Swansea's horse?" Tad inquired softly.

"Very serious. What do'ya know that I obviously don't?" Davidson asked, leaning forward.

"Know two things. I know that Swansea has a stud you covet, and I know he's about to introduce a bill that could possibly determine his chances of being re-elected. If I went to him with your word as a gentleman that you'll support his bill, I have a feeling you'd stand a good chance of improving the blood lines of your horses."

That was a typical Tad Dwyer move. Swansea initially balked at the proposal, but realizing just how much he had at stake, reluctantly agreed. Once the two men discovered just how much they had in common, the standoff between them was resolved and they eventually reached the point where they co-sponsored some vital legislation. And Ambrose Davidson got his foal.

*****

Robert E. Lee, second president of the Confederate States of America, died on October 12, 1870, two years and nine months into his term as president, with less than half his term being completed. Lee's death was difficult for the young Confederacy. Like Jefferson Davis before him, great things had been expected of Lee but little had been accomplished. Tad thought this was due to the Congress and Senate being excessively concerned with states' rights. None of the eleven states seemed willing to commit its resources to the greater good of the Confederacy.

The young nation would grieve the death of their beloved fallen leader for many years to come. Everyone, including those in political office, the ecclesiastical community, and the media, would unintentionally conspire to make Robert E. Lee, like Abraham Lincoln, greater in death than he was in life. This was the problem. Throughout the war and right up until his death, the young nation made an icon out of Lee, which, paradoxically, prevented Lee from being the dynamic leader everybody yearned for. Lee became a legend in his own time, a prophet with honor even in his own homeland. But for all the adulation and for all the placing of Robert E. Lee upon a pedestal, he was powerless in his attempts to fuse the eleven states into a single body politic that could deal with issues of national consequence, not to mention issues of international importance.

A scathing editorial, upon the occasion of Lee's death, pointed out that the way to strip a person of power was to place that person on a pedestal:

> *It is a truism that one way to avoid taking a person seriously, be it Robert E. Lee or your wife or your husband or even your boss, is to put that person on a pedestal. When we put a person on a pedestal we idolize him or her. We make that person into an object of veneration and adulation, and to that very extent we deprive that person of true humanity.*
>
> *This is what our Senators and Congressmen did to President Lee. By building him up, they actually put him down. Lee pushed*

211

hard for a general population tax, modernization of the army and navy, the replacement of sailing ships with steamships, a uniform act of interstate trade, and a national interstate transportation act calling for the building of national roads and railways throughout the South. Not one piece of legislation was enacted into law!

All of Lee's programs and proposals were a threat to states' rights. On occasion, a bill would survive the House only to die in the Senate. Several Constitutional amendments cleared both houses of Congress, only to fail the ratification requirement of two-thirds of the states.

Now, John C. Breckinridge came to the presidency at a most difficult time. He was in the unenviable position of following the Lee legend. Yet in spite of this, Breckinridge had an advantage over Lee. Lawmakers would oppose Breckinridge straight out, even attack him. Because of this Breckinridge always knew where his opposition stood. But even so, in the final analysis Breckinridge could do little better than Lee.

One evening Tad confided in his brother, "I tell you, Louis, I've become an advocate for a stronger centralized government. If the Confederacy is going to survive it must somehow move beyond rigid adherence to state's rights. And this means making some changes in the Constitution."

In his first speech before the legislature Tad stated boldly:

"Somebody must give up some authority and sovereignty, or our eleven states will be nothing more than eleven children left to play by themselves without any viable guidelines or means of cooperation and compromise. As long as the states oppose a strong central government they will be easy prey to hostile outside interests, whether it be the interests of Mexico, Spain, France, or England."

Mexico was flirting with Texas, and England was again seeking to annex the five Atlantic seaboard states. This attempt at annexation was now under serious consideration. England wanted desperately to regain a foothold amongst the Southern states. The advantages to England would be mostly economic, eliminating all tariffs on both cotton and tobacco. The advantages to the five coastal states would be protection and the extension of British parliamentary law.

The coastal states were vulnerable to such seductive propositions. They believed it would be comforting to be a part of an established social order wherein the traditions of the Southern aristocracy could be institutionalized and perpetuated. Such an alliance with mother England would afford protection to the landowners. Of course, slavery would be abolished but slavery was a dying institution anyway.

Tad didn't like to play the role of prophet of doom, yet in that vein he carried forth on the floor of the legislature:

"Gentlemen. If our five sister states allow themselves to become affiliated, in whatever manner, with Great Britain or any other foreign power, it will mark the end of the Confederacy as we know it. There is simply no way the present Confederacy could stand. We'd be forced to create yet another new nation, further depleted and weakened."

Tad then came forth with a positive attempt to intervene. He continued.

"Therefore, I'd like to propose that we, the legislature of the state of Tennessee, invite the states of Alabama, Mississippi, Louisiana, Texas, and Arkansas to join with us in writing a letter addressed to the governor and legislatures of each of the five seaboard states. This letter would petition them to give further consideration to the likely ramifications and impact of any affiliation with foreign powers upon the future of the Confederacy."

The motion passed, although not unanimously, and Tad was appointed chairman of the project. The committee did its work but none of the officials in Alabama, Mississippi, Louisiana, Arkansas, or Texas gave much input so the project became mostly a Tennessee endeavor. The letter was sent to the governors of the five coastal states and to each and every member of their state legislatures. Letters were also mailed to all of the Congressman and Senators of the Confederacy and to President John C. Breckinridge.

The Dwyer letter concluded:

Affiliation with England will mean higher rather than lower taxes, greater international responsibilities and commitments rather than fewer, and less, rather than more, local autonomy.

In short, the very champions of states' rights are now being courted by a world power that would be more restrictive than the present Confederacy, and even more restrictive than their former affiliation with the United States of America.

What, therefore, had been our purpose in fighting a second war of American independence if now the coastal states were going to undo the net effect of both the second and first wars of American independence?

213

To the signatories of this letter, it would appear that the coastal states want the security that is derived from dependency rather than suffer some of the hardships that safeguard autonomy and independence.

The Dwyer letter made sense. It didn't put an end to anything, but it slowed things down, and seemed to trigger some further thought and questioning. It also gave Tad Dwyer name recognition throughout the Confederacy.

By late '72 the issue had subsided. The statesmen and politicians of the coastal states were having second thoughts. Many were harkening to Tad's letter, now known formally as The Dwyer Petition.

Tad was now in his fifth year in the legislature and was highly regarded. He had friends from both major parties, although the Republicans still looked rather paltry compared to the Democrats.

By 1873, Tad had made up his mind to run for governor of Tennessee. He discussed it with Jane and Louis. "I think the time is ripe. I'm growing restless and increasingly tired of the legislature. I feel I've done all I can do. There'll be several contenders, but I don't think any of them can seriously challenge me for the nomination."

Tad was probably correct. Even those who opposed him on major issues did so on political grounds, not personal ones. The fact was, people liked him. Even his staunchest adversaries respected him. It was becoming increasingly clear that Tad Dwyer was a man marked for distinction.

Jane and Louis were very supportive of Tad making the run for governor. But not Elizabeth. Of course she didn't come right out and say so, but she let Louis know that she was embarrassed and ashamed of Tad's lack of educational background. "I think he's too pedestrian and common for such a high office."

Louis and Elizabeth were on opposite sides of almost everything these days. Elizabeth seemed threatened by the entire Dwyer family and increasingly jealous of Tad and Jane's close relationship with Louis. It got to a point where Tad didn't really feel welcome in Elizabeth's home.

The decision to run was made. All was set. The nomination would not be automatic, but Tad had a stronger claim on it than anyone else. He was in a solid position. He was ready to fight a strong campaign. The thought of becoming governor excited and energized him. The future looked bright.

*****

Just as all the cards seemed to be coming together for Tad to run for the governorship of Tennessee, catastrophe struck. Like a bolt of lightning striking out of nowhere, this letter transported Tad back to the final conversation he had with Robert E. Lee, in late '62, just as Tad was preparing to go to Johnson's Island.

> *Monday, March 24, 1873*
> *Mr. Taylor Arvin Dwyer*
> *c/o General Delivery*
> *Post Office, Nashville, Tennessee*
>
> *Dear Mr. Dwyer,*
> *You are hereby subpoenaed to appear as a witness for the Defense in the matter of the Confederate States of America versus William Dean Tanner.*
> *Mr. Tanner is accused of having served as a spy for the Union Army between May 1861 and the end of hostilities.*
> *You will please respond to this subpoena and make your presence known at 9:00 a.m. on Tuesday, April 15, 1873, at the National Court House, Richmond, Virginia.*
>
> *By order of the Court,*
> *Ramsey L. Feldham,*
> *Attorney-at-Law, Counsel for the accused.*

Tad just sat and stared at the letter. He reread it several times. Disbelief, bewilderment, anger, and rage raced through him. He felt nauseous and light-headed. He was jolted into revisiting his past in a way that he could never have possibly imagined. Billy Dean Tanner a spy? Incomprehensible! Absurd!

April 16 seemed like a long way off. For almost three weeks Tad had difficulty concentrating on his daily responsibilities. His enthusiasm for the hardware store declined noticeably. His pursuit of legislative matters began to drag. At this moment of his life Tad could think of little else than the forthcoming trial of Billy Dean. His mind was bursting with questions. If Billy Dean wasn't a spy how in the world did they come to suspect him, and then accuse him? Or was he some sort of innocent accomplice, having unwittingly played into the hands of sinister forces? And if he was a spy, why, why, why?

215

He couldn't help wondering if Billy Dean found the lost orders that night when they were searching through the grass and brush at the site of the craps game? But if Billy was a spy he didn't need the actual copy of the lost orders. Hell, Billy Dean knew very well what those orders said.

Tad kept telling himself that if Billy Dean was a spy he could've had the Confederate brass put the finger on Tad at any time. All Billy Dean would've had to do was to tip off the Union intelligence people and they would've found a way to accidentally-on-purpose have a coded message intercepted. A message implicating Tad in the lost orders incident.

He continued going over these possibilities and scenarios until his mind was in a state of puzzlement. He always ended up in the same place, outraged, confused, and angry. But most of all, he remained stunned. Eleven years had come and gone. In spite of the fact that they had not crossed paths again, Tad could not bring himself to believe that his very best friend in arms during the terrible war, a friend who seemed to care almost as much about Tad's welfare as his own, could've ever been a Union spy.

CHAPTER TWENTY-ONE

The trip to Richmond was uneventful, and Tad could do little to get his mind off the forthcoming trial. A single thought kept pushing itself to the forefront of his mind. It was that morning in October when he couldn't sleep and he encountered Billy Dean out in the woods by the stream. When Billy asked Tad what he was doin', Tad answered Billy's inquiry by saying he was doin' some housecleanin' and washin' off some dirt. At this, Billy mumbled something about someday he'd show Tad what dirt really looked like. Maybe that was Billy's way of sayin' not everything was bright and rosy in his own life. Now as he travelled by train to Richmond, Tad continued to ponder these things but could get no further than vague suppositions.

He booked in at the James Hotel a full day early so he could have time to talk with Billy Dean and gather as much information as possible prior to the court proceedings. He found his way to the Supreme Court. There was no way he could locate Billy Dean except through his attorney, Ramsey L. Feldham. Even then, he didn't know if he'd be permitted to talk with Billy Dean. But he had to try. He approached a policeman:

"Lookin' for Attorney Ramsey L. Feldham."

"He's probably in his law office. Feldham and Feldham. Just go down to the corner and turn onto Virginia Place. Office is right there," a cheerful voice responded.

Within minutes, he was standing in the presence of Ramsey Feldham. "Mr. Feldham, I'm Dwyer, Tad Dwyer. I'm subpoenaed for the Tanner trial." When Feldham stood to shake hands Tad saw that Feldham was an inch or so taller than him. With his receding hairline and sculpted graying beard, Feldham looked distinguished

217

and imposing.

Feldham's office was well appointed, with exquisite furniture and tasteful décor. The redwood desk was elaborately carved and contrasted well with the oak bookcases. The window was draped in red damask, which added a touch of elegance.

"Oh yes, glad to meet you, Mr. Dwyer. Didn't expect you till tomorrow, though. Tanner spoke highly of you. Said you and he were good friends during the war." When Feldham smiled his eyebrows seemed to curl upward. He seemed to Tad to be courteous, yet distant and very serious.

"As you can imagine, this subpoena came as quite a shock."

"Sorry, Mr. Dwyer. I hate to tell you this, but the prosecution has Tanner cold. I'm afraid we're fighting for his life."

"But how . . . Why?" Tad stopped short. "Still can't believe it. I must see Billy Dean. Can you arrange it?"

"Yes, Mr. Dwyer, but please don't come back here and tell me anything he tells you unless it can serve to totally establish his innocence. The case against him is so strong that I've never come out and asked him if he's guilty. I simply must assume he's innocent, and I prefer to go before the military tribunal believing that he's innocent."

"But don't you really want to know if he's innocent?" Tad asked, surprised and alarmed by Feldham's attitude.

"I want to go into this trial *believing* that he's innocent. If he starts confessing things to you because you're his best friend . . . Well, I just don't want to hear it. Make sense?" Tad nodded. Feldham paused as if to get his thoughts straight, "I'm just telling you I don't want you coming back to me and telling me stuff I don't need to hear." Tad was still confused but said nothing.

They agreed to meet at 2:00 p.m. the following day. "I need to go over the charges with you and prepare you for what's ahead. It's not going to be easy." As they parted Feldham gave Tad directions as to how to find Libby prison.

Tad felt some anger toward Ramsey Feldham, but the more he thought about it the more he began to realize that maybe Feldham was correct. In fact, maybe he should approach Billy Dean the same way. Assume from the start that Billy Dean is innocent. Inscribed in Tad's mind, as deeply as the episode of the lost orders, was the promise that he'd made to himself a long time ago to the effect that if ever Billy Dean needed him, he'd make every effort to help him.

Libby prison, located on the James River several blocks

from downtown, was the original warehouse of Libby & Sons, Ships Chandlers. The four-story chandlery was taken over by the Confederacy in 1861 when the need arose for additional space for prisoners of war. In recent years the building served mostly as an armory and a warehouse for military supplies and ordnance. A few rooms were retained as prison cells.

"Gawd, Billy, you look the same. Like you haven't aged a day."

"You too, you old rebel hell raiser. What's it been? Near ten or eleven years?"

"I can't believe any of this. Tell me it isn't true." Tad blurted out, then wished he hadn't. Then he quickly changed his mind. "No, Billy, don't tell me anything. Let me believe what I believe and my testimony'll be easier."

"Whatever you say, but it doesn't look good. They've got me up on three charges. Only one has to do with you. All I ask is that you tell the truth. Don't hide or try to color anything."

He looked Billy Dean right in the eye and asked, "What if they ask me something I need to cover up to save my own skin?" Before Billy Dean could respond, he continued, "Billy, I'll lie for you if I have to. You sure have kept my secret all these years. Lord knows where I'd be today if you hadn't."

"No lies for my sake. Just tell the truth as you see it. That'll be a great help," Billy Dean said quietly. "As far as lyin' to save your own skin, well, I gave this some thought and I think you'd better stick with your exact same testimony as the Stoesser trial. I doubt anyone could prove you weren't tellin' the truth. Do you recall your testimony, Tad?"

"Recall it? Every word's etched deep in my memory. Couldn't forget it even if I wanted to."

After about an hour of catching each other up on what had been going on over the past years, Tad began to take his leave.

"Thanks, Tad. I'm glad Feldham found you. We were fairly certain you'd still be in Nashville. I hear you're quite the politician. And that Dwyer letter! Feldham asked me if you were the same guy as the Dwyer Petition? I told him you sure as hell were."

"Thanks, Billy. You sure I can't do anything more? Like sleuthing or trackin' down last minute details?"

"No. It's all been done. Thanks anyhow."

"I don't suppose they'll let me talk to you again till after the trial's over?"

"Afraid not."

"Well, if you need to be in contact, send me a note through Feldham. All right?"

"Fine. Thanks again. You're a good friend."

Tad started to extend his hand and then realized he and Billy had never said good-bye back at the end of the war. Tad opened his arms wide to Billy. Billy reciprocated. Tad fought back his tears.

The next afternoon Ramsey Feldham briefed Tad and summarized the charges against Billy Dean.

"The first charge accuses Tanner of transmitting sensitive information to the Union War Department in the two week period preceding First Manassas. Specifically, he's accused of sending estimates of Confederate troop strength and location to his Union contacts."

Tad was silent as he thought back to the news of his brother Art's death at Shiloh and how Billy Dean was such a help to Tad when he received the news at First Manassas.

"The second charge alleges that Tanner was privy to a copy of General Robert E. Lee's Confederate Special Order 191 on the evening of September 9, 1862, and attempted to transmit a summary of its contents to his contact."

Tad hoped it wasn't Hill's copy of the lost orders. Feldham didn't mention to whom this copy of the orders was addressed.

"The third charge alleges that between October 15 and November 20, 1862, Billy Dean Tanner transmitted information regarding the Confederate Army of Northern Virginia's troop movements."

Feldham continued, "Your presence in the court is for the sole purpose of giving your own testimony. You will not be privy to the testimony of any other witnesses. If Billy Dean is found guilty on any one of the three charges, the death sentence will likely be imposed."

Tad spoke his mind with a sense of authority: "I intend to leave no doubt in the court's mind that Billy Dean had little, if any, opportunity to transmit to any source whatsoever, the contents of Special Order 191. Even if he'd made an extra copy I don't see how he could've had the opportunity to get it out of camp. 'Sides, we all knew what was in those orders anyway. We were couriers."

"I'm glad to hear that, Dwyer. I only hope the other two charges don't prove to be difficult to refute," Feldham said solemnly, then added, "one more thing before you leave, Dwyer. Ordinarily this case would be handled after the fashion of a military court martial, but since the war's been over for almost twelve years, the Confederate Congress has determined that the loci of authority should be the Supreme Court of the Confederacy. There is no military jury, only a three judge panel from which there shall be no appeal. If Tanner is found guilty his only remaining hope is to seek either a commutation or a pardon from the president."

"Is that proper, Mr. Feldham?"

"Yes. Since the end of the war there've been several espionage cases. By 1866 the War Department was weak and ineffectual and had hardly any manpower for this sort of thing. The Congress and Senate voted to mandate all these cases to the Supreme Court. The Supreme Court then appoints a military type panel of judges."

"Do you see this as being to Tanner's advantage or disadvantage?"

"Definitely to his disadvantage. Two of the three judges, when they were in the service, held the rank of major. The other judge in the case, the one who'll be the chief magistrate, was a colonel. Higher brass is usually tougher than those of lower rank."

"What's the chance of a pardon or at least a commutation?"

"Practically none at all. President Breckinridge is hard as rock in these matters. But if it comes to that, I'll try my best."

Tad left Feldham with the feeling that Billy Dean was well represented. Seems like a solid man to me. Just hope he can do it, Tad thought.

Wednesday, April 16 was rainy and cold. One of those days left over from the Ides of March. Richmond was a drab place. The buds had popped too soon due to the early April warm spell. Then the cold snap came and killed off anything that had been brazen enough to make itself known.

The roads were so muddy that in the trek from the James Hotel to the Supreme Court, Tad's shoes became covered with red clay. Tad smiled as he noted that Richmond had quite a manure problem.

He arrived early and looked around the huge edifice. He made his way to the office of the counsel for the defense, a special room used by the counsels for defense in all of the trials requiring their services.

Tad spent the entire morning cloistered in the office of the counsel for the defense. Fortunately for Tad, he'd picked up some reading matter the previous evening. Altogether there were five people in the room, including the gentleman who sat behind the small desk. Tad figured the man behind the desk was a secretary and the other three were probably witnesses. He didn't recognize any of them.

Tad's hands shook as he perused the *Richmond Daily*. His mouth felt dry and his lips stuck together. Not only was he concerned for Billy Dean, he was increasingly aware that he could slip up on some detail and easily bring suspicion to bear upon himself. After all, he kept thinking, I'm a very close friend of a man who is now accused of being a Union spy.

As he was attempting to calm himself down, a man, who looked vaguely familiar, entered the room. Tad was positive he had known this man at one time, but he couldn't place him.

"Mr. Dwyer? You are Tad Dwyer aren't you?" The intruder asked in a friendly tone of voice.

"Yes. I'm Tad Dwyer." Tad's dry mouth almost made him tongue-tied. He was fairly certain he'd crossed paths with this person sometime in the past. "You probably don't remember me, but I'm Arnold Latham. I used to work for *Harper's Magazine*. We met some years ago at the Stoesser Court Martial."

Tad's heart started to throb and his pulse quickened. This man's very presence was a threat to him. So much so that he began to perspire profusely, after the manner of the old days when he felt overwhelmed with guilt.

"Yes, I remember quite well. Must admit I wouldn't've been able to place you had we passed on the street. How've you been, Mr. Latham?"

Something told Tad to keep the conversation on Latham or any other inconsequential subject. He reminded himself that he'd refused Latham an interview after the Stoesser trial. And further, he had no trouble remembering that he didn't trust this man. Indeed, he'd surmised back then that Latham suspected him of being less than totally honest.

"I'm now with *The Southern Advocate*. I'm sure you've heard of us. I'd like to do a story about you, a feature article about your political life and your former military life. I understand you and the defendant were very close friends."

Tad interpreted this last remark as a statement rather than a question, so he didn't respond to it.

"Yes, I know the *Advocate*. No, thank you Mr. Latham. I think it best that we not converse in any manner." Tad intended to be straightforward and firm. He didn't wish to attract any attention to himself in the company of these people, either by agreeing to the interview, or by refusing to do so.

Tad continued: "Please accept my thanks. I don't intend to appear uncooperative, but I believe it's in the best interest of everybody for me to say nothing other than what I say under oath."

Tad was very aware that everyone else in the room was listening to him.

"I wish you'd reconsider," Latham replied. "Maybe at the end of the trial? I'll catch up with you at the end of the trial. Will that be all right?"

"I'll think about it." Tad felt he dare not be too negative and too unyielding. He dare not shut the door too tightly or too forcefully. He was always aware of that line from Shakespeare, or was it from the Bible? Something to the effect of *methinks thou doth protest too much.*

Tad could hardly disguise his tremendous sense of relief when Latham departed through the door and down the corridor. The others in the room had no doubt absorbed the entire conversation.

He didn't know who these people were that were seated in the same small waiting room, but he assumed they were part of Billy Dean's defense. He decided to introduce himself.

"I'm Tad Dwyer. A friend of Billy Tanner during the war."

"I'm Frank Simmons. I knew Billy Dean in the early part of the war. Pleased to meet you." Simmons was tall and gaunt with blonde hair and a short beard.

"I'm Phillip Angelucci. I met Billy briefly after the war ended." Angelucci was of medium height, with dark eyes and brown hair. He was clean-shaven, and had a scar on his left forehead.

"And I'm John Rogers. I've never met Tanner. Not quite sure why I'm here." He was short and slight of build. His nose was a bit small for his face, but when you looked straight at him you couldn't help notice his deep blue penetrating eyes.

Tad, Simmons, Angelucci, and Rogers all shook hands with each other. The ice was broken and they chatted a bit.

Except for a few interruptions and an occasional conversation, the rest of the day went by in almost total silence. None of this foursome imagined they'd be kept waiting until afternoon the following day.

On the second day, the seventeenth, upstairs in the main courtroom, the bailiff belted out the opening words: "Hear ye,

Hear ye, Hear ye. The Supreme Court of the Confederate States of America is in session. Today is continuation of *The Confederate States of America versus William Dean Tanner*."

"The prosecution calls Mr. Will Troutman."

Jacques Belleau, the prosecutor, was a man of moderate build who exuded confidence with his every move and every word. He looked to be about 40 or 45 years old. He wore a sizeable moustache but was otherwise clean-shaven. He spoke with a French accent, but he displayed an impeccable command of the English language.

"Mr. Troutman, please tell the court how you came to believe that Mr. William Dean Tanner served as a Union espionage agent during the war."

The witness for the prosecution was a man of medium height, with strong blue eyes, sagging eyebrows, and a weak cut of jaw. His moustache was sizeable and sharply trimmed. His posture was erect and his overall appearance was of a poised and self-possessed man. He looked to be a man of means. His attire was immaculate and he carried a cane.

"Some years ago, in 1859, after my wife was murdered, my only child, my son, Daniel Rutherford, who by then was 13 years old, got it in his mind to run away from home. I'm afraid I wasn't a very good father. He and I quarreled a lot. We seemed to clash about everything.

"Well, I was at loose ends for a long time. You know, losing both my wife and my son. Daniel never came back. Shortly after the war began, I sold my business and headed northward in search of Danny. I went to Kentucky and Ohio. I suppose I wasn't very methodical, but I really wasn't thinking straight. I drifted eastward into Pennsylvania. Stayed up north during the war. Spent the last six months of the war in Harrisburg. Never did find Danny.

"Then, about two years ago I decided I couldn't leave this earth without making an all-out concentrated attempt to find Danny and attempt to reconcile with him. I went to Richmond and studied the war records of hundreds of the Confederate regiments. I assumed that Danny had enlisted in the Confederate cavalry. Good on horseback. Always liked horses. Had his own mount since he was about eight. Later, I questioned my logic on this point and figured that maybe if Danny was that angry with his old man, he possibly could have enlisted in the Union army. So I went to Washington to search Union files and records."

"And what did you learn, Mr. Troutman?" Jacques Belleau

was gentle in his interruption, but it was fairly obvious he wanted to lead Troutman into more rewarding waters.

"Nothing. At least not that trip. Then I headed back to Richmond where I accidentally found something I wish I'd never discovered. Looking through the official records of the Army of Northern Virginia, I discovered my son had indeed joined up with a Confederate Cavalry, the Eighteenth Tennessee Volunteers. He was killed in the final campaign of the war as the Army of Northern Virginia made its move from Harrisburg to Baltimore. But he wasn't killed in battle. He was han . . . he was . . . forgive me, this is very hard for me," Troutman said, struggling to maintain his calm demeanor.

"Take your time, Mr. Troutman," Belleau interjected.

"He was hanged on the gallows as a Yankee spy," Troutman spit it out quickly.

Gathering his composure, he continued: "I discovered it quite by accident. In reading the roles of the Eighteenth Tennessee, I ran across the name of James Ruther Donley. The name of Ruther caught my eye inasmuch as Daniel's middle name was Rutherford. I wouldn't have thought anything about this, except his address jumped right off the page. Same as our home address in Nashville, where my wife, Elly, and I lived since Daniel was born.

"I perused the war record of James Ruther Donley until I discovered that he'd . . . until I discovered that he'd been hung as a Union spy. I then went back to the war department in Washington, and after days of sleuthing, I was able to confirm that Danny had gone northward after he ran away from home and somehow got involved in espionage. The Union people gave him the code name of *Ruff* and sent him back south to Memphis, Tennessee where he joined the Eighteenth Volunteers."

Jacques Belleau was becoming slightly impatient at the lengthiness of Troutman's testimony, although he covered himself well. "Now Mr. Troutman, will you please tell the court, what this story, this tragic heart-rending story, has to do with this trial."

"Well, in trying to learn everything I possibly could about my son's death I learned about a Union contact in the headquarters staff of General Robert E. Lee. I presume this contact would channel information to my son Daniel, who would get it to another Union plant.

"I guess the Union people figured that a young boy was no threat and would arouse less suspicion than a grown man. I don't know. All I know is that I lost my son. They took my son from me and poisoned him against me."

"Now, Mr. Troutman, can you name the person who allegedly was the contact person in the headquarters staff of General Lee?" Jacques Belleau was becoming very anxious to have Troutman name names.

"Yes, sir. The contact person was a person with the code name of *Foot*."

"And were you able to ascertain the identity of the Union espionage agent referred to as Foot?"

"Yes, sir. Foot is the accused, William Tanner."

"Will you please point him out to the court?"

"I reckon that's him right there." Troutman said, pointing at Billy Dean Tanner.

"But I can't swear to that. I never saw the man before right now."

"Thank you, Mr. Troutman. That will be all." By now Belleau could scarcely disguise his delight at Troutman's testimony.

The counsel for the defense, Ramsey Feldham, began his cross-examination.

"Mr. Troutman. How do you know that the person with the code name of Foot is William Dean Tanner? Do you have documentation regarding the charge you have just brought against Mr. Tanner?"

"No, sir. I don't have the original documents if that's what you mean. Those would be impossible to get from the Yankees. But I have copied every page reference, and every relevant text, so that everything I've said can be corroborated. The prosecuting attorney has my copy of these documents."

Ramsey Feldham was up the proverbial creek. He hadn't counted on such direct identification. He felt his case slipping away.

"Objection, your honor. Until this court can verify the accuracy of Mr. Troutman's information, especially the linking of the code name Foot with the accused, I submit that the testimony presented by Mr. Troutman is nothing more than hearsay and as such it has no validity in this court."

Feldham was clutching at straws with this objection.

At this Jacques Belleau rose quickly from his chair and attempted to speak, but the presiding judge quickly cut him off.

"Objection sustained."

"You are out of order, Mr. Belleau. This Court stands in recess until the hour of 1:30. At that time, in chambers, I will consider any evidence the prosecution wishes to submit regarding the validity of the identity of the man whose code name is Foot."

CHAPTER TWENTY-TWO

In chambers at 1:30, Jacques Belleau handed the judge a notarized letter from the district court in Washington, D.C. Because of the notarization the judge determined that the letter was legally binding. Returning to the courtroom the judge overruled Ramsey Feldham's objection. The documents Mr. Troutman presented to the court were to be accepted as credible and valid.

*****

Billy Dean had been studying Will Troutman throughout his testimony, and gradually came to realize why he looked familiar. Slowly, it hit him as events from more than a decade ago rushed through his head. The face was older, but the look in the steely blue eyes hadn't changed—hard, bitter, and mean.

Years earlier, this man, whom he had known as Ward Thompson, had changed Billy Dean's life forever. And not just Billy Dean's life. Ward B. Thompson ended the life of his wife, Elly Thompson, and indirectly ended the life of his son, Daniel Rutherford Thompson.

Billy's mind drifted back to that fatal night when he and Thompson's wife, Elly, were sharing intimacies in the Thompson bedroom. Thompson, his gun at the ready, caught them in bed, defenseless. When Billy fought with Thompson, Thompson wheeled around, took quick aim, and fired at Elly, almost point blank. Billy acted impulsively, wrestled the gun from Thompson and then threw it on the floor as he made his escape. He never returned to Nashville or to his home in Sparta. Thompson, of course, filed homicide charges against Tanner.

Tanner escaped and eventually signed on as a spy for the Union army, deserting forever his wife and two young children. He changed his name from Justin Bethune to Billy Dean Tanner. Ever since that fatal night Billy Dean lived every day in bitter regret, forever a fugitive and forever cut off from his family and his former life.

As Troutman took the stand he appeared startled when his eyes first met Billy Dean. There was no doubt in Billy Dean's mind that Troutman had recognized Billy Dean. Here at his own trial Billy Dean was certain that Troutman was really Ward B. Thompson, Elly's husband and Elly's murderer. But as Billy Dean listened to Troutman's testimony, he knew he couldn't reveal this to his attorney, at least not now. If Billy Dean were to accuse Troutman of being Ward Thompson, Troutman would counter that the only way Tanner could possibly know Troutman's true identity was if Tanner was actually Justin Alexander Bethune. Justin Bethune was still wanted for the murder of Elly Thompson. They had both recognized one another, but neither could reveal his discovery without implicating himself.

Daniel Rutherford Thompson, a.k.a. James Ruther Donley, a.k.a. Ruff.

Ward B. Thompson, a.k.a. Will Troutman.

Justin Alexander Bethune, a.k.a. Billy Dean Tanner, a.k.a. Foot.

*****

Mr. Ramsey Feldham, attorney for the defense, came forward.

"The state calls Mr. Frank Simmons."

The court deputy entered the room where Simmons, Angelucci, Rogers, and Dwyer were all sequestered. Incarcerated was more to the point.

"Mr. Simmons, your presence is requested by the court."

Simmons was duly sworn and instructed to sit in the witness chair.

"Mr. Simmons. Please tell the court how you came to know Mr. Tanner."

"I worked with Mr. Tanner during the early months of the war. Especially at First Manassas."

"Mr. Simmons, as you know, Mr. Tanner is charged with

espionage in behalf of the Union forces against the Confederacy. My question to you is very straightforward. Did you at any time have any cause to doubt the integrity and loyalty of Billy Dean Tanner in the time frame in which you knew him?"

"No, sir. I did not. I worked with Tanner as a courier in the headquarters staff of General Pierre G. T. Beauregard. I never had any reason to suspect Tanner. He always seemed to be matter of fact and businesslike in the way he carried out his duties. Everybody seemed to like him. He was quiet. Kept to himself most of the time."

"Did you ever have the slightest hint that something was wrong, or that there was something out of the ordinary with Tanner?"

"Objection. The question calls for an opinion." Jacques Belleau was firm, even as he was soft-spoken.

"Overruled. I want to hear what this witness has to say." The chief judge was likewise soft-spoken, yet firm.

"No, sir. Tanner never seemed to go anywhere, or come up with excuses about having to be somewhere. He always seemed to be alone, yet easily accessible."

"Did you ever suspect or harbor any suspicions about Tanner's loyalty to the Confederacy?"

"Objection."

"This question calls for an opinion on the part of the witness."

"Sustained." The judge seemed irritated.

"O.K. I'll ask you directly: Did you ever have any reservations about the trustworthiness of Mr. Tanner?"

"No, sir. Absolutely not."

"That will be all. Thank you, Mr. Simmons."

Simmons started to rise as if to leave.

"I'm sorry. You're not yet finished, Mr. Simmons. The counsel for the prosecution has questions for you," said the chief judge.

Jacques Belleau strode forward, acting every bit as if he was completely in charge of everything.

"Mr. Simmons, at that early stage of the war, did couriers such as yourself and Tanner have access to the substance of the various orders and instructions?"

"Oh, yes. Most of the orders were written. Very few were sealed in any formal way. A few were verbal messages. Most of these were information-type communications."

"Would you give me an example of the latter? An information-type communication."

"Well, say that the army—no. That won't do. Here's one close to the fact that I remember well. It went something like this: 'Simmons, go tell E. P. Alexander at Signal Hill to pay particular attention to the far reaches of his left flank. We must not let our left flank be turned.'"

"In your opinion, were messages, such as the one you just described, likely to have been entrusted to Mr. Tanner?"

"Probably. No reason why not."

"Objection." Ramsey Feldham rose to his feet. "The question calls for conjecture on the part of the witness."

"Objection overruled. This is a reasonable question that seems pertinent." The judge kept placing his fingers sequentially on the desk as if playing a piano. He seemed a bit irritated at Feldham's objection.

Belleau continued: "And what might be the result if such a message was altered in meaning, or not delivered?"

"Objection." Ramsey Feldham again rose to his feet. "Your honor, this question calls for an answer which must be based solely on conjecture and sheer speculation."

"Objection sustained. Please continue, Mr. Belleau." This time the judge agreed with Feldham, although he didn't seem harsh or angry with Mr. Belleau.

Belleau continued: "Could you, Mr. Simmons, in your duty as a courier, presuming you wished to do so, could you have conveyed the wrong message?"

"Yes. I suppose."

"Please give us an example."

"Well, I could've accidentally confused such words as right flank and left flank."

"Fine. And could you have made other mistakes, such as the estimated number of troop strength?"

"I suppose so. But we couriers were very careful about things like that, and we took great pride in making sure we were accurate in our transmittals."

"But you will admit, and I remind you that you are under oath, the message could be misinterpreted or misunderstood."

"Yes, sir."

"And you will also admit that if someone deliberately wanted to change the meaning of a message he could do so?"

"Yes, but that . . ."

"Thank you, Mr. Simmons. That will be all."

Tad was dozing when the deputy entered the room. "Mr. Dwyer. Mr. Tad Dwyer. You're called to the stand."

"Do you swear to tell the truth, the whole truth, and nothing but the truth, so help you God?"

Tad wanted to shout *No*. His mind was racing. *Truth? Reality? God? Self-incrimination?* I could tell the truth, he thought, but I don't know if it's the whole truth. Further, I'm not sure about this God business. Never have been. Probably never will be.

"I do."

Attorney Feldham came on as both gentle and forthright.

"Mr. Dwyer, please tell the court your rank at the end of the war, your position in the army, and what you now do for a living."

"I mustered out as a second lieutenant, Army of Northern Virginia, assigned to headquarters staff of General Robert E. Lee, under the immediate authority of Major Edward Groves Wilson. I am co-owner of a hardware business in Nashville, Tennessee. I served as a city commissioner in Nashville and am presently serving my third term in the Tennessee Legislature."

"Mr. Dwyer, would you please tell the court how you came to know Mr. Tanner."

"My first remembrance of Billy Dean was after First Manassas. We hit it off, right from the start."

"So you knew Tanner since almost the beginning of the war?"

"As I said, since shortly after First Manassas. But I didn't know him very well till after my brother Arthur was killed at Shiloh, back in April of '62."

"How did it come about that you became good friends?"

"Well, I was informed of my brother Art's death a couple of weeks after Shiloh. I guess I sort of went to pieces. This is when Billy Dean really became a good friend. He sort of took me under his wing for a while. Kept me from losing it. Helped me get my bearings. That sort of thing. "

"How well do you know Mr. Tanner?"

"I knew Billy Dean Tanner as the best friend a fellow could have during most of the war. At the time he probably knew me better than I knew myself. He's the kind of person who is non-judging and non-critical. Know what I mean? Totally accepting. He's the kind of person with whom you could share innermost thoughts and feelings. I would say that I knew him well enough to know that he didn't drink, or smoke, or run with women. He worked like a beaver, never shirking duty, and never ducking out of the really hazardous assignments."

"Did it come as a surprise to you, after all these years, to learn that Tanner had been accused of espionage?"

"Surprise? More like a bolt of lightning. I went into shock. And I want to go on record right here and now by saying I don't believe for one single second that this man was a spy. What I mean to say is that Billy hardly went anywhere or did anything on his own. I had to coax him to get him to go into town with me. Even then, he'd never drink. He'd just sit by as I quaffed down a few. Understand, I was in my younger days then. I wouldn't do that now."

There was a muffled round of laughter throughout the courtroom. Even one of the judges cracked a smile.

"Well, you know what I mean. Next to my brother Louis and my sisters, Billy's probably the most moral and the most humanly decent person I've ever known."

"Mr. Dwyer, I would like you to address anything you know about the whereabouts of Tanner on the day or evening of General Lee's issue of Special Order 191, on September 9, 1862."

Tad thought, here it is. After all these years my own foolishness comes back to haunt me. Gawd Almighty, will I never live it down? Don't say anything you don't want Arnold Latham to put in his newspaper. Get hold of yourself, Dwyer. This is it. What I say right now may make the difference between life or death for Billy. Be careful to give the same testimony you gave at the Stoesser trial. Don't embellish anything. Tell the story slow and easy just like you've come to believe it.

"I'd been given a copy of the orders, which I presume to be the orders about which you are speaking, and was told to deliver them to the headquarters of General Daniel Harvey Hill. I went directly to the livery to secure a mount. When I learned that I would have to wait quite some time for a mount, I decided to walk. It must've taken about an hour from the time I first received the orders until I delivered them into the hands of the clerk at General Hill's headquarters.

"Later that evening all of us junior officers on the headquarters staff were enjoying ourselves over a few drinks. We did this all the time. You know, swap stories, compare notes. Well, I was there and I remember distinctly that Billy Dean was there, even though he didn't drink anything.

"They was all discussing this and that. Stuff of little importance. Then, sort of out of the blue, I remember interrupting them by saying that in all likelihood we'd be headin' north. I volunteered my belief that I was pretty sure Lee had decided to divide the army and we'd be moving out the next day and that all of us would likely remain with Lee's staff.

"You know, Mr. Feldham, all of us at headquarters staff had *good ears*, as they say. We knew fairly well what was in most of the orders, even the top secret kind.

"Then, after I'd had a couple of drinks, I discovered I was out of cigars. Billy and I walked back to my tent to get me a cigar. I remember it well 'cause I was pretty keyed up. Didn't go back to the guy's drinking session though. Me and Billy just sat there quiet while I smoked my cigar.

"Well, that's about it. Must've been ten or so when Billy Dean and I were summoned to headquarters. Major Wilson then explained how Lee was dividin' his army into four sections. This was the intent of Special Order 191. We were told to be ready to leave in an hour.

"Billy Dean and I walked back to our tents. We were supposed to strike our own tents. If we didn't have time to strike our tent some enlisted men would come and do it for us and that was usually bad news. Anyhow, I don't recall seeing Billy Dean for some time after we parted. We were busy gettin' ready to be on the march."

"In your opinion, Dwyer, could Tanner have transmitted those orders to a Union contact?"

"I don't see how. There was no opportunity for any such transmission what with the army being isolated in bivouac outside Frederick with divisions getting ready to move. Hardly no way could messages be gotten out."

"Thank you, Mr. Dwyer. That will be all."

Jacques Belleau now approached Tad.

"Mr. Dwyer. You say you were in the company of Mr. Tanner from early evening at the drinking session of the junior staff officers until sometime in the later evening. After that you didn't see each other for awhile?"

"Correct."

"But, Mr. Dwyer, none of your testimony covers the period before the evening get together. Oh, yes, you completed your mission to the headquarters of General D. H. Hill, but where was Tanner during that period of time? In other words, do you have any knowledge of Tanner's whereabouts between the time the orders were issued and the social hour?"

"No, sir. I presume Mr. Tanner was involved in some official capacity during that time like the rest of us."

Pausing for effect, Belleau now hit Tad with a powerful question.

"Now Mr. Dwyer, in your opinion, is it possible that you could've been conned and betrayed by Tanner? You know, he befriended you and treated you well, but actually he's seduced you into liking him and trusting him?'

"Objection!" Ramsey Feldham jumped to his feet

"I object to the question. It forces the witness to admit that a friend in whom he trusted could've betrayed him."

"Objection sustained."

"No more questions." Jacques Belleau had done enough damage.

Upon returning to the little room in exchange for the third witness, Mr. Phillip Angelucci, Tad was downcast. That last question about whether he could have been taken in by Billy Dean was a killer one. Had Billy Dean crossed him? Had he been conned? Had he been had? It just isn't possible, Tad thought. He was a true friend. Billy'd never betray me. Besides, he thought to himself, just as I had something to keep private, so maybe did Billy.

Tad knew better than most that we believe what we believe in order to survive. He'd been over this many times, especially in the past weeks since receiving the subpoena. In order to make sense out of life and in order to make peace with the world we construct a belief system that becomes true for us.

Tad still believed Billy Dean Tanner was his best friend and held to this belief with every fiber of his being.

Neither witnesses Angelucci nor Rogers could overcome the powerful testimony of Will Troutman. In truth, none of the other three defense witnesses, Angelucci, Rogers, or Simmons, could prove the innocence of Billy Dean Tanner. All that Feldham's defense could ever hope to do was to create a reasonable doubt. But could Feldham create enough doubt to effect a verdict of not guilty?

Several hours later, Tad heard a rumbling noise emanating from the courtroom upstairs. Within minutes, the deputy entered the little room and informed Tad and the others that they were free to leave.

"What was the verdict?" Tad inquired of the deputy.

"Guilty. The judges found Tanner guilty. Not on all counts. Just the third count. Sentencing's tomorrow, 10:00 a.m."

Minutes later, Tad found Ramsey Feldham with Billy Dean. Billy Dean seemed composed as he addressed Tad.

"I'll need to talk with you tomorrow Tad, after the sentencing. Come with Feldham."

During those intervening hours, Tad was not allowed to meet with Billy Dean, so the morning papers were the only source of information available to him.

By 9:30 a.m., Friday, April 18, the courtroom was filled to capacity. Even the hallway was packed with reporters and curiosity seekers. Outside many were waving the Stars and Bars and some held up signs of derision, calling attention to Billy Dean's affiliation with Lucifer and even the anti-Christ.

The court came to order and the presiding judge prepared to read the sentence.

"This Court, duly assembled by special legislative appointment to hear the case of the Confederate States of America versus William Dean Tanner, has found for the defendant on Charge No. 1 and Charge No. 2 as specified; and has found for the Confederate States of America on Charge No. 3 as specified.

"Therefore, by order of this Court, the Defendant, William Dean Tanner, shall be executed by a military firing squad on Tuesday, April 22 8:00 a.m., at the Parade ground adjoining Libby Prison.

"This Court stands adjourned."

The pronouncing of the sentence was over almost before it began. Amidst shouts of traitor and various obscenities such as bastard, son-of-a-bitch, nigger-lover, and union whore, Billy Dean, Ramsey Feldham, and Tad Dwyer exited the Supreme Court, surrounded by a squad of military guards. The entourage embarked for Libby prison in three separate carriages accompanied by mounted military.

Once at the prison, Tad, Billy Dean and Feldham were permitted to be alone. The only room available for such a consultation was a tiny waiting room. Bare walls. Several chairs. A small table.

Feldham began: "I'm still hopeful. After I leave here I'll go back to the office and prepare all the papers for the presidential review of the case. I'll make our case for a pardon based on the fact that neither Troutman nor Jacques Belleau produced one shred of evidence concerning any alleged transmissions of sensitive material. Further, the war's now been over for more than eleven years. I'm hoping the president may be amenable to a pardon, or at least a commutation of sentence."

Tad remembered the remark Feldham made at the briefing session when he and Tad were alone. "Breckinridge was *hard as a rock* in these matters and the likelihood of a pardon or commutation was highly unlikely."

"If I get the papers to the president this afternoon, he'll have three days to study all the material. Meanwhile, let's address the issues Billy Dean has on his mind."

Billy Dean had no questions of Feldham. He didn't even ask Feldham what he thought the chances were for a pardon or commutation. Instead, he looked at Tad intently, then paused as if to collect his thoughts.

"I've asked Ramsey to be witness to everything I'm about to say to you, Tad. I hope you'll understand the need for his presence as I unburden myself." Billy spoke in a matter-of-fact way.

Tad couldn't hold back his feelings any longer as he eyeballed Billy Dean. "Want you to know I still believe you're innocent."

"Thanks, Tad. But it's too late for that. It's time I leveled with you and Mr. Feldham. I wish Mr. Feldham to take notes. And, later, a deposition. For now, let me begin at the beginning. Please don't interrupt me. I'll take your questions when I'm finished."

"My given name is Justin Alexander Bethune. I'm married to Annabeth Grimes. I have two children, Justin Alexander and Nancy Louise. Far as I know they still live in Sparta, Tennessee. By now Justin would be sixteen and Nancy eighteen.

"Back in April of '61, I was in Nashville on business. I was selling patent medicines and I traveled all through Tennessee, Alabama, Georgia, and Mississippi. I visited all the physicians in as many towns and villages as I possibly could.

"To make a long story short, about a year earlier I had fallen in love with a woman from Nashville. We were attracted to each other and our relationship became very emotional and very physical. I loved her very much. I never thought of myself as a carousing person. Until then I'd always been faithful to my wife." Billy paused, allowing this information to sink in.

"One day her husband came home unexpectedly and caught us in bed."

"I didn't know it at the time, but her husband, a man by

the name of Ward Thompson, had led quite a life of carousing and womanizing, and very much wanted to get rid of his wife. When he caught me with her he aimed his gun at me and threatened to kill me right then and there.

"Foolishly, I rushed him and went at him. But he didn't pull the trigger. We struggled for a few seconds and then at the first break in our encounter, almost as if by plan, he wheeled around and aimed the gun at his wife and pulled the trigger. Elly died almost instantly. Thompson made it appear to be an accidental shooting, but it wasn't. Elly was off in the corner with her hands covering her face. Believe me, it was no accident. Thompson aimed that gun right at her. No mistake about it."

Both Tad and Ramsey Feldham paid rapt attention to Billy's every word. Tad sat silently, taking it all in. There was so much he didn't know about his good friend. Feldham scribbled furiously in his notepad as Billy talked, his pen scratching as he tried to record the keywords of Billy's story.

"Soon's he pulled the trigger I was on him, grabbed the gun and pointed it at him."

"No matter, Thompson had me dead to rights. There I was with the gun in my hands. Thompson accused me of killing Elly. He just stood there and laughed at me. Said 'Thank you.' He convinced me I'd be a dead duck in any court of law. In my state of panic I believed him. First chance I had I managed to escape. Threw the gun on the floor and ran like hell. Hid in Nashville for two days.

"Meanwhile, Thompson was going through all the legalities and put out a warrant for my arrest. He got good newspaper coverage. That's how I knew what was going on. He even offered a reward for any tip or information that led to the arrest and conviction of his wife's killer. He did not know my name or anything about me.

"Then I made the worst mistake of my life. I know the affair with Elly was wrong and I know it was stupid of me to rush at Thompson the way I did." Billy paused, fighting back a choking feeling, "But the worst thing I ever did was to run."

Billy continued: "Well, you can figure out the rest. I went north and ended up in Cincinnati. I made contact with a government outfit. I hinted to them that I might be willing to become involved in espionage for the Union. The talk of war was increasing every day and my sympathies had always been with the Union. Slavery disgusted me. I believed the secesh to be dead wrong on the slave issue. Hell, I was a fugitive. No home. No place to go. I'd lost my wife and children. As far as anyone knew, I'd dropped off the face of the earth. If I was caught I was as good as dead. At least I felt that way. I believed at the time that I could never win a verdict of not guilty. Not in Nashville. Not in the city where Ward and Elly Thompson owned a ladies and children's clothing store.

"The authorities in Cincinnati sent me to Washington. I became a Union agent. They gave me a new name and identity and sent me back down south to enlist in a regiment that served in the eastern theater. That's where you and I became friends." Billy Dean looked Tad in the eye.

"Couple more things. At the trial I realized this guy Troutman was really Thompson. Course I never met Elly's son, Daniel Rutherford. Not till later. I was well aware he was the light of his mother's eye. All I knew was this guy Ruff was my contact. Didn't even know Ruff's alias was James Ruther Donley. When this all became clear during Troutman's testimony at the trial I felt like puking. That poor kid! He must've really hated that bastard father of his.

"Another thing, Tad. Special Order 191. Hell, you know well as I we were all privy to those orders. Trust me on this, Tad, there was never an opportunity to get that information to Ruff. Remember, Ruff was cavalry. That night we broke camp at Frederick there was no way I could make any contact.

"That's about it. I've a final request to make of you Tad, but first, do you or Ramsey have any questions?"

Tad looked downcast and forlorn. "I don't want to believe it, but I guess I've no choice. Guess there always was a question in my mind 'bout your past, but I figured you had your reasons for bein' silent. Hard for me to digest all this."

"I know. Hard to believe your ol' sidekick was a traitor. I don't expect you to understand. Hard to believe it myself."

"Tell me, your wife and kids?" Tad's voice trailed off.

"That's part of my request. Think you're up to it?"

"Up to what? Hope so." Tad nodded in the affirmative.

"First, please, sometime in the next few months go to Sparta and tell 'em the whole story. Please tell my wife that I loved her and that I had never strayed until I met Elly. Tell her the truth, that I was too much of a coward to face the music of my affair with Elly. Tell her I feared certain death if I was arrested. Tell Nancy and Justin I loved them very much, but that I honestly believed they were better off not knowing what happened to me.

"Then, this is a rough one Tad. I don't ask you to promise that you will do this, but if you get the chance, if you ever get the opportunity, I'd be mighty glad if you could somehow put the screws to Thompson. Who knows? You may never get the chance. So be it. I don't want you to go on a revenge kick and ruin your career. Don't take this on as some sort of a vendetta. But, if the opportunity ever comes maybe you could settle the score for me. The bastard beat me twice. Once with Elly, and now this . . ."

Billy Dean's voice trailed off. He became silent for a second.

"Jesus Christ, Tad, they're . . . they're gonna . . . they're gonna kill me!"

Billy Dean's voice cracked and broke as he struggled to fight back the tears. He buried his face in his hands and sobbed.

This was the first time Tad had ever seen Billy Dean lose his composure. Through endless days in the army and throughout the trial, and even after the sentencing, Billy Dean had held his emotions in check.

Tad impulsively rose to his feet, went over to Billy Dean, and put his arms around him, father and son like. They wept together. Twenty or thirty seconds seemed like an eternity for Ramsey Feldham who could do nothing except wait.

"I love you, Billy. Nothing you did'll ever change that. You're the best friend I ever had. You know damn well I couldn't've made it without you. I promise to see your wife and kids, like you asked. And rest assured, Billy, somehow, some way, I'll get that bastard Thompson for you."

They talked a few minutes more. Billy deliberately hadn't mentioned the lost orders incident. Good old Billy, Tad thought. Even now he's protectin' my ass. Not wanting to say a word in front of Feldham.

"Tad, let's say goodbye. I want you to leave and give me some time with Mr. Feldham." Billy had regained his composure and was again very businesslike.

"Tad, you're also the best friend I ever had. Never got too nosy. Never invaded my privacy. You let me be. You accepted me. I needed that. I hope you realize I never betrayed you or used you as a source. All my stuff came directly from the higher ups."

"Yeah, Billy. Thanks. I trusted you completely. But thanks for telling me anyhow. It's nice to hear it straight from you."

Billy phrased his words so that the message to Tad was clear even in the presence of Feldham who wouldn't be able to decipher the hidden message within it.

Tad had only one thought: "He's taking my secret right to his grave."

They hugged. Both fought back the tears of love and respect. Stepping back, Billy Dean extended his hand. At this gesture Tad completely broke down.

After a few awkward seconds Billy spoke:

"This's it, Tad. I don't expect anything from Breckinridge."

It was as though Billy Dean's emotions had all been spent and now he was only to the point. "Won't see you again. No sense in comin' to see me. They made it clear no visitors except my attorney."

At this, they looked at one another, eye to eye, then they hugged each other again. Tad turned and left the room. His face was red with tears. He stumbled on one of the steps outside the prison, turned around, and spoke out loud to the witnesses in the clouds, "I love you, Billy. Always have."

CHAPTER TWENTY-THREE

The next three days seemed an eternity. Tad couldn't sleep. He'd think awhile, and then he'd take a long walk. Richmond was famous for its hills and he trudged over each of them. He must have walked back and forth through the Richmond streets half a dozen times. He passed some ladies of the street and found himself getting angry that they'd even dare attempt to entice him. He passed many shops. Nothing appealed to him. He went to a fine restaurant and did nothing but stare at the walls. He could hardly taste the food.

Thoughts coursed his mind. How would he catch up with that good-for-nothing Thompson? Once he did, how would he go about settling the score with the son-of-a-bitch? Would he still run for governor? What was the point? Life's nothing but grief. Hardly worth livin.'

On Monday Tad attempted to see Billy Dean, but the warden made it emphatically clear under no circumstances would he permit any visitor to see Billy Dean unless Feldham was present.

In the afternoon he checked in at Feldham's office hoping for any bit of news, even if it was only that the president had asked a question of Feldham. "Haven't heard a word from Breckinridge. Looks bad. I keep hoping against hope. I plan to stay here in my office all night just in case. I'll see Billy early tomorrow and if worse comes to worse I'll accompany him to the parade ground. If we should get good news I'll send an urgent message to you at your hotel no matter what the hour."

Tad had two beers in the early evening but was careful not to order a third. He muttered to himself: "Got to keep my wits about me though I'm not sure why."

Tad awoke on Tuesday morning feeling wasted, almost as if he hadn't slept. He remembered tossing and turning all night long. Found himself wondering what became of that man he caught outside headquarters tent that night when Lee was outlining his final plans. Never did hear who he was. The night hours seemed to lengthen as he endured the emptiness. He imagined the objects in his room looked like gallows and then firing squads and then caskets.

By dawn Tuesday still no message came from Feldham. Thoroughly downcast, he went through the process of rising and dressing and going down to the registration desk to check for a message. He walked away from the hotel clerk with a downcast demeanor and proceeded to the parade ground much as if he were the walking dead.

Tad was surprised to see the size of the crowd gathering for the execution. He bristled with anger, spoiling for a fight. If he overheard any jeers or derogatory remarks he feared he'd not be able to control his temper. By 7:30 there must've been three or four hundred people crowded behind the restraining ropes at the far end of the parade ground. The firing squad would be about sixty feet from the nearest spectator. Far enough away so no one could get too close, yet close enough so that the crowd could feel a part of it. Billy Dean would be paraded in, surrounded by a small troop of soldiers. He'd be placed against the brick wall and then blindfolded.

A storm threatened, with ominous clouds pressing forward in an overcast sky. At about two minutes before eight, the military guard appeared, marching through the parade ground gates at the far end. While they marched smartly in clipped unison, Billy Dean walked at his own pace. The color guard held the flag of the Confederacy. The drummers sounded the long and foreboding notes of a funeral dirge. Over and over the drums declared their unrelenting message of death.

At the far wall the procession came to an abrupt halt. A drill sergeant tied Billy's hands behind his back and his feet tautly together. The chaplain approached Billy Dean and the two conversed in private. Tad watched as the chaplain nodded, then offered a short prayer and what appeared to be a benediction.

In a resounding voice, the provost marshal read the verdict of the judges and the order for execution. The provost marshal then barked out the order to blindfold the prisoner.

It was quiet except for the sound of the snare drum and a few muffled voices. At least there were no loud mouth remarks to be heard during the last moments of the life of the man he'd known and loved as Billy Dean Tanner. His parents christened him and his wife and children knew him as Justin Alexander Bethune, but they were spared this terrible agony.

Tad wanted to cry. He invited tears. None would come. Perhaps the tears've dried up. Perhaps I'm beyond the point of feeling any pain.

The firing squad was ready. Twelve men at the ready. They were standing thirty paces distant. Nine of the guns were loaded with blanks. This was supposed to create a doubt in the mind of each of the men on the firing squad so that they could always remind themselves that perhaps it was not their bullet that killed the accused. Of course this was nonsense because anybody who was accustomed to firing these weapons could easily tell the difference between a blank blast of powder and a live charge, simply by the kick of the weapon against one's shoulder.

The chaplain walked over to his place next to the color guard.

The drummer kept up his infernal dirge.

The commanding officer shouted the commands:

"Ready!"

"Aim!"

"Fire!"

The blast was enough to sever a tree from its trunk. Mercifully, the marksmen were accurate. Three bullets pounded Billy Dean's chest.

Billy Dean fell to the ground instantly. The surgeon and two officers with loaded pistols rushed to his side. There was no need to fire a point blank shot.

*****

Tad had made all the arrangements for the burial. The body was placed in a nearby cemetery used exclusively for Union dead. Tad engaged a stonemason and paid for an appropriate grave marker.

Justin Alexander Bethune
Son-Husband-Father-Friend
Rest in Peace. April 22, 1873

Tad knelt by the grave and said good-bye to his old friend.

"Thanks, Billy. Thanks for being my friend. I feel as though the only reason I'm still alive is because you safeguarded my secret. Damn, Billy, I'm sick. You always seemed so composed, so together. I never would've guessed you had a secret too."

And then, catching himself by surprise, he blurted out something he'd been working hard to deny to himself.

"Damn, Billy, I loved you but guess I'm angry too. Yeah. I'm damned angry old friend. Why the hell did'ya have to do it Billy? Why'd'ya have to be a goddamn spy?"

Tad hesitated, surprised by his outburst of anger. "Damnit Billy, you vented your anger on Thompson by turning on the South. You could've beat that murder rap he laid on you. Shit! More I think 'bout it, the more angry I get."

The thought struck him that had Billy not taken the path he did, they'd likely never have met. He felt better as he walked away from the grave. His loss was great, but he felt good at being able to spit out his pent-up anger at Billy. Damn right, Billy, Tad continued in thought, I'm fumin' with anger that you ever let this happen.

Then Tad's anger must have triggered his recall. Only now did Tad see the irony of how he and Billy had done the same thing.

They both ran.

Billy had tried to talk him out of the lost order cover up. But Tad ran. He spent his whole life runnin' from the decision he made that day to lie his way out of the lost order fiasco, and now here he was blaming Billy for a fatal decision Billy made.

No wonder Billy tried so hard to talk Tad into coming clean with his carelessness in losing the order. Billy had done the same stupid thing in running away. He spent his life regretting it ever since. Now he was trying to prevent Tad from an equally horrendous decision.

Tad imagined Billy's response: "Your'e right, Tad. It was the stupidest thing I ever did, and it cost me my life. But, Tad, that's now in the past. Whatever you do about Thompson, keep your wits about you. Hear?"

"Bet on it, Billy! Bet on me keeping my wits and bet on me gettin' that sonovabitch."

Tad smiled to himself. Yeah, if I can get that bastard Thompson, I'll at least have a measure of revenge. The way I see it that sonovabitch's responsible for three deaths: Billy, his wife, Elly, and his son. Thompson might just have well killed that poor kid straight out like he did his wife.

Tad felt a sudden burst of energy flow through his body.

The day before Tad left Richmond, he went to see Ramsey Feldham. After the execution, Feldham asked Tad to be sure to stop by his office, that there was some important unfinished business to take care of.

Feldham was soft-spoken, almost pensive. "What I feared most is the very thing that happened. I wanted to see him acquitted, or, at worst, the sentence commuted. Know he was a spy, but I really liked him. It'll take me a long time to live this one down."

"You shouldn't blame yourself," Tad interjected. "I didn't get to see the trial, but from what I heard and read, I'd say Billy Dean had fine legal counsel. After all, you did manage to get acquittal on two of the three charges."

"Thanks, Dwyer. I'm gratified to hear you say that. Still, it only took one to get him. You and Billy Dean were close friends. I know this has been very difficult." Feldham paused, sort of eyeing Tad.

"I asked you to stop by 'cause I've something I want to give you. It's from Billy Dean."

Taking an envelope out of his desk drawer, Feldham looked Tad straight in the eyes. "This is a formal deposition Billy Dean swore out and had notarized the other day after you left. This was his final piece of business. It tells the whole story of how Elly Thompson came to be shot to death. Trust me on this, you know everything that's in here so don't break the seal unless you're in a position to use it against Thompson. Even then, make sure you have Thompson and an attorney present. This is a copy. I have the original. If you ever get a chance to use this against Thompson, please send for me at once. If Thompson ever came to trial, it would help our case if I could testify as to the circumstances under which I took this deposition."

"You have my word." Tad was rising to his feet as he spoke. "I only hope the opportunity comes before life passes us by."

Feldham took another envelope from his desk. "Please give this to Mrs. Bethune. I should say his widow. Maybe she's remarried by now. It's his final appeal to his faithful wife and children to forgive him, and there's a check representing all Billy's remaining earthly assets, a considerable amount. It's also an attestation of his and your friendship and trust in one another and hence this visit."

"I trust your fee has been taken care of?"

"Yes. Billy took care of everything. Thanks for asking."

Tad thanked Feldham. Shook his hand. Started to cry. Feldham put his arm around Tad, attempting to comfort him.

Tad set to walking, and again appeared to wander aimlessly through the streets. It was near 5:00 when he arrived at his hotel and found the message in his box.

Dear Mr. Dwyer,

> *Please meet me in the hotel lobby tonight at 8:00. I very much wish to talk with you.*

Thank you. Arnold Latham

Attached to the note was a business card: *The Southern Advocate.* Arnold Latham, Correspondent.

Tad dreaded the idea of meeting Latham. In fact, meeting with Latham was the last thing in the world he wanted to do. Tad had in his mind that he'd eat dinner and then get his things ready for departure early on the morrow.

He forced himself to weigh the pros and cons of granting Latham an interview. On the plus side he could tell the whole story over again, and by so doing, he'd set the record straight once and for all. This would demonstrate that he had nothing to hide. Also, it would get Latham out of his life. Grant him this one request and that's it. Once, and never again.

Tad reasoned to himself: But, no. There is no "once and for all." Look at the negatives. One episode will simply whet this guy's appetite for more. He'll never be satisfied. Besides, what if he misquotes me, or worse, twists my words and takes things out of context. Haven't I learned all about innuendoes and how people can be made to look guilty just by association or inference? And *The Southern Advocate* certainly doesn't have the kind of solid reputation that *Harper's* has.

Tad didn't need to go any further with his list of negatives. He thought to himself, regardless of what people may conclude from my silence, I'm far better off keeping my own counsel without ever allowing myself to be quoted in public. Besides, I've testified twice under oath. It's all part of the public record. I'll never have anything more to say. Tad swore an oath to himself.

His internal dialogue now ended, Tad hastened to enjoy his

dinner before meeting Arnold Latham in the lobby.

"Mr. Dwyer," Latham appeared anxious and excited, "I'm so glad to see you."

"Received your message this afternoon," Tad replied curtly. "I came by only to tell you in person that I have no need or personal desire to talk with you."

"Oh, that would be a mistake, Dwyer. I think you know as well as I that your testimony at the Stoesser and Tanner trials leaves many unanswered questions. *The Southern Advocate* would like to help you put the record straight once and for all. You need us, Dwyer. You do realize that, don't you?"

"Mr. Latham. I will say this one more time. I've no need or desire to talk with you. There's nothing to say that is not spelled out clearly in the record. I have no further comment on the subject."

"But, Dwyer, you're a public servant. You're in the legislature."

"Thanks for reminding me. I'd almost forgotten. Good day, Mr. Latham."

At this Tad turned brusquely and started walking toward the stairway.

"I'll get you for this, Dwyer. I'll write the damn article without you and you'll never live it down. It'll cost you, believe you me."

"Is that a threat or a promise?" Tad bit his lip to keep from saying anything else. He knew he was being set up. Latham had just baited the hook. Tad kept heading to the stairway. Billy Dean must be smiling, he thought, and managed a smile himself.

Next day, Tad boarded the early train for Knoxville. At Knoxville he changed trains and headed straight west to Nashville. But at Cookeville, in the heart of Tennessee, he detrained and hired a carriage to take him southward eighteen miles to the village of Sparta.

He checked in at the Sparta Inn and freshened up. After asking directions he set out walking. Within another ten minutes he found himself standing at the front door of the former residence of Billy Dean Tanner.

"Hello, Mrs. Bethune?"

"Yes, I'm Mrs. Bethune." Tad noted that she still responded to this name. She hadn't remarried.

"I'm Tad Dwyer. I'm a friend . . ." He started again. "Mr. Bethune was a friend of mine." Tad fumbled a bit. Wondered if he should have said *is* a friend?

"Oh, please do come in, Mr. Dwyer."

Annabeth Grimes Bethune was a very attractive woman of middle years. She had brunette hair, a slim figure, blue eyes, and very prominent eyelashes. She wore a slightly shabby but tidy homespun dress. She moved about with a sense of grace. Tad's first thought was how could Billy have done what he did? Tad noticed she wasn't wearing a wedding ring. On the mantel there were pencil sketches of two children, who he presumed to be Justin and Nancy when they were much younger. A quick glance failed to reveal any similar sketch of Billy Dean.

"Please, Mr. Dwyer, have a seat and make yourself comfortable. I'm afraid you've caught me unprepared. Wasn't expecting company. I just got home from work. Haven't had a chance to get at any house work what with clerking at the dry goods store. I'm always playing catch-up."

"Your place looks fine." Tad responded with a knowing smile. There was an awkward interlude of silence.

"So you have news of Justin?"

"Yes, as a matter of fact, I do. I'm on my way to Nashville, and I stopped to see you in order to share with you, to the extent you wish to be informed, of events concerning Justin."

Tad had carefully composed and memorized these words. He would keep faith with Billy Dean only to the point of Annabeth's acquiescence. He was determined to respect her wishes. Perhaps she had no desire to know any details concerning her husband of over nineteen years. She may wish to keep the past forever out of mind.

While he was thinking what to say next Annabeth looked Tad in the eyes and asked hopefully: "Is he alive?"

"No. He is not alive." Tad paused, allowing a few seconds for this to sink in. "Mrs. Bethune," he said softly. "I'm prepared to say some things that you may not wish to hear. Please give this some thought. I've already entered your life unannounced and uninvited."

"Oh, Mr. Dwyer. You sound very protective. I have no need to think it over. For years I've been tortured by thoughts of Justin. I've been through all kinds of anger and bitterness. I must know whatever it is you have to share. I must hear it, no matter how bad it is. Maybe I'll finally be able to get on with my life. I feel like I've been treading water all these years, ever since . . . that terrible day when I heard Justin was wanted for murder." She fought back tears.

"Where are your son and daughter?"

"They'll be home within about a half hour."

"Do you think we should begin now, or should we wait for them?" Tad said, trying to be diplomatic.

"If you don't mind, I think it best to include them from the start. I'd rather they hear things directly from you. We've been very close all these years. We have no secrets. A few years ago I told them all I knew. Of course they grew up knowing their dad had left them and all that. But what I mean is, when they were older I shared with them as much as I knew about the affair with that Nashville woman."

Tad began to feel that he was in the presence of a very special lady.

Nancy and Justin came home within five minutes of each other. There was hardly time to get acquainted. After all, Tad was the newest person in their life, and he was going to share with them information that could possibly affect everything they said and did from this time forward 'til the end of their lives. It was no small thing, having this stranger in their home.

It was almost seven by the time Tad finished. He'd gone back over one or two things several times. They had questions. There were tears and laughs. Except for the truth about his dereliction with the lost orders, Tad held nothing back. He joined with them in their anger about Billy Dean becoming a Union spy. He shared his belief that Billy Dean could've beaten the murder rap, if only he hadn't panicked and run.

By the end of the evening, he was referring to Billy Dean as Justin. And Annabeth, Justin, and Nancy were referring to Justin as Billy Dean. He knew this night would be only the beginning of a long journey for Annabeth, Nancy, and Justin.

Tad discovered that he too had a great need to talk about his experience with Billy Dean. He who came to deliver somber news to the innocents now became part of both the grieving and the healing.

Responding to Annabeth's request, Tad gave explicit directions concerning the location of the cemetery where Justin was buried. Then he handed Annabeth the envelope. "Billy Dean, err, Justin, wanted you to have this. It's a personal note and the remainder of his estate. All the legal bills have been paid."

It was now time for Tad to leave. He felt as though he'd been the one who'd been helped and healed. He could not hold back his tears. They each hugged him in turn. Their tears were a mixture of pain and joy, sorrow and relief.

Tad walked to the hotel. He felt pangs of hunger, but nothing was open. He didn't sleep well. Certain things kept replaying over and over in his mind.

*****

Once back home Tad found himself unable to do anything. Didn't eat right. Didn't take any exercise. Slept fitfully. Continued to shirk his legislative duties. Spent hardly any time at the hardware store. Billy Dean and his family preoccupied his mind in such a commanding way nothing else could gain entrance. The darkness of his mood pervaded every corner of his life.

One day Jane made a special trip to Tad's house. When he didn't respond to her gentle knock, she banged on his front door. When Tad finally responded she was aghast at his appearance. Disheveled, unshaved, slouched. He looked a mess! Pretending not to notice how terrible he looked she scolded him: "Tad, I don't know what's wrong, but you've got to get a hold of yourself. Look at you! You look terrible. And your place is a mess. I know you've lost a dear friend, but life goes on and everybody's asking about you. I cover for you as best I can. Looks to me like you've given up on running for governor."

Tad said nothing. Shrugged his shoulders. "Don't rightly know. Don't know for nothin'."

After Jane left Tad slipped back into his melancholic mood. He hadn't felt this down since after he'd gotten home from the war, when he rammed the piece of glass through his hand. Doc Hayes had scolded him good. Said the problem wasn't the war, it was the bottle. "All right, Doc, tell me what to do this time. I feel like total shit and I ain't been drinkin', carousin', or gamblin. Just can't seem to get beyond thinkin' 'bout Billy Dean."

Tad fell into a deep sulk. Felt sorry for himself to the point he'd feel totally drained. Like he was sitting on his own private pity-pot. Then, after wallowing for a time, his fatigue would help him escape into sleep. When he awoke he'd start the whole cycle all over again. Think clearly for awhile and then start to feel sorry for himself.

One sleepless night, after about ten days of being hunkered down in the nasty blues, Tad had a talk with Billy Dean. In the semi-consciousness of restless sleep Tad imagined Billy Dean lighting into him something fearful, reading him up and down for his stupid and irresponsible behavior. "What you're doin' is shameful. Don't you see, Tad, you're letting yourself down and you're lettin' me down."

Then, after one more day spent in self-reproach, the vicious cycle of gloom and self-recrimination seemed to lift a bit. Wore itself out. It was as if the energy spent in maintaining his exhaustion now turned on itself, at least enough for Tad to assert himself and take some positive steps toward making himself human again. It was like his whole being rose up in rebellion and said enough is enough. He put his house in order and bathed. As he stood in front of his mirror to shave, he scolded himself: "No more of this shit, Dwyer!"

Tad had no sooner gotten his two houses in order, the house his mind lived in and the house his body lived in, when Jane again paid him an unexpected visit. This time Jane didn't even take time to comment on how nice Tad's place looked. She simply blurted out, "Tad, you must read this article in *The Southern Advocate* written by a man named Arnold Latham. Thinks you're the missing link to the mystery of some orders that were supposedly lost."

Tad felt a terrible, sinking feeling in the pit of his stomach. Taking the article from Jane, he sat down to assess the damage.

At the Stoesser trial there was one witness for the prosecution who may have committed perjury! This same person was also a witness for the defense at the Tanner trial, eleven years later. Second Lieutenant, C.S.A., Taylor Arvin Dwyer served as a junior staff officer in the field headquarters of the Army of Northern Virginia, under General Robert E. Lee. In this capacity, he also served as a courier. On September 9, 1862, when General Lee issued Special Order 191 to his divisional generals, Dwyer was entrusted with a copy to be delivered to General Daniel Harvey Hill.

General Hill claimed he never received his copy of the order. Subsequently, General Hill accused Sergeant James L. Stoesser, a clerk on Hill's staff, of having lost Hill's copy of Special Order 191. A court martial followed and Stoesser was acquitted of the charge. In his testimony Dwyer claimed that he personally delivered the orders to Sergeant Stoesser.

Last month at the Tanner trial Dwyer once again may have committed perjury. He again testified that he delivered Special Order 191 to General Hill's headquarters. Dwyer refused my invitations to be interviewed after both the Stoesser trial and after the Tanner trial. We must infer that these refusals are calculated to keep the door closed on this sensitive matter. If Dwyer has nothing to conceal why does he

*decline to be interviewed? The suspicion is that Dwyer himself lost those
orders. We find it peculiar that no one has ever brought charges against
him.*

"What does this mean, Tad?" Jane seemed agitated. "Is this
going to get you into trouble?"

Tad quickly reassured Jane. "No. It's no big deal. My
testimony's on record. Let people think what they want. One thing
for sure, if I give any kind of reply I'll never hear the end of it. It'll
make things much worse. This guy Latham is a flunky reporter who
wants to make a name for himself at my expense."

After Jane left Tad had another talk with himself, this one
out loud and to the point. He was stern and deliberative: "Probably
never gonna' get rid of Arnold Latham. Must put that mutton
thumper out'a my mind. I'll be damned if I'm gonna let him pull
me down or stand in my way. If I let him scare me out of runnin'
then I've let him win by default. I'll show that sonovabitch. My best
bet's to reshuffle the deck and go for the governor spot. I'll take my
chances. Got nothin' to lose and everything to gain."

Tad's old penchant for gambling now energized him. Instead
of Latham's article in the *Advocate* having a negative effect and
bringing him down, it had the opposite effect of stimulating him
and giving him new purpose in life. "This is for you, Billy. See your
bet, Latham, and I'll raise you clean out'a sight!"

*****

Next day Tad arranged a meeting with Jane and Louis.
There was only one back room left in the hardware store. The other
rooms were remodeled in order to accommodate Jonathan's family.
Jonathan had married Jessica back in '70 and they had a little boy
called Dwy. His full name was Jonathan Dwyer Herkimer.

"I need you both. Louis, I need you to be my campaign
manager. You're good at organizin' and hardly anything escapes
your attention. And you've a good feel for politics. And Jane, I need
you to run the hardware business by yourself till the campaign's
over."

Louis was anxious to get started. "Great! The Democratic
primary in September is wide open and the November election's
nothin' but a formality. The real fight will be the primary. We'll
have to muster our forces."

253

Louis continued with a sense of urgency and purpose: "I think you're in a great position. It's a logical step in anyone's language. Your record stands for itself. Just about right in both length of public service and seasonin'. You've certainly got good name recognition."

Age was in Tad's favor. In just a few days, on May 18, he'd begin his forty-fifth year. The prime of life. Tad looked forward to the campaign. He was good at it. While he was not a great general like Lee, Jackson, or Longstreet, he had the down-to-earth appeal of an army veteran who'd done his duty courageously throughout the war. He could tell war stories and keep an audience spellbound for the better part of two hours.

And perhaps of even greater importance, Tad could charm men as well as women. He could talk the Appalachian hill country talk as well as the softer tone of the Cumberland Plateau. Western Tennessee would receive him as one of its own because he was from Nashville rather than further east. Eastern Tennesseans were often viewed with skepticism by folks in middle and western Tennessee. There'd been a lot of Union sympathizers in eastern Tennessee and Tad would need their vote. He'd probably have to turn on a little charm: "Aw shucks, I'm just a down-home country boy like y'all. Never did own any of them thar slaves, but I reckon they've as much right to our free Tennessee air as anyone."

He figured he could handle the heat if somebody made a carousing or womanizing charge against him. Anyway, he hadn't womanized in years. He recalled that day he walked away from the two prostitutes at the Chesapeake Hotel in Pikesville when he was recuperating. Besides, if someone were to accuse him of immoral behavior, the burden of proof would be on him or her.

"But that leaves me alone in the hardware store." Jane was not sure she could spare Louis. "I can't manage the store, do the books, and still be on the floor all day."

"Just be till November." Louis really wanted to go on the road with Tad.

"Yes, but that's almost five months away."

"Tell you what," Louis responded. "I'll do all the ordering. You manage the day-to-day stuff. I'll even help with the books. And I think its time we promote Jonathan to some title like *assistant manager* and give him more responsibility. You know, he's become a valuable asset. Knows the inventory backward and forward and handles himself well. He can talk white talk and black talk. Customers like him. Jessica's a big help too."

"Can't afford to increase Jonathan's pay unless Tad accepts less." Jane was blunt.

Tad was quick with his response. "Jane's right! I think its time I became a silent partner. If I lose the election then I'll just have to find another line of work. But I'm not gonna lose! Meanwhile, use my pay line to increase Jonathan and the two of you. You both certainly deserve a big increase. It'll make Elizabeth happy too." Tad stopped and rubbed his forehead. "And there's another thing I'd like to do. Like to get in touch with Jonathan's old slave master, Caleb Herkimer, and purchase Jonathan's freedom. Give papers to Jonathan."

"Great idea. Can we do it soon? Like before the campaign starts?" Louis was thinking of the political payoff Tad would enjoy if he were ever questioned about hiring a slave.

"I agree," Jane added. "We probably should have done it long ago."

CHAPTER TWENTY-FOUR

On a sultry Tennessee night in August, Tad gave a major speech in his run for governor. This was to be his only appearance in Chattanooga and he gave it all he had. Tad was exhausted and elated as he stepped down from the speaker's platform. His audience had really given him a rousing endorsement. They continued cheering for at least thirty seconds after he'd concluded his speech and many were now milling about, waiting to shake his hand. Tad was a bit embarrassed because he was soaking wet with perspiration, but he needn't have been because everyone else was in the same boat.

"Tad! Tad Dwyer!" a strong voice called out from the side of the hall. Looking out over the heads of those pressing about him, Tad recognized the tall, redheaded man who was working his way through the crowd. When Tad waved back he saw that familiar grin sweep across the face of Red Dawkin.

He continued shaking hands with every single well-wisher. When Red, holding back until the last person had greeted Tad, reached his side, the two men embraced warmly. "You're the last man I expected to see tonight! What brings you here?" Tad's face lit up with beams of delight as he enthusiastically pumped Red's hand.

"Here on business, lieutenant, and when I heard you were speakin' tonight I decided to look y'all up. Real glad I did. That was some fine speech. You sure have the gift of gab."

"Thanks, but let's cut the lieutenant stuff. It's ancient history. And speaking of gab, I always thought you were the one called Talker."

"Yeah, but you have a way with a crowd." Red was sincere in his compliment. "Thanks, Red. Look, if you're not busy, let's go

256

over to my hotel. I could sure use a sandwich and a beer about now. Give us a chance to catch up on old times."

"Sounds fine," Red replied.

Just about this time Louis walked up and Tad introduced him. "Hey Louis. This here's one of my buddies from my time with General Lee. Meet Red Dawkin, better known as Talker. Red, this is my brother Louis. Louis's my campaign manager."

"I heard a lot about you, Red. Especially when Tad came to Johnson's Island after the fightin' was over to help me home to Tennessee. I'd lost a foot at Perryville."

"Gee, Louis, wouldn't've guessed it. You sure walk like nothin' ever happened."

Tad piped in, "You should see him dance."

"Well, believe me, it took a long time."

A half-hour later the three men were comfortably seated at a corner table in the hotel restaurant, and for the first time in months, Tad was able to sit back and laugh as Red regaled them with one war story after another. After one beer Louis excused himself. "Mind if I leave you two war heroes alone? I'm kind of tired and I could use some sack time."

After Louis took his leave, Tad turned to Red.

"Well look here now, Red, you've been talkin' non-stop ever since we got here and you still haven't told me what you're doin' here. You're quite a far piece from home aren't you? So, what kind of business you in?"

"Shoes," Red said flatly.

"Shoes?" Tad asked, raising one eyebrow. "You talkin' 'bout horseshoes, or this kind of shoes?" he asked, raising his foot to display his shoe.

"Somethin' like what you've got on your foot, but a helluva lot better. They cost a bit more, but they're worth every penny. They're more comfortable than what you're wearin' and will last you a lot longer."

"Whoa!" Tad exclaimed with a laugh. "Course if they're as good as you say they are, I'll take a couple pair."

Now it was Red's turn to laugh. "All my samples are in my hotel room, but I couldn't sell you shoes no how. I'm a drummer. I go to stores that carry a line of shoes and try to convince 'em that I've got the best shoe available, and they should carry my line. Once folks try 'em, they'll never buy any other kind."

"Never thought you'd end up as a drummer. With the line of

bullshit you hand out you must be the best salesman the company has. How'd you ever get started drummin' for shoes?"

Red turned serious for a moment, "You remember that snowball battle we had right after the blizzard? Course you wouldn't remember it like I do cause you was an officer and the snowball fight was jest for us enlisted men."

"Yeah. Sure do! If memory serves, you somehow talked your way into it. It was supposed to be for infantry only. Froze my tootsies watchin' you guys. A great day."

"Better believe it was. I tell you, after my experience that day my heart was never again in the war. It was a low time for me cause I was questionin' why the hell we were fightin' the war, and I tell you, never in my life did I feel so hopeless and depressed."

"Why? What happened? I never knew you were so discouraged and down!"

"Well, let's just say the killin' was gettin' to me. It was some time in the early afternoon, I was cold, tired, alone, and surrounded by a bunch of Yanks. Guess I just snapped, threw myself into the snow and began screamin' and yellin', punchin' away at the snow like a crazy man. But those Yankee boys didn't laugh or pelt me with snowballs. They let me calm down and then they listened to me tell how I was feelin'. I began to wonder if somehow I got poured into the wrong damn uniform.

"Well, I made a new friend that day. A Yankee friend, by the name of Corporal Nate Phillips. I still remember how he listened to me pourin' out my guts. Well, after the fight we exchanged addresses. Then, about five years ago Nate came down to Johnson City and looked me up. I'd moved to a different house, but he found me.

"Turns out his family was in the shoe business up in Massachusetts. He talked his Pa into takin' a chance on expandin' the business with a southern factory. He has a good head for business and realized that shoes could be manufactured much cheaper down here. He also knew us Southerners would never buy no shoes from the Yankees, so he was lookin' for just the right Southerner who'd be willing to invest in a shoe factory in Tennessee. It'd provide jobs for the local people, and no law said they had to know the company was partly owned by Yanks. Said when he found the right man he planned to bring him up north and teach him the shoe business from top to bottom.

"Nate asked me if I was interested. I replied as to how I was interested in *workin'* for him, but I had no big money to invest and I never wanted to be in charge of nothin' or nobody. Just wasn't my style. You know me, Tad. I don't want nobody bossin' me around and by the same token, I've no desire to be bossin' anyone else."

Tad nodded, and Red continued. "Then I remembered Major Ezekiel Shaw. You remember him, don't you Tad? He was with our horse artillery."

Tad nodded in hesitation: "I've heard of him, but I don't think I ever met him. The years've gone by, Red, and I'm really better with faces than names."

"Well, anyhow, Shaw's a fine man. A straight shooter, if'n you know what I mean. One of the best in my opinion. The thought hit me that Major Shaw just might be a good match for Nate. Know what I mean, Tad? And he didn't live too far from Johnson City, so the next afternoon Nate and I looked him up. Nate ran his business proposition by Shaw. After thinkin' 'bout it for a spell Shaw decided to throw in with Nate. The Shaw family had been raisin' cotton for years, but times changed, and Shaw decided the shoe business was such a good investment he couldn't turn it down. Shaw came from an old southern family with money, so he and Nate Phillips became perfect partners."

"I was surprised Major Shaw remembered my name, me being just a staff sergeant. Said he remembered me as Talker. Well, I thought that would be the end of it. Nate and Shaw would go into business together. But then, a few months later, both Nate and Shaw come to see me. They wanted me to go to work for them, to travel through the South and talk merchants into carryin' their line o' shoes. Said they'd even put me on salary. I told 'em I liked the idea of bein' a factory rep but that I preferred to work on commission. That way I can look out for my own ass and not have to cover everybody else's, know what I mean? Anyhow, it sounded challengin' and I like travelin', so that's what I'm doin'. Really like it. Been at it about four years now. Doin' real well. Now, aren't you sorry you asked?"

"No. Not at all. I think this is really great! Yankee design but made down here with a rebel label. I'll have to get some of those shoes. Drummin' shoes is perfect for you Red." Tad chuckled. "Could be the first step toward better relations between North and South."

"Better not say that too loud if you expect to get elected governor, Tad. Some folks might agree with you, especially in east Tennessee, but probably a lot more wouldn't," Red cautioned.

"Enough about me. What's been goin' on with you?" Red

seemed genuinely interested in hearing about Tad's career in politics.

Before long Tad had recounted all the circumstances of his elections and accomplishments, from Dwyer Hardware to the Manure King of Nashville to the Dwyer Petition. Before long Tad became sullen and soft-spoken as he described the circumstances and details of Billy Dean's trial and execution.

Both men fell silent for a minute or so, and then Red addressed his pressing concern. "Tad, I thought your speech was great. Really did. But, you're looking tired. I can tell it in your face. You need some time off! You've been through a helluva lot and your system needs time to catch up."

Tad's head came up and he looked at Red to see if the man was serious or leading up to something humorous. There was no grin on Red's face.

"Thought I'd covered it up." Tad quipped.

"You've been under a tremendous strain. Shows on your face. Oh, strangers might not notice it, but I saw it plain as day the minute I saw you. You've been pushing yourself, probably keeping busy to avoid thinking about Billy Dean. You can't run away from it, Tad. You have to deal with it. You're not doing yourself any favor by pushing yourself to the point of exhaustion. How about taking a week off! I head back home tomorrow to Johnson City. Come with me. My place is quiet and secluded. Lots of good fishin' too." Red looked him straight in the eyes.

Tad felt uncomfortable, and chuckled nervously. "God, I'm glad you're not runnin' for governor against me . . . you're awfully convincing."

"Then do as I say and come home with me. You're not gonna lose the election 'cause you took a few days off. I'm sure you can make the arrangements with your brother. Whether you want to accept the fact or not, you're gonna win the election. I get around, and I hear people talkin'. You're one of the common people, one of us. No offense. It's just that they like what you've been tellin' 'em, and they're gonna vote for you. You owe it to yourself and us to be in good shape when you move into the governor's office. Not a burned-out replica of what you used to be."

Tad had never seen this side of Red, and nobody had spoken to him quite like this in a long time. Certainly, nobody had been as solicitous about his well-being, except of course Jane and Louis. He had to admit that Red was right about his having pushed himself in an attempt to take his mind off Billy Dean. He was tired. He could use a break.

"You sure I won't be a bother? Hell, I haven't even asked you if you're married or have kids. I'm an old bachelor. Will I be a bother to anyone?"

"I'm not married. Bein' on the road, I haven't stayed in one place long enough for any gal to throw a rope round me. I live with my sister but she'll be glad to have intelligent conversation around the house for a change." Red flashed his famous Cheshire cat grin.

"After our folks passed away neither of us was married, so I bought me a bigger place and Charlyn moved in with me. Got a lot of space so we don't annoy one another. She teaches school. The kids love her and she enjoys being around 'em. Says they keep her young."

"Your sister never married?"

"Yes, Charlyn was married once. Her husband, Ben Hatcher, was killed at Carlisle. You remember, don't you, Tad? That day at Carlisle when you found me outside headquarters. I was feelin' terrible. Tears were runnin' down my cheeks and you were so understandin' and told me to be extra careful because the worst thing could happen to my sister was if I was to get killed too."

"Oh, yes. I do remember. I never met your brother-in-law, but it's all coming back now. He was a captain, wasn't he? Right in the center of the breakthrough of Jackson's middle? I'm glad I helped you some that day, Red. I should've been a lot more help than I was. People need friends. I know. Billy Dean was awful good to me when I first heard my brother Art was killed at Shiloh."

"Yeah. Poor Ben. Never knew what hit him." Red paused for a second. "Anyhow, as I was sayin', neither of us is married and the arrangement works fine. Charlyn's a mighty pretty woman. Smart too."

Red pulled his timepiece out of his pocket. "Well, if we're gonna' catch the morning train to Knoxville we'd better call it a night. Y'all better be at the depot in the mornin' or I'm gonna come a gunnin' for you. Hear?"

"It's a deal. But I'm a little uneasy about your sister. I sure hope she doesn't mind unexpected guests."

"In my business, I'm always draggin' prospects home. They take one look at Charlyn, put away one of her meals, and they're ready to throw everyone else's shoes out and just stock ours." Red flashed his wide grin.

Tad quickly made arrangements with Louis. Actually, there

were no speeches scheduled for another week and Louis decided to stay over in Chattanooga for a couple of days. Said he would enjoy the time alone.

On arrival at Red's house in Johnson City, Tad came face to face with a new experience. Charlyn was tall, slim, and attractive. A truly stunning woman! Tiny little crow's feet at the corners of her eyes were her only concession to the passing years. Her hair was a dark red and her figure certainly the envy of women much younger. Mother Nature had a big lead over Father Time.

Charlyn greeted Tad warmly, saying she'd heard much about him from her brother and had read many complimentary articles about him in the Knoxville newspaper. After a few pleasantries she excused herself, saying that if they were going to have an evening meal, she'd best be about it.

"You see, Mr. Dwyer, Red's made sure I'm the only slave left in Tennessee," she replied with a cheery smile.

"Yeah, she never lets me forget how bad a cook I am," Red said, laughing.

The meal was one of the finest Tad had eaten in a long time and he complimented Charlyn at great length. Tad never seemed to grow tired of fried chicken and mashed potatoes.

"Wait 'til you see what she does tomorrow. Her Sunday meals are a real production!" Red seemed very pleased Tad had decided to come.

"You're welcome to attend the meetin' house with us in the morning, Mr. Dwyer?" Charlyn announced hopefully.

Tad nearly burst out laughing when he saw the expression on Red's face. Red obviously hadn't made any plans about attending church. Here he was pretendin' to be makin' a face like the devil, turning his head sideways to sideways as if to say no, no, no.

"C'mon, sis. Lay off the church thing," Red exhorted.

"Red, hush up! I think it'd be the gentlemanly thing for you to do. We certainly can't have Mr. Dwyer, a candidate for governor, sittin' in our church with nobody to accompany him."

Tad looked puzzled "Heck, who needs Red. If you'll have me I'd be glad to sit with you, Charlyn. May I call you Charlyn? And no more of this Mr. Dwyer stuff. Please call me Tad."

"I'll be singing with the choir." She chose to ignore Red's obvious reluctance. "Don't pay any heed to my brother. He's an out-and-out heathen who needs religion more than any other man in the county."

Tad laughed a nervous sort of laugh. "I'd be delighted to attend church as long as the preacher isn't down on free-thinkers. I'm just not cut out to be the church-goin' type, but I reckon if I'm with you two it'll be all right. You can protect me. But please," Tad hesitated, "please don't introduce me to anyone 'til the service is over. That way the preacher won't know I'm that guy runnin' for governor."

"Turncoat! Are you sure you weren't secretly makin' snowballs for those Yanks that day?" Red interjected. "No wonder they captured our flag."

Tad felt uneasy as he sat in the pew next to Red. The smell of oiled floors and burning candles, the stain glass picture window of Jesus praying in the Garden of Gethsemane, the muffled sounds of parishioners as they waited for the service to begin. At first Tad wanted to excuse himself. Church reminded him of his past, his guilt, and his failures. It reminded him of his childhood and of his father. As a child Tad hated going to meetings and listening to preaching.

Tad knew very well he'd come here only because of Charlyn. When the choir entered he found himself almost fixated, staring at her. She was radiant and beautiful. As the choir sang he was absorbed in thought. He thought how lucky he was to have run across Red and to be sitting here admiring this truly beautiful woman. Tad didn't hear any of the anthem's words, not to mention the preacher's.

The days passed quickly. They all went on a shopping trip on Tuesday and a picnic outing on Wednesday. Tad began to wish that Red would get lost so that the threesome would become a twosome. Charlyn's voice was sensuous and he found himself enthralled whenever she spoke. He had to make a conscious effort not to gaze upon her. Charlyn was a delightful companion, and for the first time in years he felt a strong desire to become physically close. At first, he dismissed his feelings as typical male desire, but then he realized his feelings ran much deeper than that.

Charlyn was more than just an attractive woman. She was a very caring person who put other people's welfare above her own. She knew when to utilize her keen sense of humor and when to express love and concern. On a couple of occasions he and Charlyn had engaged in political and religious discussions. Tad talked freely about how he had severe struggles in accepting the concept of a personal and loving god. Charlyn seemed to accept Tad's feelings without criticizing him or passing judgement. "I tend to agree with much of what you're saying, but I enjoy the people, and especially singing in the choir." Tad was enthralled with her.

It was inevitable that the subject of the death of Charlyn's husband, Ben, would come up. "I didn't know Ben. But Red reminded me about the circumstances that day in the center of Jackson's middle. I wish I could've been of help to Red. He was devastated."

"Oh, but you were a big help! Red wrote me that you told him he should take extra good care of himself, at least for his sister's sake, so that she didn't lose both a husband and a brother. I remember crying and sobbing when I read that. Made me feel good that somebody else cared about Red. He and Ben were really good friends."

Dinner on Thursday evening was a delicious treat. But Tad could hardly keep his mind on the food. He was experiencing something he thought he'd never live to experience. He tried to push the dreaded thought of leaving out of his mind, but he had a train to catch in the morning.

Some time after dinner Charlyn came to the door of the parlor. There she found Tad sitting on the velvet Empire sofa watching the leaping flames in the fireplace. It was an unusually cool and rainy August evening and Red had suggested having a fire for old time's sake. Red insisted there was something comforting about a glowing fire in a fireplace. The fire was no sooner going full strength than Red dozed off. By the time Charlyn entered the room he was dead to the world.

"Am I intruding?" Charlyn asked, entering the room and then pausing as if not knowing whether she should.

"Please, I've been hoping you'd join me. Red retired about half-hour ago. Look at him," Tad remarked.

At this Red awoke. He apologized and excused himself. "It's time I got up and went to bed."

Charlyn laughed. "That's Red's favorite ploy." She paused and then looked at Tad. He appeared to be in a very pensive mood.

"Would you mind if I trimmed the lamp? The fire's so beautiful."

"No, please do," Tad smiled at her warmly, his heart starting to pound.

She trimmed the lamp and then sat down next to him.

They both sat in silence for several minutes, allowing themselves to fall under the spell of the glowing fire.

Tad was afraid to break the silence, but he was determined

to ask the burning question that kept pushing itself to the front of his mind.

"May I . . . may I see you again one day?" His voice was subdued from the emotion he was feeling.

"Oh, I hope so. I look forward to it." Charlyn revealed her feelings without hesitation.

Tad continued, "I've enjoyed being with you this week. I want you to know that I—" He hesitated. "I've developed feelings for you. Do you have any idea how I feel about you?" Tad whispered the question, almost afraid to hear the answer.

As she turned toward Tad her eyes met his. She answered, "I do."

Tad was caught totally and completely off guard. He could hardly believe her. She was mirroring Tad's feelings. He felt an inner surge of excitement and hope. Never felt this way before. What joy! He opened his arms as he reached over to her.

She pressed herself softly against him. Their lips joined together as they held tightly in a prolonged embrace. Little did they know the embrace would last for years.

*****

Campaigning was fun again, like back when he first ran for the city council in Nashville! Since returning from Johnson City, Tad had a smile on his face that seemed to light up his entire countenance. He moved through crowds with poise and self-confidence. He communicated a genuine desire to lead the state of Tennessee into greater prosperity. He constantly advocated closer working relationships among the eleven Confederate States.

One of his main themes was the attracting of Northern industry. "If we are to be truly united in our quest for employment for all our people we need to attract Northern industry and trade. We need more Yankee dollars invested in Tennessee." Tad always included the story of Red and Nate Phillips and Major Shaw in every speech he made. He didn't use their actual names but he used the story to his advantage. He showed little patience for protectionist policies that prevented the new nation from more aggressive trade and manufacturing.

Things were shaping up well for the primary on September 9. Tad was confident he would win. None of the other two candidates had his impact. One candidate was a popular war hero by the name of William Orr. From Memphis, Orr was well educated and a good speaker. But Orr had no government experience and no public service record. The other candidate, Clarence Marlowe, had served in the Tennessee legislature, but was relatively unknown outside of his home district in Maryville. Marlowe had not served in the Confederate Army and was thus at a disadvantage with both Tad and Will Orr.

The day after the primary the final results pointed to a November election between Dwyer and a Republican by the name of Ralph Conway. Tad had won a plurality of the Democratic Party votes, winning almost 45 percent of the total. Orr garnered 37 percent and Marlowe a surprising 18 percent. Tad particularly liked Will Orr and planned to offer him a high-level position in his administration, partly in exchange for his enthusiastic support in the November election and partly because Tad really believed Orr to be a solid man with sound ideas and good judgment.

On Tuesday, November 4, 1873, Tad easily won the race for governor.

In the days following the election his decision to involve Will Orr among his appointments proved to be a masterstroke. Orr was determined to justify the governor's faith in him and he knew serving in Tad's administration would give him invaluable experience. Tad had no truck with the practice of surrounding oneself with sycophants and persons of mediocre ability. To his way of thinking, the higher the quality of his appointed officials, the better he looked.

Back home in Nashville, Jonathan also received a position of status. He was now legally a free man. Caleb Herkimer had pushed hard to get a good price for Jonathan, once he learned who he was dealing with. Tad had offered 30 dollars Confederate money. Herkimer insisted on 50. "Let's meet his price and get this over with." Jane not only wanted freedom for Jonathan, she was worried about bad press possibly connected with employing a let-go Negro, and negative implications for Tad as governor. "We can take the money out of profits from the store. Goodness knows we've done very well this past year."

Jonathan was surprised and elated when Tad, Louis, and Jane called him and Jessica into the office and presented him with his papers. The papers gave legal ownership of Jonathan to the Dwyers, but then the Dwyers signed off, thus giving Jonathan his absolute freedom. "This's got to be the happiest day of my life. You folks been like parents to me and I'm grateful and mighty proud to be part of

Dwyer Hardware. If'n its all right with y'all, I'll be spendin' the rest of my life workin' for Dwyer Hardware."

By late January, Tad, with Louis as his chief of staff, was satisfied he had made all the right appointments. Yet there was still one person missing, one key position open. That position would be filled on Saturday, June 6.

CHAPTER TWENTY-FIVE

"I, Taylor Arvin Dwyer..."
"I, Charlotte Lyn Hatcher..."

On Saturday, June 6, the social event of 1874 took place in Johnson City, when Governor Taylor Arvin Dwyer and Charlotte Lyn Hatcher exchanged wedding vows. It seemed as though every friend, relative, and politician in Tennessee crowded into the little Federated Church or made it to the gala reception that followed. Louis served as best man and Red escorted his sister down the aisle and gave her in marriage to Tad.

Not surprisingly, Louis's wife, Elizabeth, upstaged everyone by wearing a maroon and white striped walking dress complete with fringe and an enormous bustle. But things like that didn't bother Charlyn in the least. Charlyn wore a more tasteful gown of mauve silk trimmed with pleated ruche and delicate blond lace. In place of a veil on her head, she wore a lovely Spanish comb which had belonged to her mother. This was her day and no outlandish, tasteless dress by her future brother-in-law's wife would detract from Charlyn's radiant beauty and captivating demeanor. This tall woman with the radiant smile, dark red hair, and youthful figure had captured everyone's fancy.

Beautiful within as she was without. Charlyn moved among the guests with a sense of grace and charm. Tad felt he couldn't have been more fortunate had he lived seven lifetimes. He basked in the warmth created by the congratulations heaped upon him by all his friends.

On an earlier trip to Johnson City to finalize arrangements, Tad announced to Red that he and Charlyn had made plans to honeymoon at a nearby hotel in Kingsport. But Red would have none of it. "A couple should have a little privacy on their weddin' night. Why don't you two go to my place, in the foothills of the Smokies less than twenty miles from here. I use it for huntin', fishin', and when I just want to get away by myself. Heck, if you stay at the hotel there'll be someone pounding on your door all day and probably all night. Charlyn's never been to my cabin. It'll be new to both of you."

Charlyn quickly replied, "That's just the problem Red, I've never seen it! Only heard your stories about it. Heaven only knows what it's really like."

Without giving Tad a chance to speak, Red continued, "Give my place a try and if you don't like it you can always go back to your hotel idea. My cabin's well stocked, though I don't s'pose you'll be much interested in food 'til Monday at the earliest. I'll even get spring water hauled in just in case you get too weak to lug water. Got a little boat and there's always nice trout in the brook."

Tad didn't know what to think. "How do we know you'll keep our secret? Sure don't want anybody findin' us."

"You'll have to trust me on this one, soon-to-be brother-in-law."

"Red, I don't know whether to run you outta' here or hug you." Tad chuckled. "You're sure a thoughtful pain in the behind."

Tad thought the reception would never end. There were toasts and short speeches. Even a formal resolution of best wishes from the Tennessee State Legislature. Finally the time came for Charlyn to throw the wedding bouquet. She saw Jane standing next to Betty and Blaine out of the corner of her eye and threw it over her shoulder right in Jane's reach. Jane caught it, and then blushed.

They arrived at their honeymoon cabin at about half past seven. The eighteen or so miles in the small carriage on the rutted dirt road was very tiring, especially after the stress of the wedding and the reception. But the cabin proved to be everything Red had promised, and more. He'd obviously arranged with someone to come in and ready the place. It had been aired out and a large kerosene lamp illuminated the interior. One end of the large cabin served as the kitchen and was set apart by a worktable. Charlyn took note of the iron wood-burning stove and the ready supply of water. Her practiced eye assured her the place was practically spotless. Foodstuffs and provisions filled the panty. Wood was carefully laid in the fireplace in addition to the firebox.

"Let's light the fire," Charlyn suggested. "I'll never forget that last night of your first visit. You looked so deep in thought. I was afraid you didn't share my feelings. I was hoping you wanted to hold me as close as I wanted to hold you."

"For me a night to remember and treasure," Tad replied. "I was taken with you. Ever since that Sunday service when I watched you in the choir I knew you were the one for me. 'Course I was worried you wouldn't feel the same about me."

Tad took her in his arms. They kissed long and deep, and she melted in his embrace. There'd be plenty of time for a fire later.

*****

A popular governor, Tad was unopposed within his own party when he came up for re-election in 1877. He faced only token Republican opposition. Tad often commented that his greatest asset on the campaign trail was Charlyn. She accompanied Tad on each of his trips. She could mix with anyone at any level. She used her attractiveness in a positive manner. Never a flirt, but always gracious and charming, she was as tactful and diplomatic, as she was beautiful and intelligent.

She had a remarkable ability to put a new slant on almost any event or problem. She could redefine the smallest crisis. When a committee chairman was moaning and groaning about losing a battle with a Congressional committee, Charlyn commented: "Look at it this way, this wasn't a defeat, it was but an opportunity for you to go through this other door where you can be more creative and more assertive."

To Charlyn a defeat was never a defeat—it was a redeployment or a planned retreat. A setback was an opportunity for reassessment. A strong criticism served as a buoy in the water helping one to navigate. She was not one who would make light of serious issues, but she was one who had the knack of helping people by changing the way they looked at things.

On May 16, 1877, a day that Tad henceforth claimed to be the second happiest day of his life, Charlyn gave birth to Arthur Isaiah Dwyer. Of course, when anyone dared to ask what was the happiest day of his life, Tad would simply point to Charlyn and say, "When that lovely lady became my wife."

Everybody said Arthur looked just like his father, even though he had reddish hair and his mother's eyes and nose. Little

270

Arthur quickly became the most spoiled, if not the most loved, of any child to bear the Dwyer name. Sometimes Tad wondered what he'd ever done to merit such good fortune. Charlyn was all that he could ask for in a wife, and more. And now, with the birth of Arthur, Tad's sense of joy knew no bounds.

Except for developments in Richmond.

Alexander Hamilton Stephens of Georgia was elected to succeed John C. Breckinridge as president of the Confederacy in the election of 1879. By the time of his retirement, Breckinridge had become the most popular of the young nation's presidents, finishing the last four years of Lee's term and then being elected to his own six-year term running from 1874 to 1880.

Now, after nearly one full term, Stephens expressed no interest in running for a second term in the election of 1885. Robert E. Lee's second oldest son, William Henry Fitzhugh Lee, better known as Rooney, was rumored to be the frontrunner for the country's highest office.

Things had not gone well for the Confederacy and no one was more aware of this than its past presidents. None had spoken favorably of their years as chief executive. The Confederate Constitution didn't give much power to its president or its House and Senate. Consequently, the office of the presidency was beginning to be looked upon as an exercise in futility. On the occasion of his retirement John Breckinridge was quoted as saying, "The frustration of being president is due to the very structure of the Confederate Constitution. We are not a republic. We are a free association of states. This is our glory and our peril, our strength and our weakness."

Grover Cleveland, the first Democrat to be elected president of the United States since before the War Between the States, was attempting to increase trade with several of the Confederate states. This was something Tad believed in and strongly endorsed as governor of Tennessee. Unfortunately, it often resulted in bidding wars, wherein the states were pitted against each other to see which one could come up with the most attractive offer to induce a Northern company to expand its manufacturing or move its corporate facility to the South. When this happened the only real winners were the Northern bankers and industrialists because often the states, in their efforts to outbid one another, gave away too much.

Tad nominated C.S.A. Tennessee Senator Howard Pennington for a second term. Pennington, however, quickly informed Tad that he did not wish to continue in the C.S.A. Senate.

He complained to Tad, "The Senate's near a total waste. Being a Senator is like being a valet to the best man at your brother-in-law's wedding. Most of them see the Senate as a place to hang their hat while they go and play fox and hounds. It's a club for overindulged playboys who don't give a damn about the plight of the common people. Most of 'em are aristocrats. Born with silver spoons in their mouth. Bunch of spoiled losers in my opinion."

Midway through his Senate tenure, Pennington introduced three pieces of legislation. He wrote a short column for the *Nashville Guardian* describing the three bills that he had introduced.

> *The first program was aimed at creating a national relief organization. The legislation was designed to put homeless and starving people to work for the public good. I was committed to the program and worked very hard to get it out of committee.*
>
> *I introduced a second bill designed to raise revenue for the central government. I proposed a one-half percent tax on all goods, excluding food products. I proposed that all monies raised in this manner be spent on rights of way for a national rail system, harbor and waterway improvement, and our nations' road system.*
>
> *My third bill provided for the granting of property tax relief over the first five years for any new business or industry from any foreign nation wishing to purchase property in any state within the Confederacy. This tax relief package would range from 100% the first year with a 20% decrease each ensuing year.*
>
> *I regret to inform the citizens of our state that each of these bills died in committee.*

Tad had great respect for Pennington. He also had sympathy with Pennington's thoughts and beliefs about the C.S.A. Senate because he himself shared many of these thoughts. Tad was becoming increasingly discouraged about the future of the Confederacy. Speaking to an open forum in Nashville, Tad pulled no punches about what he saw happening. "If the present course is stayed and the eleven states are left to their own devices they'll evolve into eleven separate countries. Each of these *state-countries* cling to their prized autonomy, and each wallows in its own inability to provide opportunity for jobs, commerce, food, clothing, and shelter for its own people. Prosperity is only for the well-born few."

Tad kept company with a few neighboring governors who were beginning to realize that if the states were not willing to cede any power to the central government or allow the central government to take any initiative to get the country out of depression, the Confederacy would soon go under. States' rights had been the celebrated *cause* in winning the great war, and now the cause of states' rights was becoming the underlying reason for the lost peace.

*****

In 1883, midway in his third term of office, Tad was surprised to learn that there were between nine and twelve state legislators who were holding a semi-secret caucus dedicated to the idea of Tennessee bolting from the Confederacy and petitioning to rejoin the Union. This bit of information really caught Tad off guard. He'd often entertained such thoughts but never spoke of them to anyone except Charlyn, Louis, and Jane. He'd often thought to himself that since Tennessee was the last state to secede from the Union it surely would be fitting if it were the first state to rejoin.

The caucus was supposed to be an open caucus, but there was never any official publicity about it. No one from the press was invited, nor did anyone from the press find out about it. Invitation was by word of mouth and the attendance seemed to increase by one or two at each successive meeting.

Soon after learning about the caucus Tad decided to "drop by." "Am I permitted to attend your deliberations?" Tad asked before he presumed to enter the room.

"Certainly, governor. As a matter of fact, we've been discussing about whether or not to extend to you an invitation to join with us. I think we're to the point where we need your guidance." Tad recognized John Alcort, a legislator from eastern Tennessee.

Before long the chair of the caucus, Clarence Marlowe, Tad's old opponent back in his first gubernatorial primary, called upon Tad to speak at the next meeting of the caucus, asking him to address specifically the process they should follow if they decided to rejoin the Union.

Thus it was, at the next meeting of the caucus, Tad carried forth. "Returning to Union statehood requires two things. First, there needs to be a petition to the Confederate Congress for the dissolution of the relationship presently existing between Tennessee and the Confederate States of America.

"Secondly, a state desirous of joining the Union would follow the identical established process as any other prospective state must do, as set up and required by the Constitution of the United States."

"Maybe I shouldn't ask, but I'll stick my neck out and ask anyway." James Cranford was always very blunt and often outspoken. "I have two questions: First, How do we know we are within our rights to secede?"

Governor Dwyer responded: "The first sentence of the preamble to our Confederate Constitution states: *We the people of the Confederate States, each State acting in its sovereign and independent character* . . . " Is the central government sovereign or is each state sovereign? Our Constitution answers that question once and forever. Tennessee is sovereign and our affiliation with the central authorities is by our choice. Yes, we have the inherent right to secede from the Confederacy."

James Cranford then asked his second question: "My second question is: Where do you stand on this issue of secession? How do you feel about it? Are you with us or against us?"

The very question brought a hush as Tad thought carefully before responding. "I know practically nothing of your past deliberations. I confess I only recently heard about this caucus. Today is only my second exposure to your thinking. At this point I will not commit myself, but I will state without reservation that I am *open* to the idea. I think a lot of open discussion and public debate needs to precede such a decision. I think every step needs to be carefully thought out. For instance, assuming we as a state elect to do this, should we simply go it alone or should we pass some sort of resolution and then share our action with the ten other governors and state legislatures?

"If our legislature should vote to leave the Confederacy, I think we should work directly with the other governors and legislatures rather than the Richmond folks. The Richmond people are actually powerless in this matter. Further, I believe we should let those in authority in each state know what we intend to do before we actually do it. That way, they'll all have a chance to converse with us about our reasons and motivation. Who knows, maybe two or three'll want to join with us? But one thing, in my opinion, is absolutely necessary. That is, if we are really serious about our intentions, these meetings and deliberations should not give any appearance of secrecy, not even a hint."

"Governor, when you say 'assuming we as a state elect to do it' does that mean a popular vote?" Cranford asked.

"Yes. As you will recall, before Tennessee seceded on June 8,

1861, there were two popular votes. In February of '61 the popular vote was negative. It was defeated by nearly 10,000 votes. Then, in June of '61, after Governor Isham Harris refused to accept the results of the February referendum, there was a second popular vote that strongly favored secession. If it hadn't been for Governor Harris' determination to secede, we would still be Yankees."

At this there was noticeable rumbling throughout the room.

Tad continued: "If the governor should veto the bill authorizing a referendum, the legislature would need a two-thirds majority to overrule the veto. A referendum is the only way we can really determine the will of the people. But before we rush into a referendum, I think it's imperative that every attempt be made to determine the people's state of mind on the matter."

"I take it from the tone of your remarks that you think there's merit in approaching the other states?" Sam Nottingham was one of the few Republicans in the Tennessee Legislature.

"Sam, I firmly believe that the more states expressing their resolve to leave the Confederacy in order to return to the Union the stronger and easier the entire process would likely be. If only one or two states wished to leave, it would likely be much more difficult, especially if those states were not presently contiguous with any of the existing states of the Union. For instance, what if Georgia or Florida or Arkansas were the only ones to vote for disunion with the Confederacy? They are contiguous only with other Confederate states. We in Tennessee are, of course, contiguous with Kentucky.

"Also, if reunion were ever to be sought by any Confederate State, it would be much more advantageous if the current Union president was a Democrat, especially one who exhibited a conciliatory attitude toward the Confederacy. I believe Grover Cleveland would be more amenable to such an overture than any recent Union president."

Long discussions ensued over the next several weeks. The caucus took Tad's advice and openly advertised its weekly meetings, inviting any interested legislator to attend and participate in the deliberations. Of course, once the meetings were advertised, the press would play its role in any forthcoming drama of secession.

During the next few days and weeks Tad came to a firm decision. He'd come to believe, with every fiber of his being, that reunion was the only chance the people of Tennessee had for economic survival.

By early 1884 the news had traveled far and wide that the

state of Tennessee was seriously considering removing itself from the Confederacy in order to rejoin the Union. Tad was bombarded with hundreds and hundreds of letters, most of which indicated some degree of support. There were, of course, many hate letters. He was called every name imaginable, and there were several outright threats to his life.

By June it was clear that there was great concern throughout the South about Tennessee. Rumors abounded. There were messages of support and alarm. Almost every response indicated a desire for Tennessee to hold back any formal petition until the states had sufficient opportunity to discuss the matter.

Tad suspected that one way or another Tennessee would petition to rejoin the Union. The real question was whether or not Tennessee would be acting alone or in concert with others.

Clarence Marlowe was appointed by the caucus to meet with Tad.

"As you know, there's a lot of interest out there. The caucus has received a great range and volume of response. Most of it seems to indicate a wish for us to withhold our petition 'til it can be properly discussed and debated. The caucus passed a motion asking you to call a meeting of all the Confederate governors for this purpose. The caucus has agreed to serve as host to all who come."

Tad liked the idea. It certainly would be good for Nashville and for Tennessee. He intended to play the governors in such a manner that they'd have the opportunity to study and debate the wisdom of Tennessee's action. "Perhaps," Tad said to Charlyn, "we're just imagining all of this. Maybe the Confederacy's really on firm ground and it's just me that's seein' these things and thinkin' this way. Could be there'll be strong sentiment against what we've done and little sympathy for our position. Maybe all the other states will be hostile toward us. I doubt it, but we must find out."

Tad acted quickly to implement the will of the caucus. In April 1885, in the last year of Tad's third term as governor, the Tennessee Legislature passed a resolution inviting the governor and two state legislators (preferably one from each party) from each of the other ten Confederate states to attend a conference in Nashville, Tennessee. The expressed purpose of the conference: to solicit viewpoints and counsel regarding the Tennessee Legislature's proposed intention to call for a statewide referendum on the proposal for Tennessee to exit from the Confederate States of America and petition to rejoin the United States of America.

The conference attendees would be asked specifically to discuss, evaluate, and critique the following two resolutions.

> *The people of Tennessee, voting in referendum, hereby petition for the dissolution of the relationship presently existing between this State and the Constitutionally authorized Confederate States of America, effective midnight, December 31, 1887. This resolution authorizes the Governor of the State of Tennessee and its Legislature to initiate these proceedings.*

> *This resolution was followed by a second resolution:*
> *The people of Tennessee, voting in referendum, hereby petition for admission to the union of states known as the United States of America, effective January 1, 1888. This resolution authorizes the Governor of the State of Tennessee and its Legislature to initiate these proceedings.*

As a matter of practical politics the sending of copies of the Tennessee Resolution to the governors and legislators would have the effect of circumventing the Confederate Congress and Senate in favor of working with the governors and legislatures of the other ten states. Tennessee was accused, and rightfully so, of spearheading a flanking movement wherein the eleven CSA states simply bypassed the central government.

The first meeting of governors in the history of the Confederacy was called to be held in Nashville, Tennessee, July 5-8, 1886. "Of course," Tad said somewhat sheepishly, "come November of '85, I may no longer be governor. A fourth term may be out of the question. As a matter of fact, the election may give us a clue as to the thinking of the folks of Tennessee. If they're against the whole idea of secession and re-union they sure as heck won't be voting for me."

*****

Tad looked up as Louis entered the room. One look at his brother's face was enough to convince him that Louis was the bearer of bad tidings.

"Look at this! You ought to file charges against this son-of-a-bitch," Louis raged as he thrust the latest copy of *The Southern Advocate* toward his brother.

"Must be my friend Latham again." Tad sighed wearily as

he caught sight of the banner head.

Tad leaned back in his chair, put his feet on his desk and commenced reading: "I'll be damned!" he exclaimed suddenly as his eyes picked up the name that had haunted him for so many years. He'd often wondered if James Stoesser was still alive, and if so, would he ever contact Tad or attempt to blackmail him in some way. After all, Tad had clearly done this man a rank injustice, testifying under oath that he'd indeed delivered those special orders personally to Stoesser.

The article was written under the heading: *Deathbed Indictment of Governor Dwyer* under Latham's byline.

> *This reporter recently took a statement from a man who sustained fatal injuries as the result of a fall while making repairs on the roof of his barn. James Stoesser, age 56, died only two days after telling this reporter that Tennessee Governor Taylor Arvin Dwyer committed perjury while serving in the Confederate Army. Dwyer told General Daniel Harvey Hill that he had personally delivered Special Order 191 to Sergeant James Stoesser, staff sergeant in charge of General Hill's headquarters. Inasmuch as those orders were never received by General Hill, General Hill brought court martial proceedings against Stoesser, claiming Stoesser and his staff mishandled the orders.*
>
> *At the trial, Dwyer testified that he handed the orders to Stoesser. Stoesser and his two subordinates testified that Dwyer had never set foot inside their headquarters tent. The Court Martial Review Board exonerated Stoesser of the charges, but no charges were ever brought against Dwyer.*
>
> *Dwyer obviously lied about delivering Special Order 191 to Stoesser, but the question that haunted Stoesser until the day he died was what really happened to those orders that were never delivered? James Stoesser told this reporter that he still believed Dwyer was lying through his teeth and that he knew more than he was telling, and he found it strange that no charges had ever been made against Dwyer.*

Tad groaned out loud as he finished reading the account.

Louis interrupted. "Who's this guy Stoesser anyway?"

"Don't you remember me telling you about Stoesser and his two buddies? They're the ones who ambushed me and bagged me that night."

"Oh yeah! Just never really associated the guy's name."

Tad considered carefully his next words to Louis. "Latham

just won't let go. Somehow I knew Latham was trouble right from the start. A hungry reporter looking for a story. Did I tell you he came up to me after the Stoesser trial and wanted to interview me. I refused politely, but that's why he's still after me. Then he came after me at Billy Dean's trial. Same deal. Wanted to interview me to let me tell my side of the story. 'Course I told him I'd just told my side of the story in court and that was the end of it." While it pained Tad to do so, he was very careful not to tell Louis the whole truth.

Tad then thought to himself. At least I now know Stoesser can't hurt me. He's the only other person besides Billy Dean who could deny my story. Come to think of it, Latham's done me a favor. How else would I ever've known Stoesser was dead?

"Don't you think we should sue this guy Latham?" Louis asked. "I mean he's committing libel. He's actually accused you of losing those orders as well as having committed perjury."

"If I were a private citizen I think I would, but as governor I just can't be bothered with petty stuff like this. Mustn't stoop to his level. Latham's been after me for years and for me to file suit wouldn't be in the public interest. I think my best bet is to ignore him. Remember, November '85 is just around the corner."

"I don't know. Seems someone ought to put him down." Louis gave a look of total disgust.

Tad hated to lie to Louis. The thought of withholding the unspoken part of the story from Louis bothered Tad. He knew Louis would be deeply hurt and angry if he knew that Tad hadn't told him the whole naked truth.

When Tad was alone he mumbled to himself, "Guess this thing'll be with me till I kick. Seems like I never finish paying the price."

CHAPTER TWENTY-SIX

Monday, July 5, 1886 and Nashville was filled with an air of excitement and expectation. All the other ten governors were in attendance, and Tad, now in his fourth term as governor, put feelers out to learn as much as he could about where they stood. He picked up a sense of enthusiasm as well as profound frustration. He heard endless rounds of complaining, mostly about the weakness of the Confederate Congress. When he reminded them that the Confederate Constitution was designed so that the states would not lose their sovereignty to a strong central government, they replied that states' rights, or states' sovereignty, had now become the core of the problem.

Governor Harold Latimer of Georgia complained that without financial help from the central government, there was no way an individual state could take care of the thousands upon thousands of homeless—black and white. Latimer moaned, "We can't tax our people to death. We need help. Financial help. Our roads are horrible and our railroads are even worse. We have only one way to raise money. Direct taxes for goods and services. And you know what a burden that becomes."

"It's no wonder we've got so many vigilantes in Mississippi," complained Erich Friehoffer. "We have little or no money to pay constables and sheriffs, and so the people just band together and form their own law. We have hundreds of vigilantes roaming the countryside, and we have terrible poverty. Apathy is everywhere. No one seems to give a damn about anything."

"Well, let me tell you," opined the South Carolina Governor Roger Franklin, "if this current state of affairs continues much longer, South Carolina will be in bankruptcy. If that happens we may be forced to petition England for relief."

Franklin's last remark was not calculated to bring a laugh. It was an open secret that South Carolina was still in talks with England about becoming a Protectorate of the British Empire.

The formal session was much the same. First on the agenda was a short introduction by the governor of Tennessee. After giving a brief history of the caucus and explaining why the Tennessee legislature was perhaps planning to seek dissolution with the Confederacy, Tad asked for questions.

"What do y'all in Tennessee expect to gain by going back to the Union?"

Tad answered straight out: "We were far better off as part of the Union than we are now. Our standard of living has decreased steadily since 1861. We're trying to draw as much manufacturing from the North as we can, but the investors are afraid of us. They maintain we lack the ability to ensure the security of their investments simply because we have such a weak central bank and a huge war-debt with terrible credit. They're afraid we're going to hit them up for taxes. I honestly believe if we were back in the Union, Yankee industrialists would be standing in line to invest in factories and manufacturing."

"But the biggest reason," Tad continued, "is not commerce, believe it or not. The biggest reason is that we came to the conclusion that the Confederacy had degenerated into an every-state-for-itself type of thing, and frankly gentlemen, we're scared. Plain and simple. We don't fit into the Atlantic seacoast states or the Gulf of Mexico states. We're caught right in the middle."

"Mister Chairman," Governor of Virginia Lance Jenkins rose to speak. "I move that this council of governors request the governor of the state of Tennessee to convey to the Tennessee Legislature that we, the governors of the remaining states in the Confederacy, do humbly and respectfully request that Tennessee postpone its timetable for action until such time that our respective legislatures have opportunity to give due thought and consideration to what course of action they might like to take."

"Second the motion." Rising to his feet, Harold Latimer of Georgia gave an emphasis to the motion that was unmistakable.

Tad was quick to respond. "Gentlemen, this is an open forum. We have no legal status, so I question whether or not we have any authority to make motions. I have no legal status to chair this meeting. Perhaps it would be best to elect a chairman who then could lead us through this kind of business, more or less as a consensus type of resolution which would convey the sense of the motion."

"I nominate Erich Friehoffer of Mississippi to be our chair, and Harold Latimer of Georgia to be our secretary." John Paul Logan of Florida was persuasive simply through his tone of voice.

"Second," Governor of North Carolina Sullivan Truax responded.

Since there still was no chairman to receive this motion, Tad thought it would do no harm for him to handle this one item of business. After all, he'd been the one who'd called this meeting.

"All right. There's a motion on the floor to elect Erich Friehoffer of Mississippi as chairman, and Harold Latimer of Georgia as secretary of this meeting. Are there any other nominations?"

Tad paused. "Any other nominations or discussion?" Seeing that no one had any questions, he put the question. "All those in favor of the motion, please say yea."

The room was full of yeas.

"Opposed please give sign by saying nay."

There were no nays.

This business having been attended to, the Mississippi governor, Erich Friehoffer, went to the front of the group. He asked Lance Jenkins to restate his motion and to put it in writing. Then he asked for reconfirmation of the second. Harold Latimer of Georgia obliged. This being done, Friehoffer asked for discussion on the motion.

"Before we vote on this motion I would like to hear Tad Dwyer speak to it. Would the gentleman from Tennessee give us his reaction to this motion?" Roger Franklin of South Carolina was soft-spoken in his request.

Tad rose to his feet. "I will be very pleased to transmit your request to the Tennessee Legislature. While I can't predict their response, I do think they'll be most eager to hear what transpires here over the next several days. After all, the Tennessee Legislature called us all together for this meeting. My guess is that their response will be favorable, unless the waiting period becomes too drawn out."

Stuart Williams of Alabama inquired: "In other words, Mr. Dwyer, if several of us, or even more than several, should happen to be in sympathy with Tennessee's petitions, it might be possible that Tennessee would temporarily postpone its timetable until others of us could act in concert?"

"Yes. I think that is a very reasonable assumption, Mr.

Williams. I can't promise, of course, but my best guess is that the Tennessee Legislature would postpone its referendum regarding a dissolution petition, at least for a time. As governor, I would certainly recommend it."

"Do I hear other discussion?" Friehoffer was careful to make certain that if anyone else wished to speak, they'd have the opportunity.

"There being no further discussion, let us bring the motion to a vote. All in favor please say yea."

The room resounded with the sound of yea.

"All those opposing the motion—"

The room was dead quiet.

"Abstentions?"

"Tennessee abstains." Tad didn't feel he should vote for or against this particular motion.

"All right, then," spoke Friehoffer, "Tennessee has been officially requested to postpone its timetable until such time we all, in our own legislatures, have opportunity to give due thought and consideration to the matter of whether or not we might be willing to join with Tennessee."

The tone and intensity of the deliberations began to change. Not only were the governors more relaxed with one another, they seemed to desist from the lethal political pastime of trying to impress one another.

The conversation kept coming back to the Confederate Constitution. Sullivan Truax of North Carolina asked Tad to explain his understanding of the procedure that would be necessary if Tennessee, or any other state, wished to dissolve its relationship with the Confederacy.

"First and foremost," Tad responded, "the Constitution of the Confederate States of America is an extension of its preamble." Tad was well prepared. He had a copy of the Constitution in front of him. "The very first line of the first sentence states:

We, the People of the Confederate States, each State acting in its *sovereign* and independent character . . .

"The important word, gentlemen, is the word *sovereign*. Each of us is a sovereign state. There is nothing illegal in what Tennessee proposes to do. Until now, no one has ever expressed a desire to dissolve the relationship existing between their state and the central

John F. Crosby

congress of the Confederacy. My assessment is that the process would be a rather simple one. There is no specific clause in this Constitution forbidding dissolution of the existing relationship by any of us. Each of us is absolutely sovereign."

Tad carried forth: "This is what the war with England was all about. England with its king and Parliament were sovereign. The colonies were not. This is what the *Articles of Confederation* of the thirteen original colonies was all about. Each colony or state was sovereign and the centralized government was nothing but a compact. Something like the *Mayflower Compact*.

"Here we are again: The states and the federal establishment cannot both be sovereign. Either one or the other—but not both. No compromise on this issue has ever been found. Not even in Ancient Greece."

There was a hushed stillness. People were caught up in the irony of what he was saying.

"The answer to the question about procedure in separating ourselves from the Richmond government is quite simple and straightforward: There is absolutely nothing in the Constitution that can be interpreted to imply, or even hint, that each of us is not free to leave the Confederate compact if and when we should so choose. Who can deny that this is exactly what the war was all about, the right of a state to separate itself."

Vincent Bellcamp of Texas took the floor. "Seems to me we need some sort of document wherein we can list those problems and forces that we appear to be reacting to. Even in the *Declaration of Independence* there's a list of reasons given as to why the colonies were separatin' themselves from the mother country. Can we create a committee to draw up such a document so we can discuss the points, one by one? No big formal document, but something we could react to?"

"Second that motion." Sullivan Truax thought it was a very good idea.

"Call for the question." John Paul Logan of Florida saw no need to discuss the motion.

Friehoffer put the question. "O.K., but our time together is short. We will need the report by tomorrow morning."

"All in favor of closing debate say aye." Many ayes resounded.

"All against say nay." The room was silent. The question was called. There would be no more debate.

"Fine. We shall now vote on the motion by Vincent Bellcamp

284

of Texas. All in favor please say aye." Again, there was a loud chorus of ayes.

"Opposed please say nay." Again, the room was silent.

"Fine. The motion is carried. I appoint Andre Gilbert of Louisiana, Lance Jenkins of Virginia, and Frank Delaney of Arkansas to draw up a list of particulars. Could you three gentlemen please have your report ready by tomorrow morning? Doesn't need to be elaborate or in fancy language like the *Declaration of Independence*, just a listing of the basic problems and issues facing the Confederacy with just a little bit of explanation for each point."

The three agreed, excused themselves, and retired to a private room. Gilbert and Delaney prevailed on Lance Jenkins to serve as chair of their committee.

At 10:00 a.m. the next morning a copy of the report was before each of the eleven delegates.

Tuesday, July 6, 1886
ISSUES AND PROBLEMS FACING THE CONFEDERATE
STATES OF AMERICA
Compiled by Lance Jenkins of Virginia, Frank Delaney of Arkansas,
and Andre Gilbert of Louisiana

   Your committee identified a list of issues and problems and then attempted to categorize them. Each of the five categories is thematic in that it serves as a repository for issues and problems that are interrelated and tend to recur again and again. We tried to pare the list down so as expedite discussion.

   1.   [The Principle of State Sovereignty] States' rights, or state sovereignty, constitutes the basic underlying philosophy of the C.S.A. Constitution. The committee is in unanimous agreement that the original thrust of the Constitution for state sovereignty was well intended. Implicit in this philosophy, however, is an absence of authority on the part of a national congress. Without such national or federal authority, the eleven sovereign states *lack the ability* to cooperate fully to establish the necessary tenets and structures of an effective centralized government.

   2.   [Business, Trade, and Industry] The power of the Confederate Congress to *promote business, trade, and industry* is severely limited, almost non-existent. And, further,

while this was supposedly done in order to protect states' rights and state sovereignty, the states lack any authority to command the cooperation of other states. As an example, we have been unable to agree on interstate tariffs and tonnage duty, except on sea-going vessels for the improvement of sea ways and harbors.

3. [National Bank and Banking System] This is related directly to the preceding. There is little faith in the monetary system, the banks, and the national treasury. There is little confidence in the established procedures for backing up paper currency. There is no provision or mechanism for the collection of monies with which to underwrite roads, waterways, or railroads. Again, it is as though we were eleven separate nations.

3a. The depression of the late seventies has set the C.S.A. back even further than the immediate post war years. We are slowly investing in localized textile factories rather than shipping all of our cotton abroad or up north. Tobacco is the most promising industry. In 1881 a machine was patented which is capable of rolling cigarettes. This has proved to be a very welcome invention and we need to capitalize on it, but so far not a single state has been able to secure financing.

3b. A few rail lines are expanding and this will open up many more industrial opportunities for the smaller towns. We still lack standardized gauges on our many railroads, rendering them practically useless in many instances. Financing is a huge stumbling block. There is no public financing. Private financing suffers from a lack of faith in Southern currency and this fact alone keeps us from competing with the people up north.

4. [National Military Presence] Although the Constitution permits a standing army and navy, none such exists. Further, the Confederate Constitution prescribes for each state its own militia and its own funding of this militia. There is no national protection of coastal land, harbors, or waterways. In the matter of self-defense it is as if we were eleven separate nations prepared to go to war with each other but totally unprepared to deal with any international adversary or belligerent. What if Mexico or Spain should attack New Orleans? Or England attack Hampton Roads?

5.[General Welfare and Education] The Constitution of the Confederate States, contrary to the Constitution of the United States, does not contain a *general welfare clause.* In the Confederacy the problems connected with the poor, the homeless, and the unemployed, whether they were persons of color or not, is the exclusive responsibility of the eleven states. This places an unbearable burden on the states and their citizens.

5a. Each state is left to its own devices as to how it handles the homeless and the starving. Disease, oftentimes due to malnutrition, continues to wipe out entire families. Slavery exists only on the few cotton plantations that have survived the depression. The problem of homeless and unemployed freed-slaves and let-go slaves continues to undermine the peace and security of our cities and towns.

5b. The poor are largely illiterate. Schools are the responsibility of local cities and towns and are funded from taxes levied on local commerce and residential real estate. Only children whose parents paid real estate taxes are permitted to attend.

5c. Along with the strife there is growing resentment among the lower and middle classes toward the Confederacy and its system of government. Increasingly one hears people saying that common folk were much better off before secession.

End

Reaction to the committee's report was subdued. Deliberations continued into the late morning of July 7.

Lance Jenkins attempted to clarify the possible alternatives facing the governors. "Gentlemen. As I see it the entire question eventually boils down to a choice between three alternatives. We could all go home and leave things as they are, which then, I presume, would mean that Tennessee would go it alone. Or, we could attempt to revise, change, and create a new Confederate Constitution. Lastly, some of us could follow the example of Tennessee."

As soon as Lance Jenkins finished speaking, Stuart Williams of Alabama introduced a motion. "I move we create a standing council of governors and that Erich Friehoffer of Mississippi be appointed official coordinator of the council as well as chairman for a period not to exceed two years from this date."

After a second by Truax, the motion passed unanimously.

John Paul Logan of Florida stood up. "I think we should find out where we stand on this whole thing so that we can use our remaining time in these deliberations in the most profitable manner. I therefore propose a straw vote. Nothin' in writing. Not even recorded in our proceedings. Let's find out where each of us presently stands. Could we just ask for a show of hands of those governors who think they'd like to pursue further the issue of dissolution?"

Vincent Bellcamp stood up. "I don't think this is a good idea. What if we were to change our mind later?"

"That's just why Logan's proposal for a straw vote is a good one." Andre Gilbert of Louisiana interjected. "With a straw vote no one is committed to anything because it's not official. It's just a means to find out which way we may be leaning. With a straw vote we'll at least have an idea of how each of us is presently thinking."

Bellcamp continued his objection: "I still don't think we should vote on this."

Friehoffer responded, "Thank you, Mr. Bellcamp. I appreciate your candid opinion. Are there any other objections to a straw vote?" Friehoffer was not one to hem and haw, or waste time beating around the bush.

Hearing no objections, he declared: "All right, then. We will do a straw vote. No need to write any of this down. Here is what we will do. I'll give you three options. You can vote only once."

"First option: Those presently thinking they would like to *consider further* the idea of their state's possible dissolution with the Confederacy. If this is your position I'll ask you to stand to be counted.

"Next, I'll present option two: Those presently thinking they are *not at all sure* of their position on the matter.

"Then the third option: Those presently thinking that they *do not wish to pursue* the issue of dissolution any further. Remember each state has only one vote."

"Any objections to this procedure? Remember this's only a straw vote. Nothing'll ever be written down in any official way and nobody is bound to anything. We're all free to change our minds as often as we like."

Friehoffer, although somewhat humorless, took firm control. His manner indicated a sense of purpose, so that others felt secure in following his suggestions.

"O.K., gentlemen, once again—three options. One—

consider further. Two—not at all sure. Three—do not wish to pursue."

"Option one: Those thinking they would like to *consider further* the idea of their state's possible dissolution with the Confederacy. If this is your present position please stand to be recognized."

Six men stood, including Tad Dwyer.

After the six sat down, Friehoffer stated the second option: "Those thinking they are *not at all sure* of their present positions. Please stand."

Two men stood—Lance Jenkins of Virginia and Andre Gilbert of Louisiana.

After these two sat down, Friehoffer presented the third option: "Those thinking they *do not wish to pursue* the issue any further. Please stand."

Three men stood—Roger Franklin of South Carolina, Vincent Bellcamp of Texas, and Frank Delaney of Arkansas.

After a short recess, Friehoffer asked for more discussion.

Lance Jenkins, the governor of Virginia, said one of the key reasons he had reservations about dissolution, followed by re-admission to the Union, had to do with the veto power concerning appropriations. "Contrary to the U.S.A., our Constitution gives the president the authority to sign into law a budget and yet veto certain items *within* that budget. Article I Section 7, 2 says: 'The President may approve any appropriation and disapprove any other appropriation in the same bill.'"

"I'm afraid of the way it's done in the United States," volunteered Frank Delaney. "I believe the president should have this power and in this case our Constitution is definitely superior."

"I agree. And another thing I would hate to give up," Harold Latimer appeared to be agitated as he continued, "is this idea that when a bill comes through our Congress it can relate to only one specific subject, and the title of the bill must reflect that subject. In the Union they attach all sorts of crazy riders to their bills which have nothing to do with each other, except the rider is usually a piece of pork going into somebody's barrel. I'm not sure just where it is in our Constitution, but it's there."

"Article I Section 9," Tad interjected. "I can't remember the clause."

"Shame on you, Dwyer. You should know these things!" At this everyone laughed. Latimer enjoyed picking on his friend.

Tad quickly thumbed through his well-worn copy of the

C.S.A. Constitution. Finding it, he blurted out: "Clause 20. 'Every law, or resolution having the force of law, shall relate to but one subject, and that shall be expressed in the title.'"

Sullivan Truax rose to speak. "Gentlemen, I sense that we could continue to sit here all day and pour out our beefs. I think it's time to proceed to deal with formal motions. Therefore, Mr. Chairman, I move that we set aside tomorrow, Thursday, July 8, for the purpose of debating and voting on motions and that these motions be drawn up by you and one other person of your choice."

"Second," Logan responded.

The motion carried unanimously. And so it was that Erich Friehoffer and Harold Latimer came to formulate three motions that were clear and forthright in their intent. These motions were distributed on Thursday morning. Chairman Friehoffer asked if someone would care to move the motions in turn, inasmuch as the chairman was not empowered to make motions.

The motions were simple and straightforward. They were hardly debated. A point here, a change there. Nothing substantive.

> **Motion 1**. "Each state is to discuss the issue of dissolution in any and all ways appropriate to it. By utilizing legislative motions, state conventions, and/or referendums, each state is to respond by *formal resolution, pro or con*, by February 1, 1887."
>
> **Motion 2**. "One month later the governors of those states which stand for dissolution will gather in Atlanta, Georgia, in order to adopt all the necessary resolutions which will then be submitted to both the C.S.A. Congress and the U.S.A. Congress."
>
> **Motion 3**. "The effective date for dissolution with the Confederacy is set for midnight, December 31, 1887, and for readmission to the United States at 12:01 a.m., January 1, 1888."

Chairman Friehoffer made it abundantly clear that no one here gathered was under any moral or legal obligation to carry through in any way, except to notify this committee of their intentions by Feb. 1, 1887. If any of the states or perhaps several or all should decide not to go through with dissolution that certainly was their prerogative.

Each of the motions was passed unanimously.

"Mister Chairman." Governor Franklin of South Carolina rose to speak. "Through these four days I've come to feel a great admiration for my fellow governors. I want you all to know the esteem and respect in which I hold you. At this late hour, however, I must declare to you that South Carolina, *in all likelihood,* will elect to remain in the Confederacy, even in the event the Confederacy is nothing more than three or four states."

In turn, Frank Delaney, Vincent Bellcamp, and Andre Gilbert rose to echo the sentiments of Roger Franklin. If things did not change, South Carolina, Arkansas, Texas, and Louisiana would remain in the C.S.A.

When they finished speaking, Chairman Friehoffer paused to reflect. "Gentlemen. This is not a time for formal speechmaking, but I feel compelled to say a few words. We came here to explore our alternatives. I think we've done a creditable job. I have great respect for Mr. Franklin, Mr.Delaney, Mr. Bellcamp, and Mr. Gilbert. It may be that others will remain in the Confederacy. It may be that one or more of you who stand now in favor of dissolution from the Confederacy will go home to face enormous opposition. Or, who knows, it is entirely possible that one or more of the four of you who now stand opposed will eventually decide to rejoin the United States. Whichever way it is, whatever happens, let it never be said we did not listen to one another or confide in one another in a spirit of honesty and cooperation. I salute each of you."

Sullivan Truax of North Carolina seemed to speak for all when he said: "I feel terribly sad. Our victory cost us thousands and thousands of lives and untold heartache. And when we finally won our freedom we weren't able to live up to its promise. In spite of all our work and sacrifices, we just couldn't go it alone. Guess we had to do it this way. At least it's easier to live with myself knowing we tried everything humanly possible. Who knows, maybe we all misread what we thought was some special plan of Providence?"

Stuart Williams of Alabama then asked to be recognized.

"Gentlmen, when I stop to think about all the terrible difficulty we have had in Alabama I feel both a sense of sadness and joyful anticipation. I have felt utter devastation, even bitterness, through my term of office. I believe our Southern constitution is almost worthless. Oh, yes, I know it works better for others than for us. Yes, it has some good things in it, but I now realize what a god we, at least we in Alabama, have made of the concept of state sovereignty. In Alabama we have held to this doctrine to the point of self-destruction. Our state sovereignty has done nothing but contribute to increasing poverty and apathy and a sense of despair. Now, after this experience of attempting to do something constructive, I want you all to know how overjoyed I am regarding the outcome of our time here together and how proud I am to be part of this endeavor."

There were several shouts of "Hear! Hear!"

At this, the Chairman thanked Stuart Williams for his heartfelt statement and asked if there were others who wished to speak.

After several more statements it appeared that the day was spent.

Governor Friehoffer then invited everyone to meet one final time for a grand banquet. "Regardless of what each state chooses to do, let us all, even those who remain with the Confederacy, plan to attend a grand banquet in Washington on December 31, 1887."

The conference adjourned at 3:20 in the afternoon, Thursday, July 8, 1886.

*****

February 1, 1887, and the resolutions were all in Chairman Friehoffer's hands. Somewhat surprisingly, Virginia and Louisiana joined with the other six states in declaring for dissolution with the Confederacy and reunion with the USA. South Carolina declined, and would therefore constitute with Texas and Arkansas the Confederate States of America.

*****

In the next issue of *The Southern Advocate* Arnold Latham didn't hesitate to castigate Tad. Writing his article based on tidbits of information garnered here and there, Latham concluded:

> *Governor Dwyer of Tennessee is the driving force behind the proposed dissolution of the Confederacy. How else would we expect him to act, considering that his best friend was executed as a Yankee spy? If Governor Dwyer has nothing to hide, why then has he refused to answer the charges I've repeatedly made against him? I maintain Dwyer has betrayed the Confederacy and should be tried for treason.*

CHAPTER TWENTY-SEVEN

I n early September of 1887, Tad received a letter from the last person in this world he would have expected.

Mr. Taylor Arvin Dwyer
Tennessee State Capitol Office Building
Nashville, Tennessee

September 2, 1887
Dear Mr. Dwyer,
        I request to see you in your office one week from today, Friday, September 9. I hope this is convenient for you. Please confirm the time.

William Troutman
P.O. Nashville, General Delivery

Tad could hardly believe it. William Troutman, also known as Ward B. Thompson, father of Daniel Rutherford Thompson and husband of Eleanor Thompson, wanted to see him. He read the letter several times, trying to fathom its meaning. Wonder what he's up to? Don't like the feel of it, he thought.

To his knowledge he'd never met this man. During the Tanner trial he'd been sequestered with the other defense witnesses and didn't see any of the witnesses for the prosecution. Even though he was eagerly looking forward to finally meeting him, his gambler's instinct warned him that he might be going up against a stacked deck.

Thompson would never approach me unless he was attempting to confront me with something. Tad mused half aloud as he drummed his fingers on the top of his desk. "Well, I can't even cut the cards unless I ante up," he said with resignation, and reached for his pen.

He replied to the address Troutman indicated and said he'd be available to see him on Friday, September 9, at 3:00 p.m.

Pressure began to build as the week passed. He grew increasingly irritable, having little or no patience with anyone. "Damn!" He said out loud even though he was alone at home, "I haven't felt like this since the war." Tad recalled how tension always mounted just before a maneuver or an engagement.

On the afternoon of the ninth Tad was ready. He'd arranged for his attorney, Sheldon Armstrong, to be present. Even though he had no idea as to the reason behind Thompson's desire to speak with him, he thought it best to be prepared for a high stakes game. As a precaution he'd placed Billy Dean's sealed deposition in Armstrong's hand. "This's my hole card." He grinned as he spoke. "To my knowledge, Sheldon, I've never met this man. All I know is what I've already told you." Tad had briefed Armstrong on all the things Tad felt Armstrong should know, omitting, of course, the finer details of the lost order incident.

Armstrong was as tall as Tad but his portly mid-section created a presence of being bigger and tougher. Some folks would consider him to be intimidating. He was balding, had a small goatee, and appeared to be continuously frowning.

"Just keep your wits about you. We'll have to see what develops." Armstrong's advice reminded him of how Billy Dean used to talk to him.

When Thompson arrived at Tad's office, Tad experienced one of the greatest shocks of his fifty-eight years. The man who stood before him was the very same man he'd seen in Harrisburg back in '62 when he'd delivered the surrender ultimatum to the mayor.

Here was the man with a face he could never forget. He was of medium height with strong blue eyes, sagging eyebrows, and weak cut of jaw. His sizeable mustache was sharply trimmed. His erect posture reflected an intimidating demeanor.

Well I'll be! He thought, so this is Thompson! Then he recalled the second time he'd seen him. It was in Harrisburg on his way to the depot with the two nurses, Sandra and Nancy, after that terrible beating.

"My name is Will Troutman. I have an appointment with Mr. Dwyer." Thompson, aka Troutman, had the edge on Tad because he had sat inconspicuously in the back of the courtroom during the Tanner trial, listening to Tad's testimony while Tad had not been so privileged to hear Troutman's testimony. Somehow Tad missed seeing Troutman when Tad was in the witness chair . . . understandable because of the pressure upon Tad as he gave testimony.

"I'm Tad Dwyer. Please come in."

"This is my attorney, Sheldon Armstrong." Tad spoke with a matter-of-fact tone of voice.

At this, Troutman seemed to draw back. "I don't want an attorney present. What I have on my mind is only between the two of us," he announced firmly.

Tad was not about to let Thompson dictate the terms. "Standard procedure when I'm not informed as to the nature of the business, Mr. Troutman. If you find it offensive, I'm sorry. Tell you what. I'll have Mr. Armstrong step outside so that you can tell me what's on your mind. After that, I'll decide if his presence is necessary." Tad could spin a fib as good as ever.

"Guess that'll be acceptable," Thompson conceded.

Tad's mind was on fire. His pulse was racing. His heartbeat was rapid. So this is Ward B. Thompson. The man who murdered his wife while scuffling with Billy Dean. The guy who not only testified against Billy Dean, but the very person who pinned his wife's murder on Billy, forcing him to flee. This man is the father of Daniel Rutherford Thompson, known to the men in his outfit as James Ruther Donley, known to the Yankee spy system as Ruff.

Tad maintained his composure.

"Please, have a seat." Tad waited patiently for Troutman to take a chair. As soon as he sat down, Troutman pulled several pieces of paper out of his coat pocket. "Dwyer, I'll get right to the point. I read this article in *The Southern Advocate* by Arnold Latham. No doubt you've seen it." He handed it to Tad.

Tad paused before answering. "Yes, I've seen it. What about it?"

"Well, I've studied up on you, and I'm quite positive you're the guilty culprit who knows about those missing orders. You're a spy just as much as that yaller belly Tanner."

And your own son, you bastard! Tad thought to himself.

"Sorry, Mr. Troutman," Tad said, rising to his feet, "but if this is why you've come it's imperative that Mr. Armstrong sit in. If this is not acceptable, then our conversation is finished."

"I don't see why one man can't talk to another without some damn attorney being present," Troutman protested.

"Because, Troutman, you've just accused me of being a spy, that's why. There's no way I'm going to stand here and be accused without a witness present."

Crossing the room, Tad opened the door. "Please come in Mr. Armstrong. This conversation cannot continue without you."

Within seconds, Armstrong entered the room. By this time Troutman was on his feet ready to bolt. Tad knew he had to act quickly or Troutman would be gone.

Addressing Armstrong, Tad said, "Mr. Troutman has just accused me of having been a Yankee spy. He read an article in *The Southern Advocate* and claims I have knowledge of what happened to General Lee's lost order."

Troutman made a move toward the door.

"I'd advise you to remain right here, Troutman. You've just made a serious accusation. Unless you wish me to bring charges against you immediately, I suggest you sit down and give me your full attention." Armstrong sounded most intimidating.

It was obvious to Tad that Armstrong was playing a heavy hand. In truth, Armstrong had no legal right to detain Troutman. Nevertheless, this was a two-sided charade and the duo of Dwyer and Armstrong was beginning to lay a trap for the unwary Troutman.

Tad took the offensive: "Ward Thompson, you just walked into an indictment."

"I what?" Then he caught himself. "My name's Troutman, not Thompson."

"Cut it right there, Thompson. No more games. We both know who you are. You used the name Will Troutman as an alias while you were up north. Your son's name was Daniel Rutherford Thompson. Your wife was Eleanor Thompson. Even your store was named Thompson Dry Goods. Matter of record."

"What's that got to do with anything? I've never denied that my given name is Ward Thompson."

"Guess my hearing isn't so good." Tad said with a grin. "Now we can get on with it."

"Get on with what?"

"Let's begin with the fact that Billy Dean Tanner recognized you at the trial. He kept quiet about it, but he informed his attorney and me that you were the man he wrestled with the night your wife was killed."

Tad continued to bait Thompson: "We have it on good authority that you also recognized Billy Dean Tanner as being Justin Alexander Bethune."

Tad had no such evidence. He was playing a hunch.

"Yes, there's no sense in hiding the fact I was able to place that traitor's face as the same person who killed my dear wife," Troutman confessed.

"Well, Thompson, we've got a surprise for you." Tad nodded to Armstrong.

"Attorney Armstrong here has something he wants to read to you."

Armstrong reached into his coat pocket and pulled out the sealed envelope.

"You'll notice, Mr. Thompson, that this envelope is sealed." Sheldon Armstrong showed the sealed envelope to Thompson.

"I don't like this. What's this got to do with me or with anybody for that matter?"

"Just this, Mr. Thompson." Armstrong opened the sealed envelope and began to read.

Deposition
Libby Prison, Richmond, Virginia.
April 18, 1873.

    The following deposition was duly subscribed and sworn by Justin Alexander Bethune, alias Billy Dean Tanner, on the 18th of April, 1873. Deposition was made in the presence of Ramsey Feldham, Attorney at Law, and counsel for the defense in the matter of The Confederate States of America versus William Dean Tanner.

    I, Justin Alexander Bethune, alias Billy Dean Tanner, do solemnly swear to the accuracy and truth regarding the matters about which I now speak.

    Beginning in the spring of 1861, I had occasion to share the favors of an intimate nature with Eleanor (Elly) Thompson of Nashville, Tennessee. One night in late October of 1861, Mr. Ward B. Thompson, husband of Eleanor Thompson, returned unexpectedly to his residence and discovered his wife and me in a compromising situation. Mrs. Thompson and I loved each other very much. Elly felt trapped in her marriage and I was lonesome, being on the road so much.

    He accused his wife of playing the harlot and me of being a pimp and a gigolo. We quickly became embroiled in a physical scuffle.

He pulled a gun on me and as I sought to bring him down he wheeled, took careful aim, and shot his wife in the chest. At this, I was able to grab the gun from him and hold him at gunpoint.

I immediately realized the hopelessness of my situation. Thompson was quick to claim that I had killed his wife. Even as I held the gun in my hand, I denied that I had possession of the means to do so. Thompson and I both knew who pulled that trigger and we both knew that it was no accident.

I was faced with the prospect of admitting my adulterous affair to my family and attempting to exonerate myself from the charge of murder that Thompson threatened to bring against me. In court it would be Thompson's word against mine, and I feared the odds were too strong against me.

I quickly determined on an alternative course of action that I regret to this very day because it cost me the loss of every person whom I ever loved or loved me, and has now cost me my life. Without due forethought I made up my mind to flee from Thompson at my first opportunity. This I did, leaving the gun behind.

I request that this deposition be used as evidence against Ward B. Thompson (alias William Troutman), and that he be charged with the intentional murder of his wife, Eleanor. Of these three things I am absolutely certain: (1) Eleanor Thompson was not shot accidentally while Ward Thompson and I scuffled. Her death was the result of Thompson taking a deliberate shot aimed directly at her chest while she was huddled in the corner of the room, her head buried in her hands. Thompson took deliberate aim at his wife, much as a person intent on taking the life of another. (2) I did not handle the weapon until after Elly Thompson was shot. (3) Immediately after Thompson pulled the trigger, I wrestled the gun from him.

I attest to the truth and veracity of the above statement. I further reiterate that I have always regretted the cowardly manner in which I endeavored to handle the entire incident. I go to my death ashamed and repentant for my foolish decisions. Most of all, I beg forgiveness of my faithful wife and my two beautiful children, none of whom I ever saw again. They deserved far better.

Finally, I have entrusted this deposition to my attorney, Ramsey Feldham, and to my dear friend and comrade in arms, Taylor Arvin Dwyer, who knew me only as a fellow Confederate officer by the name of Billy Dean Tanner.

Signature of Deponent: Justin Alexander Bethune, (alias, Billy Dean

Tanner)
Signature of Deposer: Ramsey Feldham, Attorney–at-law.

Thompson remained expressionless. He had a deadpan face. When Sheldon Armstrong finished reading he looked over at Thompson. "That's it Thompson. We'll be filing the necessary paper work on Monday morning. You'll be arraigned on a single count of murder in the first degree."

"You can't touch me. Haven't you slippery lawyers ever heard of the statute of limitations?"

"There are occasions when the statute of limitations can be waived, especially in capital offenses such as this. Rest assured, a brief for waiver of limitations will be included in our paper work," responded Armstrong.

"You know Bethune's lying through his teeth, don't you? Just because he's dead don't mean he's telling the truth. It's perfectly clear he's out to get me in order to save his own sk . . ." Thompson's voice trailed off.

"Go ahead. Finish your sentence. To save his own what?" Tad exclaimed eagerly.

Thompson was silent.

"Please tell us, Thompson, if Bethune was about to be executed when he gave this deposition, how will his lying serve to save his own *skin*?"

"Well, it's obvious he's out to get revenge for my testimony against him."

"I have no idea about that. I do know that Justin Bethune had no reason or motive to kill your wife," Tad responded.

"You bastards," Thompson exclaimed. "The whole thing was an accident. The gun was meant to threaten Bethune. If he hadn't hit me just at that instant the gun wouldn't have gone off. It was an accident. I can explain everything. Just you wait and see."

"Yes. We'll do just that," Armstrong replied. "In the meantime, you're free to leave. However, if I were you I wouldn't attempt to leave the city of Nashville. If you skip town now it will be a sure sign of your guilt."

When Tad was alone he pondered the irony of Armstrong's last sentence. He quickly thought to himself that running was exactly the tragic mistake Billy Dean had made. He mumbled in a half audible voice, "Me too. Both of us should've fessed up right early. Could've avoided a lot of pain and heartbreak all these years for both Billy and me."

After the court hearing on Monday, September 12, Sheldon Armstrong sent a letter to Ramsey Feldham of Richmond, requesting his presence along with the original copy of the deposition to present to the next grand jury.

*****

Washington was crowded. Military reunions were everywhere. Tent cities lined the open areas for as far as the eye could see. Almost every company, of every regiment, of every division, of every Confederate and Union army was encamped somewhere in the environs.

Jane, Lucy, and Red accompanied Tad, Charlyn, and young Arthur. Lucy was now a widow. Jane appeared to be sweet on Red, but Red didn't seem to notice. Or if he noticed he was not letting on. Louis was present with his grown children, Blaine and Betty. Elizabeth Ann's absence was conspicuous. No one seemed to care. Even Jonathan came. He was a great help to everyone. Jessica stayed home—Dwyer Hardware was in her capable hands.

Festivities were going on everywhere. Whether the regiments were from Wisconsin, Mississippi, or Georgia, this was going to be the social event of the century, the culmination of a war that all but decimated the resources of the South and caused bitter division amongst people everywhere.

The next two days would be a time of remembrance. Americans were again to be truly brothers. It was a time for rejoicing and celebration. This was to be an occasion for gaiety and laughter, and the recounting of former days, both in their tragedy and in their glory.

Everybody had war stories to tell. Some were already saying that this war gave definition to the American people, and that in spite of Southern victory, the ultimate triumph was fulfillment of the dream and vision of Lincoln himself.

Sprinkled between the parties and the reunions were the memorial and remembrance services. There were broadsides everywhere in sight advertising regimental *Calling of the Role* and *Services of Divine Commemoration of the Dead.*

At 7:00 p.m., the final State Dinner of the Confederate States of America was scheduled in the Palace, the largest indoor facility available in downtown Washington. Every governor, every state official, every congressman and senator of the C.S.A., together with state legislators, cabinet, judicial and diplomatic personnel, and their families were invited. Attendance was expected to be well over a thousand.

There had been heated debate about whether or not United States President Grover Cleveland should be invited to attend, and if in attendance, should he be asked to speak. Many people felt strongly the final hours of the Confederacy were not a time for representative dignitaries of other sovereign powers. It was finally decided that this was to be the final grand state occasion of the Confederacy and there would be no invitation extended to any outside person or power, including the president of the U.S.A. The press, however, would be welcome.

Following a jubilant songfest, ending with the final chorus of *Long Ago*, the assemblage joined in a sustained and wild cheer. The shouting, yelling and applauding filled the Palace and rose to an exuberant crescendo. Only the continued shouting of the master of ceremonies had any impact on the crowd.

The featured speaker of the evening was Eric Friehoffer of Mississippi.

"Misssterrr Chairrrmannn."

The words carried the deep resonance of a bass voice adept at stately and sometimes funereal intonations.

"Misssterrr Chairrrmannn."

"Misssterrr Chairrrmannn." Slowly the crowd managed to quiet itself.

"Misssterrr Chairrrmannn, I have the honor of presenting to you the Honorable Eric Friehoffer, governor of the state of Mississippi and chairman of the Governors Council of The Confederate States of America."

Again, the introduction was met with enthusiastic applause.

"This is indeed an occasion worth remembering. First, and of greatest importance to all of us, I have recently heard directly from Governor Frank Delaney of Arkansas and Vincent Bellcamp, governor of Texas. They both inform me that their respective legislatures have recently approved bills calling for a referendum on the issue of dissolution and reunion."

At this, the Palace broke out in thunderous applause and cheering.

In his speech Friehoffer was down to earth and practical in his exhortation for all Southerners to commit themselves to the New

United States of America. His talk went a bit long at fifteen minutes.

After greetings from various dignitaries, Tad Dwyer was scheduled to give the final speech of the evening. By this time, as Tad expected, everyone was becoming very tired of the long-winded rhetoric.

Nevertheless, the crowd greeted Tad with robust applause and cheering. He came to the podium and approached the lectern. Again, there were frenzied shouts and cheers. He waited patiently for the crowd to quiet. He then used the ensuing silence to increase the sense of anticipation leading to his first remarks.

"We shall proceed tomorrow, Monday, January 1, 1888, to the official reunion ceremony without blame or reproof. We shall not look back with remorse, nor shall we look forward with dread. We shall not look back with shame, nor shall we look forward with fear.

"Rather, we shall look backward with honor, and we shall look forward with trust. We shall look backward with pride, and we shall look forward with hope."

People started to cheer, but Tad continued.

" . . . A hope rooted in the firm belief that only a reunited and strong United States of America can take its rightful place amongst the nations of the world and in the affairs of mankind.

"And if we have learned nothing else from the scourge of division, war, and bloodshed, let it be this:

"We are Americans before we are Southerners or Northerners, Easterners or Westerners. We shall always have need for one another. And in this need lies our strength. And in this strength lies our future.

"In truth I submit to you.
Divided we stood, for twenty-seven years.
But now, let it be known to the whole world,
Henceforth and forever,
United we shall stand."

Then, after a short pause, Tad concluded with his final salute to the Confederacy.

"I salute you my fellow citizens and comrades in arms:

From the laurels of victory
In the Cause of Freedom,

To the memory of faded banners
On the field of battle.
The hopes of the Confederacy,
Forever lost in the ashes of glory."

With these last words the Palace fell silent. One second. Two seconds. Three seconds. Tad turned to take his seat.

And then, much as before but with even greater passion, the crowd roared its approval. Pandemonium broke out. The rebel yells and cheers increased in intensity as Tad returned to the lectern to acknowledge the ovation by waving to the crowd a final goodbye.

A long night of revelry ensued. Washington was lit up in all its splendor. Everyone was anticipating the formal reunion ceremony scheduled for 10:00 in the morning. Tomorrow would be another long day of rejoicing and celebration. Tad, Charlyn, and Arthur returned to their rooms in the Regency Arms about midnight.

In the morning when Tad opened the door of their hotel room he noticed a magazine lying on the hallway floor. Attached to this latest edition of *The Southern Advocate* was a printed note. "Dwyer—see page 19."

The article described how one of Latham's earlier pieces about Tad had caught the eye of a man by the name of Mario Conti. Conti, as quoted by Latham, stated:

> *I think I remember Tad Dwyer. It was at a craps game the same day we all moved out of Frederick, Maryland. I have no idea of the date. All I know is this guy was throwing sevens and elevens, and I was losing. I left the game shortly after he did. Then, later that evening, he and this other fellow somehow located me. This guy, the one who won at craps, said he'd lost some kind of letters wrapped around two cigars at the craps game and wanted to know if I'd found them. 'Hell' I says, 'if'n that's all you lost today what's the big deal? I lost a pile of dough and you complain about two or three lousy cigars.' Then this guy says it isn't really the cigars that're important, but the letters were something he valued because one was from his brother serving in the west. The other was from his sister telling him of his brother's death. Then I felt bad for him. I assured him I hadn't found any letters or cigars.*

Latham went on to assert that the letters mentioned by Dwyer were in fact the lost copy of the Special Order 191, and that the letters were probably Dwyer's fictitious invention to cover himself. Latham went on:

> *I maintain that charges of treason and perjury ought to be brought against Tad Dwyer. Also charges of neglect of duty.*

Charlyn couldn't help but notice how upset Tad was at reading the article. "What's going on? Why is Latham still on such a vendetta to get you, Tad?"

Tad gave Charlyn an answer, short of the secret truth, keeping his own counsel about the real events of that afternoon. "About two weeks after Arthur was killed at Shiloh I received a letter from him. He'd written it on April 2. Then, after another couple of weeks, Jane wrote me and told me Art was killed at Shiloh on April 6. Of course these letters took on special meaning for me and I kept them on my person. I remember wrapping them around my pack of cigars I always carried with me."

"I don't get it! What's Arthur's letter got to do with the lost orders?"

"Latham believes I didn't deliver those orders at all. I guess he thinks the papers wrapped around the cigars are not Art's and Jane's letters but the copy of the orders. Can't be sure about his suppositions. All I know is he's after my hide. Been on my case for years. Still hoping for a scoop."

Tad hated lying to Charlyn more than anything in the world. He silently scolded himself. God, I feel like such a shit! Such a terrible, stupid mistake I made back in September of '62. I should've fessed up right away. Was overcome by fear. Just like Billy Dean. We both made the same stupid mistake by running and not facing up to the truth.

Tad held fast to his belief that nothing would come of this latest revelation. He was greatly relieved by the fact that by noon today he would no longer be a part of the Confederate States of America. Therefore, short of extradition, there would no longer be the means available to handle such a case even if somebody pressed charges against him.

"So what are you going to do?" By this time Charlyn was visibly upset.

"I think I'll call a press conference for later this afternoon and give a formal reply to Arnold Latham."

After breakfast Tad stopped at the front desk to check for messages.

"Oh yes, Mr. Dwyer. I have a letter for you. Came in early this morning." The clerk handed an envelope to Tad marked *urgent*.

Tad looked at the return address. Why would Sheldon Armstrong send him a letter? Must be bad news, thought Tad, because good news is never marked urgent. He ripped open the envelope.

Dear Tad,
Wed. Dec. 28, 1887

Caught this in yesterday's paper. Tried to get in touch, but you'd already left for D.C. Thought you'd appreciate it.

Congratulations.
Yours,
Sheldon Armstrong.

Tad's hands were shaking as he read.

The Nashville Guardian, Tuesday, December 27, 1887
LOCAL BUSINESSMAN HANGS SELF

Well-known local businessman of the 1850s, Ward B. Thompson, was found dead at his residence yesterday. The coroner determined the death to be self-inflicted by hanging. On November 17 of this year Thompson was indicted by the Davidson County Grand Jury for the murder of his wife, Eleanor, in October of 1859. At that time, it was thought she had been killed by a male acquaintance, Justin Alexander Bethune. Bethune was charged with the crime but escaped, never to be captured.

Recently, a sworn pre-death deposition from Justin Bethune, brought to light the accusation that Thompson, not Bethune, turned the gun onto Eleanor Thompson. Bethune, alias Billy Dean Tanner, swore the deposition just before he was executed by a military firing squad, having been found guilty of participating in the Union espionage network during the war. Bethune had served as a courier on the staff of Robert E. Lee.

Ward and Eleanor Thompson had one son, Daniel Rutherford Thompson, who was also executed as a participant in the Union espionage network while serving in the Army of Northern Virginia.

Funeral arrangements were not complete at this writing.

A huge smile came across Tad's face as he handed the article to Charlyn. "Maybe revenge is for suckers, but I have to admit it sure feels good." He hastened to send word to Ramsey Feldham and to Annabeth Bethune.

CHAPTER TWENTY-EIGHT

Even though the temperature was a chilly thirty-nine degrees, the sunshine was warming. Even before 8:00 a.m. the crowds began filling the mall beyond the Capitol steps. By about 9:15 the grounds were crowded. Bands were everywhere and the streets were lined with men of the Blue and the Gray.

The ceremony was scheduled to begin promptly at 10:00. There would be an invocation and a medley of familiar songs from the war. Except for very brief remarks by President Cleveland, there would be no speeches. The official flags of the eight reuniting states were displayed with prominence. The Stars and Stripes flew high above, a new flag with thirty-five stars.[1]

After a prayer commemorating the fallen in the war, the president of the United States gave the official proclamation.

"As of 12:01 a.m., January 1, 1888, by act of the Senate and the House of Representatives and sealed by my signature, I declare that the states of Tennessee, Georgia, North Carolina, Virginia, Florida, Mississippi, Louisiana, and Alabama, having fulfilled all the Constitutional requirements for statehood, are now welcomed as fellow states within the United States of America."

Following the proclamation, President Cleveland spoke for about seven minutes, concluding with a quotation from the Tad Dwyer speech of the night before, as printed in the morning

---

1 After the secession of eleven states in 1861, there remained 23 states in the USA. West Virginia (1863), Nevada (1864), Nebraska (1867), and Colorado (1876) were admitted to the Union prior to December 31, 1887, bringing the total U.S.A. states to twenty-seven. With the eight re-admitted states the reconstituted nation would consist of thirty-five states.

newspapers.

> *"If we have learned nothing else from the scourge of war and division let it be this:*
>
> *"We are Americans before we are Southerners or Northerners, Easterners or Westerners. We shall always have need for one another. And in this need lies our strength. And in this strength lies our future . . .*
>
> *"Let it be known to all the world, henceforth and forever, united we shall stand."*

After the benediction the band played *The Star Spangled Banner*. The ceremony concluded with a twenty-one gun salute followed by loud and sustained applause and cheering. The reverie continued well into the afternoon and evening, with gala celebrations throughout the city.

After the ceremony Tad informed the gathered press that he would make a public statement at a press conference in the lobby of the Regency Arms Hotel at 4:00 p.m. He politely refused to answer any questions.

Charlyn, Tad, Arthur, Red, and Jane had a splendid dinner after which they hired a carriage to take them around Washington. They rode past the President's Home and the Supreme Court and all sorts of government buildings.

At 4:00 p.m. at the Regency Arms, Tad, accompanied by Charlyn, Louis, Jane, and Red, broke his silence of many years and offered a response to an article by Mr. Arnold Latham in *The Southern Advocate*.

> *"First, I'd like to say that the events as described by Mr. Mario Conti as reported by Arnold Latham in the most recent issue of The Southern Advocate are accurate. Latham reports that a Mr. Mario Conti had written a letter to him telling of an incident involving myself at a game of chance on the afternoon of September 9, 1862.*
>
> *"Second, I would like to affirm that my brother Arthur had written a letter to me several days before he was killed. He was serving our Confederate Cause at Shiloh. I kept it with another letter I received about two weeks later from my sister, Jane Dwyer, informing me of Art's death in the Hornet's Nest at Shiloh on April 6, of '62. I treasured these letters and always kept them with me during the war.*
>
> *"Then, in the early evening of September 9, I realized I'd lost*

the letters. As best as I remember, I'd wrapped the two letters around several cigars. Must have put them in my top shirt pocket where I always kept my cigars. Best I could figure was they probably dropped out of my pocket somewhere in the area of the dice game that afternoon.

"Billy Dean Tanner and I set out in hopes of finding the letters. The only person from the game we were able to locate was this man by the name of Mario Conti. Until Latham's article I never knew his name. I remember he was a sergeant. He looked rugged and fatigued. Like most of us. I explained to him what had happened, how I had lost two important letters wrapped around a couple of cigars. I enquired of him if he had seen or heard anything about anybody finding them. It's also accurate to say, far as I know, I left the game before he did.

"Finally, in the matter of Special Order 191, my testimony at two different trials is a matter of Confederate war records. I would like to thank Mr. Mario Conti for recalling the events of April 9, 1862, so that I could use this occasion to set the record straight about losing my brother's and sister's letters.

"Thank you, gentlemen. I have nothing more to say on the matter."

Tad would take no questions. The subject was closed. He was feeling very tired, and he told Charlyn he wanted to go back to their room and lie down for a spell. Charlyn went with him.

Tad was absorbed in his thoughts as he and Charlyn walked up the stairway to their room. While he seemed calm and composed at the press conference, in truth he was extremely strained. He scolded himself for thinking all these years his secret was safe and that the only one who truly knew anything was Billy Dean and Stoesser. Tad never gave a thought to Sergeant Mario Conti.

Once back in the room, Tad undid his tie and loosened his collar. He sat on the bed ready to stretch out when it hit him—at first it was pain in his left arm. And then he felt a heavy load pushing down on his chest. The pain rose up to his throat and centered in his jaw. He was helpless and unable to speak. When the pain subsided he called out to Charlyn. Within another minute, as Charlyn held him, another pain shot down his left arm. Tad fell back on to the bed. He appeared lifeless.

Charlyn ran down to the front desk. "Quick, can you find a doctor? Governor Dwyer has collapsed. He's in great pain."

A physician arrived within another twelve minutes. After a hurried examination, he gave a tentative diagnosis to Charlyn. "Far as I can tell, all the evidence points to a heart attack. We dare not move him."

"How bad is it? Will he be all right?" Charlyn was beside herself.

"Can't really say. Sometimes these things give the appearance of being worse than they really are."

"When will you know?"

"Next few hours are critical."

Tad was now fully awake and alert. The doctor insisted that Tad rest and try to sleep. Tad slept for about an hour and, upon awaking, appeared to be feeling much better. As he struggled to sit up, he experienced another attack similar to the first. This time the pain in his chest was excruciating and it left him in a terribly weakened condition.

He would appear to lapse into a coma and then come out of it. In and out. In and out. His speech at times seemed quite lucid and rational, yet the next minute he would be incoherent. Charlyn, Arthur, Louis, Jane, and Red were gathered around the bed.

After one such lapse into delirious mumbling, Tad began to speak clearly. The words began to flow and, for the most part, they made sense, but at other times Charlyn and Louis exchanged questioning glances, hoping that someone knew how to understand what Tad was saying.

He called out for Charlyn. Taking her hand, he said, "I love you, my dearest. I love you very much. You're the best thing ever happened to me." His voice then trailed off.

Then, almost as if in a different time and place, he suddenly called out: "Billy, you've got to help me find those cigars. They must've fallen out of my pocket while I was shooting craps."

Charlyn shrugged her shoulders but before she could make any comment, Tad began speaking again.

"Arthur, Arthur, are you here?"

"Yes, father, I'm here."

Tad looked in the direction of Arthur's voice, and although his eyes appeared glazed, he began speaking again.

"Son, don't ever get hooked on gambling. I should've listened to my father. He warned me about drinking and gambling, but I wouldn't listen."

Again, his voice trailed off.

"Please now, you just rest, Tad darling," Charlyn said softly.

"I'm sure a lucky man. Don't deserve it though. Wonderful

310

family, beautiful wife, good friends, and now our country back together again. Ohhhh, if only this pain would go away. Damn pain."

His hand grasped Charlyn's as he felt himself weakening. "Water. Water."

After taking a few sips, Tad lay back on the pillow and closed his eyes.

Occasionally he seemed to rouse and speak. At one point he was back in the past, speaking angrily at Billy Dean for being a spy. Then, a few minutes later he was in the present, telling Billy how good it felt to settle the score with Thompson.

He was breathing easier in spite of the tremendous energy the pain had extracted from his body. Arthur, Louis, Jane, and Red left his bedside and joined Lucy and the doctor in the next room.

Tad drifted off for almost three quarters of an hour, and he awoke he seemed rejuvenated. He looked more alert. He smiled at Charlyn and told her she looked radiant at the state dinner and he sure was proud to have been her escort. Charlyn's hopes were buoyed by his apparent return of strength. "Oh joy!" she whispered to herself.

She took his hand. Then, as he started to move to sit up, in a split second, quicker than the blink of an eye and without a sound, Tad's head turned toward Charlyn and he slumped over.

Charlyn held his hand tight as she moved to reposition him. She felt the unsupported weight of his lifeless body.

His eyes closed. There was no pulse.

*****

He was witness to birth, and then death, and then birth again. He experienced the pangs of birth of the Confederacy and then was spared to witness its sunset. And now, he was witness to the sunrise of a new nation. But, like Moses of old, he was denied entry into the promised land. It would forever remain his legacy to those whom he loved and to his fellow Confederates.

The morning newspapers told the world of Tad's death. "Taylor Arvin Dwyer, governor of the state of Tennessee, died at 1:38 a.m., January 2, 1888, at the age of 58."

The funeral was the biggest funeral ever held in Nashville. Dignitaries from all over the South with governors of all the recently re-admitted states, in addition to the governors of Texas, Arkansas, and South Carolina, joined with others from Washington in a grand funeral procession all the way to the small cemetery in LaVergne. Tad was laid to rest next to his father and mother.

*****

After a fortnight of grieving, Charlyn set out to go through Tad's belongings. One afternoon she was in the attic going through Tad's old war stuff. After going through the contents of his haversack she picked up his knapsack. After removing some rusted eating utensils and a box of cartridges, she came across two pieces of paper folded neatly together tucked away in an inner pocket. They appeared to be very old and well worn. Charlyn unfolded the pages to discover two letters addressed to Tad. The first letter was in pencil and it was badly smeared.

April 2, 1862,
Dear Tad,

Thought I'd drop you a line or two before we go into battle and something happens to me! We've been marching day and night. Right now we're north of Corinth, Mississippi.

I don't know what to expect. By that I mean I don't know if a big engagement is just around the corner or not. I hate to admit it but I have a funny feelin' that I may not come out of this one. I don't know why I feel this way. It's sort of a premonition, a feelin' of dread. It's probably nothin'.

At any rate, I 'm proud to be serving under Albert Sidney Johnston. There's none finer in my opinion. I hope you and Louis are both all right. I have no idea where Louis is.

I must confess I'm beginning to think this war is wrong. I'm beginning to believe that slavery is truly a terrible thing. I don't have a single friend who owns slaves.

Please take good care of yourself. Don't go tryin' to be a hero. I think of you and Louis often and wish we could be together.

Your loving brother,
Arthur Hayes Dwyer

The second letter was better preserved. It was written in ink.

Second Lieutenant Taylor Arvin Dwyer
C/O Major General Joseph Johnston, Army of Northern Virginia
April 18, 1862

Dear Tad,
  Yesterday Father and I received word from the War Department that Arthur was killed at Shiloh on April 6, at a place called the Hornet's Nest. We are grief stricken. Am attempting to write Louis also but am not at all sure of his whereabouts. Please, dear brother, take care of your self.

Your loving sister,
Jane H. Dwyer

Charlyn read both letters. She held them in her hand as she fell into a deep, melancholic mood. How terribly sad. Arthur, the youngest Dwyer, killed before he really lived. She thought of her first husband, Ben Hatcher, losing his life in the center of Jackson's lines at Carlisle. Then she pictured Tad saving these letters and keeping them safely in his possession throughout the remainder of the war.

Then, suddenly, Charlyn gripped the dirty arm of the old rocker in which she was sitting. The thought came to her like a bolt of lightning piercing her head.

O My God!
How could this be?
These letters . . . these are . . . these are the lost letters!
Just before he died. At that press conference.
These are the letters Tad told everybody he'd lost. Wrapped around the cigars.

Charlyn gasped for breath. She stared at the floor.

Can it be?
No it can't be!
But I'm holding the letters here in my hand!
Oh Tad! Dearest Tad, tell me. What am I to think?

She sat in silence.
Oh my dearest how you must have suffered.

She sobbed and sobbed, pounding her fists on the arms of the chair. She cried herself out.

Finally, when the truth had settled in her mind, she arose from the rocking chair. With resolve in her step she held tight the two letters and went downstairs to the giant wood stove in the kitchen.

She reread both letters one last time.

Thinking clearly now, Charlyn cobbled together all that she had been given to know about the lost orders, including Tad's last news conference on January 1, 1888, when he confirmed his run-in with Mario Conti after the dice game on that fateful day in 1862.

She took a match and set them aflame. First one letter and then the other. The flames quickly engulfed Art's besmirched handwriting and Jane's neat penmanship.

When the flames dwindled down she dropped the last unburned corner onto the top of the wood stove.

With the back of her hand Charlyn gently swept the blackened ashes into a small coffee tin.

*****

On a Sunday in early spring with buds showing signs of new life beneath the sunny skies, Charlyn and Arthur rode to LaVergne. Since it was Sunday, Jane would be at home. Charlyn visited a few minutes and then explained to Jane and Arthur that she wished to be alone at the cemetery for a short period of time. And so, leaving Arthur with Jane, she rode on to the cemetery by herself.

The grave was newly landscaped and crowned with a headstone.

TAYLOR ARVIN DWYER
May 18, 1829 – January 2, 1888
Beloved
Husband - Father
Son - Brother - Soldier - Statesman

Taking a small garden trowel in her hand, she knelt down and dug a little hole just under the front of the headstone.

Opening the coffee tin, she carefully deposited the ashes.

She thought to herself that now there was no way anyone could ever prove that the papers Tad lost at the dice game were anything other than the letters from Art and Jane. After filling the

314

hole and smoothing over the soil, she remained on her knees, pausing as if in prayer. She spoke out loud.

"Dearest Tad,"

She paused again.

"I know now these weren't really the papers that were lost at the dice game.
These were your alibi, your cover-up for something else you lost.
So be it. I understand.
You spent a lifetime hiding an unfortunate decision of your war years.
Since then you've done what you had to do.
You redeemed yourself.
You lived your life courageously.
And with honor.
I love you as much now as I ever did."

"Dearest Tad,
Today and henceforth,
Your burden is now my burden.
Your secret is now my secret. Until my life is over and I join you here."

DIVIDED WE STOOD

John F. Crosby, Ph.D.

THE HISTORICAL SETTING

In the autumn of 1862, Gen. Robert E. Lee decided to cross the Potomac, go through Maryland, and launch a campaign into southern Pennsylvania. On September 9, encamped with his army at Frederick, Maryland, Lee gave orders dividing his Army of Northern Virginia into four separate fighting forces.

Special Order 191 included plans for a three-pronged assault on Harpers Ferry: Gen. Thomas [Stonewall] Jackson and three divisions would capture Martinsburg, Virginia, swing southeast, and attack Harpers Ferry from Bolivar Heights, its western entry. Meanwhile, Maj. Gen. Lafayette McLaws would strike from Maryland Heights, across the Potomac in Maryland, and Gen. John Walker from Loudoun Heights, across the Shenandoah River to the east. Gen. J.E.B. Stuart would detach a squadron of cavalry to go with these divisions, but keep most of his men to protect the rest of Lee's forces and do reconnaissance.

Gens. Lee, James (Pete) Longstreet, and D. H. Hill would start moving the remaining divisions, ordnance, and supplies toward Boonsboro, south of Hagerstown, Maryland. After Martinsburg and Harpers Ferry were taken, Jackson, McLaws, and Walker would reunite with Lee, Longstreet, and Hill near Hagerstown, and thence move north and east into Pennsylvania.

Col. Robert H. Chilton, Lee's chief of staff, made certain that copies of the order were sent to Jackson, Longstreet, McLaws, Stuart, Walker, and Hill, in addition to a file copy. Jackson, always conscientious about all communications, was uncertain whether a copy had been sent to Hill, his brother-in-law. Since Hill's division had been attached to his own, Jackson wanted to make sure Hill understood that his division would be separating from Jackson's. To rest his mind, Jackson made another copy and sent it to Hill.

Jackson's precaution proved fortuitous: The Staff-Chilton

copy of Special Order 191 that was intended for Hill never reached him. An unknown Confederate staff officer entrusted with the document evidently had carefully wrapped the order around a couple of cigars and placed it in one of his shirt pockets or haversack or courier pouch of some type. It remains a matter of historical fact that no one has ever learned exactly how the orders became lost.

On Friday, September 12, three days after the order was given, Union troops including Sgt. John M. Bloss and Corporal Barton W. Mitchell of Company F, 27th Indiana, and two others, were resting in the vicinity of the same campground that Lee's army had occupied just south of Frederick, on property close to the Monocacy (1864) battlefield. Taking his ease in what had been a wheat field, perhaps near a locust tree, Mitchell noticed a small packet lying on the ground and picked it up to examine it. As he unwrapped what at first appeared to be two sheets of paper protecting cigars, he realized that he had found something quite extraordinary. At the top of the page was written: Special Order No. 191, Headquarters, Army of Northern Virginia. It was the copy of Lee's orders that had been addressed to D. H. Hill.[1]

Mitchell and his sergeant hurriedly took the discovery to their company commander, who sent it up the chain of command, from company to regiment to corps and finally to General McClellan, Commander of the Army of the Potomac.[2] McClellan now knew that Lee had taken the dangerous step of dividing his army into four units separated by up to 40 miles. It is commonly believed that he then commented to one of his generals, "Here is a paper with which if I cannot whip Bobby Lee, I will be willing to go home."

Upon learning that a copy of Special Order 191 had fallen into Union hands, Lee canceled plans for the northern invasion and prepared for battle against the Army of the Potomac. After limited but fierce fighting at the South Mountain gaps, the two armies met in the woods and the cornfields adjacent to Antietam Creek, east of Sharpsburg, Maryland. Between them, they would lose more than 4,700 men on September 17, 1862, the deadliest day of the Civil War.

Tactically, the Battle of Antietam was a stalemate, since neither army prevailed in a persuasive manner. Strategically, however, it was a Union victory, because it reversed Lee's northern movement. Antietam was the first battle in the eastern theater in which the Union army drove the Confederates into full-scale retreat. President Lincoln fumed because McClellan failed to pursue the retreat of Lee's army.

A major result of the Battle of Antietam was that the recognition of the Confederacy by either England or France was no longer a viable possibility. The Union rationale for fighting the war had taken a dramatic and decisive change: As long as the people and governments of both North and South held to the official line that the war was to determine whether states could secede, England would have no moral compunctions against recognizing the Confederacy. Once emancipation became law, however, secession and slavery became inseparable issues. President Lincoln released the Preliminary Emancipation Proclamation nine days after the battle of Antietam. He had written and informed his cabinet of it in July, but would not formally release it until the Union army had, in his opinion, won a significant victory. Formal release and publication of the Emancipation Proclamation was January 1, 1863.

When the Emancipation Proclamation was published, English Prime Minister Henry Palmerston abandoned the idea of bringing the issue of recognition before his cabinet. He had no viable option. Having abolished its slave trade throughout the Empire in 1807 and the practice of slavery itself in 1833, England could not hypocritically aid a rebellious bloc of states fighting for the right to own, buy, and sell slaves. And France seemed steadfastly unwilling to recognize the South unless England did.

So much for historical fact. *Divided We Stood* is the author's fiction of what might have happened had Mitchell and Bloss not found the copy of Special Order 191. Would England and France recognize the Confederate States as a sovereign power? Would the South win the war? If so, what would the postwar South look like? Would it establish itself as a strong, powerful political force? Could it solve its internal differences over harbors, forts, waterways, militias, taxation, trade, tariffs, and the myriad substantive issues necessary to viable national government and international sovereignty? In short: Could the South win the peace?

*****

With the exception of several prominent American and English statesmen, noted military figures, and the Short brothers, all other characters are fictitious. Dates and circumstances of death for Stonewall Jackson, J. E. B. Stuart, and Abraham Lincoln were altered in order to enhance the telling of the story.

(Endnotes)

1 The Sentinel. "A Local Slant on Lee's Lost Order #191", Monroe County Civil War Roundtable, June, 2014, Bloomington, Indiana. Review and commentary by Stephen Rolfe, editor, of a speech by Scott Schroeder, delivered to the Roundtable on June 10, 2014.

Stephan W. Sears. Landscape Turned Red: The Battle of Antietam. New York: Ticknor & Fields, Houghton Mifflin, 1983. Chapter Three: pp. 74-113.

2 Stephen W. Sears. Landscape Turned Red: The Battle of Antietam. New York: Ticknor &Fields, Houghton Mifflin, 1983. pp. 112-113. "The two men delivered the find to their company commander, Captain Peter Kop, who took one look at it and hurried them off to regimental headquarters and Colonel Silas Colgrove. Colgrove did not stop at brigade and division, the next links in the chain of command, but took the document straight to corps. General Alpheus Williams ... and his aide, Colonel Samuel E. Pittman, examined the paper closely... And there was every reason to believe it was authentic. It just so happened, Colonel Pittman explained, that he had been stationed with Chilton on a tour of duty in the prewar army and knew him well—and knew his handwriting. He would vouch for the fact that the writer of the document was General Lee's adjutant."

James M. McPherson, Antietam. Oxford and New York: Oxford University Press, 2002. pp.106-109. McPherson prefaces his remarks about Col. Pittman with the words: " By one account..." (p. 108) There are other hypotheses but no one has fully discredited the Pittman connection with Chilton.

CPSIA information can be obtained at www.ICGtesting.com
Printed in the USA
LVOW11s1612180815

450597LV00002B/167/P